The HomeScholar Guide
TO
College Admission
and Scholarships

Homeschool Secrets to
Getting Ready, Getting In, and *Getting Paid*

LEE BINZ
The HomeScholar

ISBN-10: 1482320487
ISBN-13: 9781482320480
Library of Congress Control Number: 2013902022
CreateSpace Independent Publishing Platform
North Charleston, South Carolina

You will see quotes throughout this book from two invaluable tools for homeschooling
high school – The Bible (NIV) and The Princess Bride (DVD). There are riches to be had
in both, although only the first is truly inspired.

Printed in the USA
Published by The HomeScholar LLC

www.TheHomeScholar.com

Disclaimer: Parents assume full responsibility for the education of their children and for the
accuracy of all homeschool records in accordance with state law. College requirements vary,
so make sure to check with the colleges about specific requirements for homeschoolers.
We offer no guarantees, written or implied, that the use of our products and services will
result in college admissions or scholarship awards.

Table of Contents

Facing Reality

Resources

Find Online Resources and Links for

The HomeScholar Guide to College Admission and Scholarships

www.TheHomeScholar.com/CollegeAdmissionBook

Foreword

The HomeScholar Guide to College Admission and Scholarships is a treasure trove for college bound homeschoolers! Planning timelines and guides, helpful tips on selecting a college, attending college fairs and finding scholarships, personal stories, resource lists, and step-by-step suggestions to make the most out of the junior and senior year are just a few of the treasures found in this book. Whether you are looking at college entrance for your first graduate, or have already assisted several children in their search for college "true love," you are likely to unearth treasures in this new book. Our family has successfully cheered on five students through the "college match-up," and yet, I discovered several helpful gems that will benefit our current and future students.

In *The HomeScholar Guide to College Admission and Scholarships*, Lee is the guidance counselor of our dreams as she leads us through the maze of college selection and acceptance. Lee's family stories provide a spark of humor and reality to what can become a rather dry and mind-boggling topic. This is no "cookie cutter" approach to education. I especially appreciate the chapter on how to determine our child's specialization, and how to document annoyance on a transcript. Detailed chapters on both the junior and senior year prepare your student to cut through the maze of college application with "ease." Chapters on writing scholarship essays and application essays are brimming with practical, easily implemented tips.

Some will read *The HomeScholar Guide to College Admission and Scholarships* when their child is in kindergarten and will chart a well-planned course to college with the information they discover. Some will find Lee's "Senior Year Last Minute 12 Step Emergency No Panic Plan" to be the life preserver they have been searching for. In either case, this book may well be one of the best investments you will make in your homeschool.

~ De'Etta Goecker, Military Mom and Chaplain's Wife, Homeschool Parent of 9

Preface

I have some great news: Colleges <u>LOVE</u> homeschoolers! Many successful homeschoolers have passed through their gates, and yours can too! In my years of work as a consultant helping parents homeschool through high school, I've come across hundreds of homeschool parents who don't realize this good news, or don't believe it's true for their child. I'm here to tell you that IT IS possible, and after you read this book, you'll understand not only HOW to help your child get into the college of their dreams, but also how to help them earn BIG scholarships to pay for it.

How do I know, you might wonder? Because not only have I helped thousands of parents across the country succeed in college admittance and scholarships, but my own family has also experienced this truth. As the parents of two homeschooled sons, we were scared and uncertain, just like you, when it came time to think about college. The high cost of a college education weighed heavily on us, and we realized that unless our sons received some big scholarships—and I mean some REALLY BIG scholarships—it would be very difficult to provide a good college education for them. Let me encourage you in your journey as I share my own family's story.

OUR STORY

Several weeks had passed since our children had spent the day at their first choice university, taking part in a full-tuition scholarship competition. Getting the invitation to compete was shocking. The university had over 2500 applicants that year, but only the top 108 students were invited to compete for 10 full-tuition scholarships, and two of those students were ours! Imagine, one family with two boys (ages 16 and 18) being invited for a day of intense scrutiny. Just making it to the top 108 was both a thrill and an honor.

Of course, we were hopeful. We had to hope, since we hadn't saved nearly enough money to pay the whole cost of tuition for each child. Our boys were nervous and excited, since they knew it would be up to them to shine through during the competition.

We were also realists. The odds of winning even one of the awards were slim. I mean…who were we? Just humble homeschoolers, armed with nothing more than mommy grades on a homemade transcript, competing with some of the top public and private high school students from around the country.

We also had to deal with the "parental nightmare scenario." What if one son got the award and the other didn't? It would be hard enough if the older boy won and the younger boy didn't. But what if (horror of horrors) the younger son won and the older one didn't? How would we spin that? I can't remember the exact talking points, but I do remember they were pretty lame. There was simply no way we could have protected our eldest from crushing disappointment. Despite our financial situation, I remember praying, "Lord, make it both, or none at all."

The first call came at about 10:00 AM. They asked to speak to Alex (the younger). He was out of the house, so they asked for his cell phone number. We gave it to them, and then asked pathetically if we could "take a message for him." "No," they said, "we need to speak to him personally." There was no hint in the caller's voice whether it was good or bad news. We didn't have to wait long. Alex got the call and then raced home. "I GOT IT!!" he shouted as he burst through the door from the garage. I'm sure the neighbors were alarmed by all the shouting and carrying on that morning!!

Then came the second call. "Is Kevin there?" "No," we said, again asking, "is there any message you'd like to leave?" "No thanks," they said, chuckling at our transparency. We assumed Kevin would soon get the call. While we waited for him to contact us, my husband and I practiced our lines in case we faced "the nightmare." Our anxiety grew with the passing minutes. After 30 minutes, we called Kevin. His phone was off. As the minutes grew to an hour, our panic and disappointment increased. After two hours, we were thoroughly resigned to consoling him when he returned home that evening. As is my custom when dealing with disappointment, I made chocolate chip cookies.

"I'm home," Kevin yelled when he returned at 7 PM that night. Matt and I ran at him like blitzing linebackers. "Well…" we gasped! "What??" he said, clearly startled by our greeting. "THE SCHOLARSHIP!!!!" we yelled in unison!

"Oh, that…Yeah, I won………I thought I told you already."

In the Binz family highlight reel, there is no greater display of shock, joy, relief and gratitude than at that moment. We were (and still are) amazed at God's faithfulness, and shocked about how this happened to our family. That was the day we became fully convinced that ANYONE can homeschool high school and make it into college with scholarships. Our homeschool journey ended in a way that surpassed our wildest dreams.

This book will share what we did to get there.

Blessings,
Lee

Acknowledgements

My biggest thanks goes to my husband, "Mr. HomeScholar" Matt, for his support and encouragement over the past thirty years. Matt, I really appreciate your daily help in my mission to help parents homeschool high school. I truly could not do this without you! Your inspiration and reassurance have given me the strength and perseverance I needed.

I thank my faithful editor, Jill Bell, for her tireless work and patience. You have a wonderful eye for detail, and it has been a joy to work with you on our projects together!

Finally, I want to thank the parents who have shared their homeschool with me. Thank you for your willingness to share your experiences, both good and bad, so they can be used to encourage others. This book is dedicated to homeschool parents facing the great unknown of college admission and scholarship. I have been in that difficult position, and it can be pretty scary!

My prayer is that God will grant you success in your journey through the next few years. Be confident and courageous! The love you have for your children will truly ensure their success. Your child was given to you, so you must be the right parent for the job (Psalm 139:13-16). You know you are capable, because you can do ALL things through Christ who strengthens you—even this (Philippians 4:13). The love you have for your child will cover any missteps along the way (1 Peter 4:8). God's plans will prevail, and you won't mess up your child's life (Jeremiah 29:11).

Introduction

"So do not fear, for I am with you; do not be dismayed, for I am your God. I will strengthen you and help you; I will uphold you with my righteous right hand."

Isaiah 41:10

"Have fun storming the castle!"

Miracle Max, ~ *The Princess Bride*

How do you find a college? Better yet, how do you pay for college? These are two of the most challenging tasks for high school students and their parents. Finding that college, the one that both parents and students are enthusiastic about, is something like finding the "love of your life." At its best, this "true love" should value the academic achievements of your student, support your years of homeschooling, adore your homeschool transcript and records, and understand your desire to give a homeschool diploma.

This book will help you to find a college to love, a college that will be equally satisfying for both parents and students, and a college that will love your student and do all in their power to court you and persuade you to choose them. We will cover a variety of topics, including how to search for colleges and interpret college statistics, how to visit the colleges and evaluate what you discover, how to prepare your kids to receive merit-based scholarships, and how to market them effectively to the colleges of their choice. Through it all you will learn to navigate the high school years with confidence. You can give your students their best shot at finding the "Love of their Life" —a college who will love them almost as much as you do.

Preparing for College

C H A P T E R   1

The Best Guidance Counselor

> *"How much better to get wisdom than gold,*
> *to get insight rather than silver!"*
>
> **Proverbs 16:16**

> **Man in Black:** *"You're that smart?"*
> **Vizzini:** *"Let me put it this way. Have you ever heard of*
> *Plato, Aristotle, Socrates? Morons."*
>
> **~ The Princess Bride**

One of the scariest roles that parents adopt when they decide to homeschool high school is the position of guidance counselor. I've known some wonderful public high school advisers, people with a heart for kids, advanced communication skills, and an encyclopedic knowledge of post high school options. Then I've known others who demonstrated an extreme dislike for teens. So how do you stack up?

The average guidance counselor in a public high school has 350 students. Unless a child gets in trouble or excels frequently, the adviser may not know a child at all. When a student goes in for advice or consulting with the counselor, the counselor typically knows very little about that student or their family. But what exactly does a high school guidance counselor do for these students? According to statistics, 92% of high school guidance counselors do these five things: use college catalogs, counsel students individually, utilize computerized career information, arrange and interpret tests, and use non-computerized career information.

Even if you as a parent are only half as good as a typical high school guidance counselor, you will still be far more effective, because you know your student so well. You know their interests and abilities, their aspirations and weaknesses. This is not to minimize the value of high school counselors; rather it is to show how, as your child's parent and teacher, you are completely capable of equipping your student with everything they need to get through the college process.

> *You are the best guidance counselor for your child. You have all the tools you need.*

Let's look at that college counselor list again, and see how a parent can provide the same things as the typical counselor.

1. **Use of college catalogs**. You can find catalogs like the *US News and World Report Ultimate College Guide* at the library, buy it at the bookstore, or at used bookstores. If you know how to find your local public library, then you can do this.
2. **Individualized counseling sessions**. How many times have you been alone in a room with your child and talked about what might come in the future? You can do this.
3. **Use computerized career information tools**. If you have used a computer before and searched for information, you can also do this.
4. **Arrange for and interpret tests**. Two websites are all you need to figure out high school tests. The College Board (www.collegeboard.com) gives you complete information on the SAT, PSAT, SAT Subject Tests, AP, and CLEP tests. The other website is the ACT (www.act.org), which provides information on the ACT, PLAN and COMPASS tests. With these two websites, you can arrange for and interpret all the tests that you need to know about.
5. **Use non-computerized career information**. This means that you allow the child to have some work experience and learn about different careers. If you do allow your child to do these things when they're sixteen or seventeen, then you can do this as well.

The very things that most high school guidance counselors do are things that you are completely capable of doing. You can be the best high school guidance counselor. You have all the tools you need.

A PUBLIC SCHOOL CONTRAST

When I was getting my hair done recently, I overheard two moms talking about their experience dealing with guidance counselors in their local public school. One mom was upset because her son was struggling with math, and he had almost failed Pre-Algebra. The mom was concerned and asked the guidance counselor to place him in Pre-Algebra again the next year, because she knew he didn't understand things, and she didn't want him to move on and be lost in Algebra 1. The counselor insisted that the student stay with his age-mates and not fail a class. Therefore, he was moved on to the next class the following year. The mom thought that she had no choice in the matter, and that the opinion of a professional educator was more valid than her own perceptions.

By the second week of the new school year the son was becoming more distraught, and his mom asked him how math was going. He said that he wasn't getting it, and that he didn't even understand what the symbols meant. The two went to talk to the guidance counselor, and they discovered the problem. The counselor had accidentally placed the student in a Pre-Calculus class instead of an Algebra class. Oops. Pre-Calculus instead of Algebra 1? There is not a homeschool parent on the planet that would make that mistake.

In a different situation and a different school district, another parent was thinking about putting her homeschooled child into public school for his senior year. She went to talk to the guidance counselor, and told them that her child was ready for Calculus. The guidance counselor explained that the Calculus class was completely full for the year, so the student could not take Calculus. Instead, the student was placed into a Business Math class for students who couldn't succeed in Calculus. It is a fine choice for a math class, but it doesn't look as academically rigorous as Calculus on a transcript.

PARENTS PROVIDE SUCCESS

Homeschool parents make great guidance counselors because we know what our children need, and our classes are never full. We can find any curriculum to teach any class that we need. We can cover core classes and create classes that encourage delight directed learning in any subject. The point of these stories is that your love for your children will go a long way towards ensuring their success in the college process. If you prepare well and learn what you need to know to help your children, you will feel confident.

Dana in Oregon expressed her confidence this way: "I am not worried about missing test dates. I know when to start communicating with colleges. I know generally what courses my daughter will need to complete. Scholarships are not a big mystery anymore. Transcripts will be a labor of love instead of a necessary evil. And if we prepare well, we may save thousands of dollars by obtaining college credit in high school. Yes, high school is a lot of work for both student and teacher— but what a difference it makes to have a plan and to know the game rules."

> *You can ensure success. You know what your child needs. Your classes are never full. You can find curriculum to teach anything. You can cover core classes and capture electives from delight directed learning.*

As parents we care deeply about our child's best interests. We are deeply invested in their success, both emotionally and financially. We want them to do well. The high school guidance counselors work to the best of their abilities, but they don't actually know a student as well as a parent does. You can feel confident in your abilities to advise and encourage your students in their college preparation. You are the best person for the job.

EXECUTIVE SUMMARY FOR BUSY PARENTS

PARENTS ARE THE BEST GUIDANCE COUNSELORS

- You have the tools you need.
- You can find the information you need.
- You know and love your children.
- You know your family and financial situation.

CHAPTER 2

Plan a Rigorous Curriculum

"Anyone who competes as an athlete does not receive the victor's crown except by competing according to the rules."

2 Timothy 2:5

"You rush a miracle man, you get rotten miracles!"

Miracle Max, ~ *The Princess Bride*

A primary goal of homeschooling high school is to keep your student's college and career options open. You want to always be prepared. I don't know if you've noticed, but the one constant in teenagers is that they change their minds—

> *Warning! Teenagers can change their minds! Be prepared for anything, by planning a college prep education.*

frequently and without warning! A child who one day appears perfectly content to begin working in a trade may stun you the next day by declaring they want to be an engineer or a doctor. If this happens to you, as it did to my best friend, you are destined for many sleepless nights.

My friend had a son that loved motors. He was always bringing home little stray engines the way other kids might bring home little stray puppies. She was convinced that her son would become a mechanic. Positive that her child wouldn't go to college, and therefore wouldn't need math, she was never concerned about pushing him along. He loved engines so much, it was an obvious fit, right? And then one day he announced that he wanted to be an engineer! He had math through Algebra 1, and now he needed Calculus!

Children change their minds, and sometimes even parents can't assume that things will end as expected. What is the best way to prepare for such potential teenage flakiness? Plan a rigorous curriculum! This is a critical step in the college quest and shouldn't be rushed. Planning a rigorous curriculum doesn't mean that your child must do calculus as a sophomore. It simply means that you keep your child challenged. Give them classes that aren't easy, not overwhelming of course, but not easy. This approach will keep your student challenged throughout their high school career.

CORE CLASSES

Most colleges have some specific courses they want to see on a student's transcript. With these classes, your child will appear well educated on the transcript.

Most colleges like to see four years of English, which you can accomplish in a variety of ways. Your student could study literature and composition through a prepared curriculum, or you could simply have them read and write a lot every year. You could consider a speech class as an alternative. Keep in mind what really matters: ending up with a student who enjoys reading, communicates well in writing, and knows how to learn.

Include three to four years of math. Math is such a cornerstone for other subjects, careers, and college majors that I believe it's important to have four years of math. Most colleges want at least 3 years, and many want 4 years of math. They especially like to see math taught during senior year.

Cover core classes: 4 years of English, 4 years of math, 3-4 years of social studies, 3 years of science, 2-3 years of foreign language, plus physical education and fine art.

Include three to four years of social studies. Colleges like to see three to four years of history and social science. Some colleges will further specify what classes they particularly want to see. They may want students to cover world history, American history, American government, and economics. Remember that you aren't confined to choosing the "expected classes" for social studies either. In our family, one son took a course in Russian history and the other chose psychology.

Core classes include three years of science. Three years is expected for college preparation, with at least one of those classes including a lab. Each area of science is so different that a child may really hate one but really love the other, so it's helpful to expose them to different branches of science. For selective schools, you might stick to biology, chemistry, and physics. You can also try unique subjects: geology, astronomy, computer programming, etc. Colleges love to see unique courses, so don't be afraid to delve into another area of science if your son or daughter is interested.

Cover two to three years of a foreign language. Many colleges require a foreign language for admission. Most of those demand two or three years of a single language, so the student becomes reasonably fluent. Whatever curriculum you choose, practice at least a little bit every day. A daily 15 minute study period is much more effective than once a week for an hour. Use a foreign language curriculum designed for homeschoolers so you aren't expected to already know the language. Find a good curriculum, let the student learn independently, and check on their progress now and then.

Core curriculum includes two years of physical education. Some children find it very easy to get the required two credits of PE, while others really balk at physical exercise. Some unique ways to obtain physical education credits are yoga or weight lifting at a YMCA. Some kids who "hate" PE will love swing-dancing or computer games requiring movement. Any physical activity that breaks a sweat counts, and you can also focus on first aid, nutrition, or health. Military academies require more PE than other universities.

Plan to cover one year of fine art. Colleges like to see some fine arts in the transcript, but usually one credit will suffice. Fine art includes music, art, theater, and dance. You can study just one or blend them into a survey of fine arts.

A rigorous curriculum includes enough electives to add up to at least 24 credits. Elective classes may be subjects required by your unique family. For example, some families require Bible classes, Home Economics, Auto Mechanics, or Critical Thinking. Elective classes may be subjects required by your state if it's not something in the other subject areas. For example, some states require Occupational Education, and others require a credit of Volunteer Service. Finally, elective classes can be collected from delight-directed learning.

These are subjects your child learns for fun, and your only job is to count or estimate the hours spent on the subject, and collect their experiences for course descriptions. Your child can have as many or as few elective credits as they accomplish during high school. For college bound students, make sure the total number of credits is at least 24 overall.

In every single area, make sure that you meet the highest possible criteria required by the colleges you're interested in. In some areas you will exceed those requirements. In other areas, especially in your student's areas of interest, you may greatly exceed them. A rigorous curriculum like this will get you noticed by the colleges.

OVER AND ABOVE

For big scholarships, you want to be an overachiever in your core curriculum, and go above what is expected. In order to reach for those really selective colleges, you should exceed the 24-credit amount. It is not uncommon for public, private, or homeschooled students who are applying to high-achieving universities to have up to 35 or more credits in high school. While not required, accruing credits that exceed expectations is a win-win situation. Nothing could possibly go wrong if you do more than required! Be sure to avoid burn-out of course, but if your student earns more than the requisite 24 credits, that's a plus when applying to selective colleges.

ELECTIVES OR CORE?

What is the proper mix between core and elective credits? Essentially, once you've fit in the core courses listed above (math, English, fine arts, etc.), everything else can be elective credit. Electives can be thought of as "delight directed learning." They center on the interests of the child. Some electives are family requirements, like auto mechanics or Bible classes. While there may be some electives that parents mandate, most electives can be things your children learn because they're interested in them. Some common valuable electives are driver's education, typing, logic, and computer skills. These are skills adults need every day. People either have these skills or wish they did! The next chapter goes into elective credits

> *Electives can be delight directed learning, family requirements, or subjects required by your state.*

in greater depth, and discusses how important they are for college admission and scholarships.

READING LIST

A reading list is an important complement to high school curriculum. Colleges are interested in what your student is reading, as well as the coursework they have completed. Colleges want to know your student, and providing a reading list tells them a little bit more about the interests and specialization of your child. Reading lists also indicate your student's reading level, how much they can get done, how fast they can read, and what they read for fun.

Colleges are interested in students that have a wide variety of reading experience. Sometimes they get frustrated when homeschoolers demonstrate an over-emphasis on classic literature, and they prefer that students also include popular literature. Students should consider selections from reading lists for the college bound as well as popular literature, books from the best-seller lists as well as books that are in the news. The key is to create a reading list that is broad. There are many helpful reading lists available online. I have a College Bound Reading List on my website to assist you (www.TheHomeScholar.com/college-bound-reading-list.php).

SCHOLARSHIPS

If your student is hoping to win a merit-based scholarship, planning a rigorous curriculum will certainly improve his chances in every situation. If two students both play first base equally well and the college needs a first baseman, they will choose the student with the best academic preparation. If two applicants have the same test scores and GPA, when a college must choose between them, they will choose the one that followed a rigorous curriculum.

To earn big scholarships, exceed expectations when possible.

In the Appendix, you'll find a chart that outlines a suggested college prep plan. Again, if you're looking for big scholarships or applying to very selective universities, you need to exceed the maximum requirements in the areas that you can.

There are many ways to stack up those additional credits and create a rigorous curriculum. My own children met the planning guide requirements, but they also really loved the social sciences. My son Alex had many years of economics, probably six or seven credits worth. He exceeded the suggested credit maximum because he studied economics all the time for fun! He also exceeded the fine art credits because he took piano every year. While these were rigorous courses, they were also fun for him because they were areas that he was passionate about.

GREAT EDUCATION

Even if your student is not in the running for a big scholarship or a prestigious college, pursuing a rigorous curriculum will still help him in the long run. At the very least, he will be smarter and better-educated than his peers! Simply by studying topics in more depth, he may be able to pass college level exams such as AP or CLEP tests, which will earn him college credit and can reduce the number of years he has to go to college. Saving money on college like this can be as valuable as winning a scholarship!

EXECUTIVE SUMMARY FOR BUSY PARENTS

MINIMUM COLLEGE PREP REQUIREMENTS

- English: 4 years of literature and composition.
- Math: 4 years, particularly senior year.
- Social Studies: American history, world history, economics and government.
- Science: 3 years, with at least 1 lab science.
- Foreign language: 2 or 3 years of a single language.
- Physical Education: 2 years.
- Fine Art: 1 year of music, art, theater, dance, or combination.
- Electives: enough so the student has 24 or more credits.

CHAPTER 3

Specialization, Passion, and Delight Directed Learning

"In the same way, let your light shine before others, that they may see your good deeds and glorify your Father in heaven."

Matthew 5:16

Man in Black: *"Oh, there is something I ought to tell you."*
Inigo Montoya: *"Tell me."*
Man in Black: *"I am not left-handed either."*

~ The Princess Bride

Your best investment in homeschooling high school—the one that will pay the biggest dividends—is encouraging specialization in your child. Many football players get big scholarships in college because football is their area of high school specialization. They are wonderful at it and many colleges are searching for that. In the same way, colleges are also looking for the gifts in your child, even if it isn't being a star quarterback. Colleges look for passion in kids.

WHAT IS SPECIAL?

When we as parents look at our child's specialization, it can be difficult to feel like it's valuable. My older son is very into chess. To me, chess is a game much like Monopoly or Scrabble. However, colleges looked at this skill and said, "Wow! He is a top-ranked player. He must have amazing critical thinking skills." Other organizations gave him

> *Specialization doesn't look like school. It often looks like fun.*

scholarship money because his chess had value to them. Even though it was difficult for me as a parent to understand, it still had value. Encourage the specialization in your child.

For some reason, perhaps God's wonderful sense of humor, the things kids are passionate about seem to frequently frustrate their parents. In my own home, this is typically how it played out: Mom says, "Will you PLEASE put that down and do your work!" For one child, "that" was the chess piece. For another child, "that" was usually an economics book. For each child, "that" was the thing they were passionate about and spent time specializing in.

It's hard, too, to recognize specialization when it is so much fun for our students. Shouldn't they be working instead of enjoying themselves? It doesn't look like school; it looks like they're just having FUN! If you are really struggling with specialization, remember that colleges love to see a student's passion. They see unique specialization in homeschoolers and they love it!

What do your children do that drives you nuts? Could it be their specialization? An interest they are passionate about? Now, I admit that sometimes they might just be wasting time, but if they are actively engaged in something, pay attention. Put aside your pre-conceived notions about which interests are valuable, and be open to the possibility of specialization.

SPECIALIZATION IS ANNOYING

For whatever reason, I notice that parents sometimes see their child's faults more easily than they see their strengths. But think for a minute: a gift can be something children will do repeatedly, over and over, to the point of annoyance! Check yourself the next time you feel annoyed at your children. What are they doing when you say, "Will you knock that off!?" Ask yourself, are you looking at their gifts? I know parents who have "pooh-poohed" some really wonderful activities because they thought they didn't have value.

Some parents didn't think an activity was academic enough, others thought it was "too narrow." Some have dismissed an interest because it wasn't a college-level interest, it was just "messing around on the computer" with programming languages.

One parent recently told me, "My son doesn't seem to have any interests at all. He is not interested in math or writing or science. I don't know what to do. He doesn't have an area of specialization." Later on in the conversation it kind of spilled out. She said, "But you know, he drives me crazy because all he ever does is play his guitar. I can't get him away from the guitar." I said to her, "That's it! That's his specialization." Sometimes you need to look at your child and see what drives you crazy, and then decide if that could be their area of specialization, or if it could be made into an area of specialization.

> *Specialization can be annoying. Annoyance may indicate specialization and high school credits.*

ANNOYANCE ON THE TRANSCRIPT!

Use the information you gain from your annoyance to give your students credit on their transcript. Let your frustrations be your guide in course titles, grades, credit values, and activity lists. Encourage their interests, as long as it's something they are actively involved in and not just laziness. Feed into their passionate pursuits.

The things that bother us often become our subconscious grading criteria. Our frustrations can indicate what course work we have assigned. Think about this statement: "Aren't you done with your spelling words YET?" This indicates that you consider spelling a part of their English class. What about this: "Is that all you want to read about?" This could demonstrate that your child is working on a delight-directed course, and learning without any assignments at all! Can you figure out a course name for that delight?

And then there is the classic phrase, "You simply HAVE to put that down now and do some school!" That statement can help you determine credit value for your delight-directed course. How often do you say it? Once a week? Once a day?? Once an hour??? It may mean your child is spending more than 5 hours a week on the activity, and you might be able to make it a high school credit. (And yes, I know for some kids it's more like five hours per day!)

Evaluate this statement: "I expect you to do a better job!" This can indicate your grading criteria. If they repeat the assignment until we decide it's acceptable, then they are working within some very high expectations. Success with high expectations should provide some very good grades on a transcript!

ANNOYANCE FOR COLLEGE CREDIT

Sometimes a child will annoy us with a skill that can be measured in some way. If your child has an interest in an academic subject, consider having their knowledge assessed. Even if they aren't "studying" a class, the student may be learning material because they are interested. I experienced this with my economics-loving son. I noticed that I was annoyed with his economics study, so I thought I should probably include it on his transcript. Although it felt like he read economics all day and every day, I felt too unsure of myself to give him a whole credit. On his transcript I decided to write Economics 1, Economics 2, and Economics 3, all with a ☐ credit value. Then I thought 'just perhaps' he could pass an exam in economics.

This turned out to be a fateful decision. I discovered through CLEP exams that he knew a college amount of information about economics (and other topics I never taught him at all). Based on those test results, I revised his transcript. I put Economics - 1 credit, Macroeconomics - 1 credit, and Microeconomics - 1 credit. I gave him "honors" for all three classes. The CLEP exam provided information about class titles, grades, and credit value. If your child has an academic interest, look into SAT 2 Subject tests, AP exams, or CLEP tests to see if their annoying interest can be measured as college credit.

ANNOYANCE INDICATES ACTIVITIES AND AWARDS

Some things aren't so much "core annoying" but are more "extracurricular annoying." If you have a child who competes or receives honors in an area he loves, put it on the activity and awards list. Sometimes parents will laugh a little when they explain their child's interest and say, "You're not going to believe this but he actually won a contest!" Perhaps the child has actually sold some CDs with his band, or won a huge cash prize for playing video games or winning chess tournaments!

Some interests and activities may be core classes, and others may be extracurricular classes.

All of these things can go on a student's activity and awards list, and the more the better! Colleges love passion, which means they love to see a LOT of a particular interest over all four years of high school. We may want our kids to be well rounded (I know I did!), but it also helps for them to have some activities they do ALL the time: lacrosse for four years, youth group, or Eagle Scouts. When it comes to applying for college, four years of an activity is ten times better than one year!

ANNOYANCE FOR CAREER PREPARATION

As your child grows, often their interests will change. Yes, passion for a subject during all four years of high school is great, but it's also important to expose your child to MANY interests so they can shape their ideas about a career. My son loved playing the piano, but after years of playing, he realized he liked it "for fun" but didn't want it to be his career. Allow your students to change interests and move their focus from one activity to the next.

It can be amazing when they put all these pieces of the puzzle together. As a senior in high school, my older son couldn't decide on a college major. Finally he decided chess was "problem solving" and electrical engineering was "problem solving," plus he loved math. He decided to be an engineer because of his interest in chess and math. Each activity seemed isolated until he put them together, with a straight line pointing straight to his college major and career interest! So encouraging specialization, even when it changes, can ultimately help with career choices.

FREEDOM TO SPECIALIZE

You might wonder how your student can possibly fit the normal core curriculum into their schedule in addition to the hours they want to spend on their specialization. The way we achieved this in our homeschool was to focus on heavy-duty academics four days a week. The fifth day was spent studying what my sons wanted to study, doing what they wanted to do. That fifth day, one son taught chess in the local area. Our other son studied college-level economics books and lectures on tape.

That fifth day wasn't always devoted directly to one specific area of specialization. Sometimes our boys would do something slightly different. One son might pick up his pencils and do some artwork, which ultimately came into play with the different scholarships that he received. Schools wanted to see some art and he showed them art. One time our son became very interested in Napoleon's invasion of Russia, so he read up on it for hours and hours on his "day off." We finally realized that he needed to get a half credit in Russian History. That is a very unusual class. It is a very different social science and it really stood out on his transcript. You need to have this important time that is available for your students to fill with academic and nonacademic areas of specialization.

> *Delight directed learning and specialization take time. Allow time each week for students to pursue individual interests.*

In *Stanford University Magazine*, author Christine Foster writes about gifted homeschool students in her article, "In a Class by Themselves." I love this quote of hers: "It's the spark, the passion that sets the truly exceptional student—the one driven to pursue independent research and explore difficult concepts from a very early age—apart from your typical bright kid. Stanford wants students who have it. Looking very closely at homeschoolers is one way to get more of those special minds, the admission office has discovered." As Foster explains it, "Homeschooled students may have a potential advantage over others in this, since they have consciously chosen and pursued an independent course of study." I love the emphasis on independent homeschooling!

Specialization will help your child stand out from the crowd. Remember that colleges don't particularly want just another cookie-cutter kid. They see that all the time. You want your student to rise above the crowd and be different. If their specialization is something that the college has never heard of, sometimes that can be of more value. You want your student to be a unique individual, a character, something colleges have never seen before.

Rather than try to squelch your student's area of passionate interest, invest in it. It might pay huge dividends during your college search. Our sons drove us crazy at times with their single-mindedness about chess and economics. But if we had prevented them from having an outlet for their passions, we would have missed some of the best opportunities in their young lives.

EXECUTIVE SUMMARY FOR BUSY PARENTS

ANNOYANCE CAN INDICATE ONE OR MORE OF THE FOLLOWING:

- Specialization or "passion."
- Classes on a high school transcript.
- Possible college credit.
- Information for activities list.
- Uniqueness in your child.
- Career and aptitude.

CHAPTER 4

Preparation Beyond Academics

"I have become all things to all people so that by all possible means I might save some."

1 Corinthians 9:22b

"What are our assets?"

Westley, preparing to storm the castle, ~ *The Princess Bride*

Preparing for college involves more than equipping our children with a strong academic background. Colleges also want students who are well-rounded. Not just well-rounded in their rigorous curriculum, although that is important, but also well-rounded as individuals. Why do colleges care?

Colleges are businesses. They make an investment in your student when they award admission and financial aid. It is an investment in the future. They believe these students will be the movers and shakers in society, and will in due time shine a bright light back on the university from where they came. As they make their decisions, they consider some key questions: "Will they succeed and make the college proud?" "Will they go on to leadership positions in society?" And most importantly, "Will they ultimately earn enough money to leave an endowment?"

> *Colleges want well-rounded individuals as well as strong academics.*

These questions play a significant, if perhaps subconscious role in admissions decisions. Clearly, colleges want to admit students who appear to be well-rounded and show potential for success. Demonstrated experience in such areas as leadership, volunteer work, and employment all contribute to a student's development as an individual, as well as the development of character, self-motivation, and socialization. These attributes will help the colleges see that your student is someone worthy of admission!

LEADERSHIP

Colleges want to see leadership demonstrated in a student's life. Leadership experience may come through Boy Scouts, 4-H, youth groups, sports, or teaching others piano, guitar, or chess. Leadership comes from passion, experience, and a desire to share interests with others. In other words, to be a leader, one must first want to be a leader.

When dealing with college applications, it is pretty easy for extroverted teens to highlight leadership. Identifying leadership in the quiet teen is a bit more of a challenge. The quiet ones may not recognize their leadership at all. In such cases, you may need to gently point it out to them. But whether or not they see it in themselves, it is often recognized by outsiders. By the time our youngest applied for college, he had amassed quite an impressive resume of leadership positions. But our oldest demonstrated his areas of quiet leadership by teaching classes to others, and during the full-tuition scholarship competition, he also came away with the big prize.

VOLUNTEER WORK

Colleges love to see students who give to the community, and students will also benefit from volunteer work. Encourage your children to volunteer for community service. This could be through a faith-based organization, in your local community, through a sports league, or just within your own neighborhood. The possibilities are endless. One way to find a good fit for your children is to encourage them to volunteer in their area of passion. Are they excited about gardening? Maybe they could volunteer with the local gardening club. Do they enjoy building model rockets? Perhaps they can volunteer with a local science camp and help others learn all about it. Whatever your child does that is helping others can count towards volunteering.

EMPLOYMENT

Students also become well-rounded through employment experiences, including internships and apprenticeships. Colleges will be impressed by students who demonstrate the skills needed to be employable, and your students will also benefit from work experience. Internships are a very popular option for homeschoolers to "test drive" a vocation or profession. Whether these are paid or unpaid internships, they can be valuable, if only for the insights they provide. Students who successfully complete an internship may even eventually land a full time position at the same company. But even if they don't, internships can yield some valuable letters of recommendation used for college admissions. Finally, apprenticeships are a wonderful way for students to get some work experience. These opportunities often grow out of the passionate interests that develop as students reach the teen years, and begin to discover more about themselves. All of these employment experiences will show the colleges that your student has what it takes to succeed in the real world.

> *Help your student demonstrate leadership, volunteer work, character, self-motivation, and socialization.*

SOCIALIZATION

Homeschoolers have the advantage in socialization, since they spend their childhood socializing across a broad spectrum of ages, classes and cultures. They are not limited to narrow socialization, segregated by age and status common in a typical American high school. Consequently, when they are called on to interact with adults in the college admission process, they often feel right at home.

Socialization was, in fact, the deciding character feature when my boys brought home two full-tuition scholarships. Every applicant invited to the full-day scholarship competition had great grades and test scores. The college admissions staff told us that they were looking at social skills as the deciding criteria. How well did these young scholars interact with one another, with the faculty, and with the staff on campus when they thought no one was looking? This seems so ironic when a common question about homeschooling is, "What about socialization?" My homeschoolers took two of the ten scholarships awarded, based on socialization! Socialization is important to colleges, so make sure you demonstrate your student's accomplishments in this area!

CHARACTER

Closely related to socialization is character. Colleges want to admit students with strong character who will go on to reflect well on their alma mater. How well have your family values been absorbed by your kids? Growth in character development is directly correlated to time spent with your kids. The "quality time" is not nearly as important as "face time." Face time can be accrued by the bushel load when you are teaching your kids for hours a day at home, shaping and molding their character day by day. The reason you don't hear about the negative effects of peer pressure in homeschool families is that the "peers" are typically siblings who are all being nurtured by the same loving set of parents.

In college admissions, character may come through best in the application essays. Encourage your teens to write about experiences that highlight their character. Brainstorm with them on the ways that they have given themselves away to others during their childhood and adolescence. Did they come with you when you volunteered at church or in the community? If so, what did they learn? Did they ever visit shut-ins with you? How did that affect them? Character is one of those traits that is caught rather than taught, so make sure your students can convey these experiences in their application essays.

> *Socialization and character qualities can be demonstrated in college application essays.*

SELF-MOTIVATION

Self-motivation is one of my favorite attributes, because of the delightful serendipity involved. Busy with my household chores, I was unwilling to re-educate myself on higher-level high school math and science. After a while, it became clear that my children had to become self-motivated and learn higher-level math and science on their own, since my husband and I felt incapable of teaching it.

And they did learn it. With the right curriculum and video tutorials, my boys basically taught themselves calculus and physics. The results were twofold. First, they learned how to be self-taught. Second, they experienced the satisfaction associated with doing it independently. When you encourage self-reliance and self-teaching, you are doing your teen a favor that will pay dividends when they go to college. Ironically, a favorite expression university professors use with their freshman students is, "I am not your parent." This is supposed to underscore the point that no one will be nagging the students to complete their work. If your student already knows how to learn on their own, they will start college with a tremendous advantage over their spoon-fed peers.

IMPERFECTION

Can you really have it all? No! Although it is important to be well-rounded, please remember that nobody has it all. When you fill out college applications, it becomes clear that your student may excel in one thing and not another. Don't despair. My students had great SAT scores, but they only had tiny amounts of volunteer work. They were employed and involved in sports, so there was hardly any time for community service. My son would occasionally play his piano at nursing homes or at church, but volunteer work was really not our area of strength. Nobody has it all. If your students are strong in some areas, but not so strong in others, that's okay. It just means they are human!

FACING FAILURE

When you complete a college application, one of the things they ask for is a list of "activities and awards." In addition to being a way for you to help your kids stand out from the crowd, there is another, little appreciated aspect of this exercise: what you record is entirely up to you! The activity and awards list is only for successes, and failures don't go on the list!

- Worked at a fabulous job? On the list!
  - o 28 job interviews followed by rejection? NOT on the list!
- Awarded $200 in scholarship money by the community? On the list!
  - o Applied to 10 big-money scholarships, but rejected by each one? NOT on the list!
- Member of the wrestling team? On the list!
  - o Never actually won a match? NOT on the list!

No homeschool is perfect, and nobody has it all.

As homeschool parents, the failures of our children and ourselves are always right in front of our eyes. Our failures may look huge and discouraging. Failure is negative feedback, telling us what we do NOT do well, and an encouragement to keep trying. But in the face of failure, remember that we also have some success. Only things our children do well are put on the activity and awards lists. Don't list the bad things, just the good things! Remember to write down those wonderful activities and awards when they happen so you won't forget anything. You don't want to be facing the application form and suddenly draw a blank.

EXECUTIVE SUMMARY FOR BUSY PARENTS

PREPARE FOR COLLEGE AND LIFE

- Colleges want more than academics.
- Leadership, community service, and employment are important.
- Social skills, character, and self-motivation are valuable.
- Nobody has everything, no homeschooler is perfect.
- Failures do not go on the activity list.

CHAPTER 5

The PSAT for Fun and Profit

> *"But seek first his kingdom and his righteousness, and all these things will be given to you as well."*
>
> **Matthew 6:33**

> *"There's not a lot of money in revenge."*
>
> **Inigo Montoya,** ~ *The Princess Bride*

I was at my husband's softball game doing what I love doing—talking about homeschooling. My friend Kathy said to me, "I never took the PSAT in high school. I don't think I knew anything about it. Suddenly all my friends were taking it one weekend, and by then it was too late to sign up!"

Some things never change! Every year I talk to students who are in the same situation that Kathy was decades ago. They don't realize the test is available or that they should register. Or they're like the parent who recently told me, "The whole concept of PSAT totally overwhelms me!" If these parents aren't careful, they will be spending the day alone while all their friends are taking the test. Because it's only offered once a year, the PSAT is really easy to miss. The <u>only</u> way to make sure your student can take the test is to plan ahead. Sound intimidating? Let's break that information down into bite-sized pieces.

The complete name for the test is PSAT/NMSQT, which stands for Preliminary SAT/National Merit Scholarship Qualifying Test. Don't just think, "Wow! That's the biggest acronym I've ever seen!" The name can help you decipher the two functions of the PSAT. The first name, PSAT, means it's a practice test that you can take "for fun" to learn about the SAT. The second name, NMSQT, means National Merit Scholarship Qualifying Test, which means you can take the test "for profit" as a junior. Either way can benefit your student. Let me describe the functions of the PSAT so that you feel completely comfortable with it.

TAKE THE PSAT FOR FUN

The first name of the test is PSAT. That's the portion of the test that is the preliminary practice, or pre-SAT. You can take the test for practice in tenth grade. I call this aspect of the test the "take the test for fun!" aspect, because your scores don't matter. The results are just for you, with no negative repercussions at all. You can use it as a starting point before you study for the SAT. It is also used to estimate your SAT scores. The PSAT also provides firsthand practice for the SAT.

The PSAT measures reading, writing, and math. Each section is given a score of 20 to 80, with about 50 being an average score. When you get the results, add a zero to the score of each section and that will estimate your score for

Have your child take the PSAT in 10th grade for fun.

the SAT. For example, if you get a 62 in the PSAT reading, it is likely that you will get around 620 in reading on the SAT. When you get the score results, they will tell you what score range you are likely to have on the SAT, and that will help you find a college that will match the academic rigor of your student.

The PSAT also provides practice in taking standardized tests in a really rotten environment. In a sea of contagious diseases surrounded by tattoos, body piercings, and smelly teenagers, my sons sat in alphabetical order in a public school cafeteria. Certainly not as cozy as sitting around the kitchen table, but it was definitely good to see the setting of the SAT before the test counted! Taking a timed test around strangers is difficult. It's more difficult when you haven't practiced it first. The PSAT can provide practice in taking a test in "less than perfect" non-homeschooling conditions.

COMPARATIVE PURPOSE OF THE PSAT

Taking the test for fun will give you a percentile score, which compares your student against other bright college-bound students of the same age.

One of the few drawbacks about homeschooling is that we sometimes lack a sense of where our students fit with the norm. We know perfectly well the foibles of our students and their weak areas, but we often don't realize exactly how smart they are compared to the rest of the gene pool. This test can be a startling reminder of how efficient and effective homeschooling can be! Even struggling learners in a homeschool environment will often test average or above in standardized tests that compare them to other high school students.

The comparative function of the PSAT will also give you a helpful "data point" about your student if they simply do not test well. Nobody is perfect, and of course there are students that won't test well even though they may be quite bright. Taking the PSAT for fun, without the risk of negative repercussions, can help you determine whether to use standardized tests scores at all when applying to college. If your student does very poorly on the test, you can decide to use other things to document your homeschool achievement. Based on the "for fun" score, you could decide to submit a portfolio instead of a test score. You might also decide to take community college courses to prove college readiness. More options will be available when you have this information from the test.

The test is good for comparison because it's standardized, and that means that states requiring a test from homeschoolers will often accept the PSAT. Better still, this is a very inexpensive test, so you can save money if you use this test over some others. As far as tests go, the PSAT is an inexpensive way to meet your state's requirement if you must do annual testing.

COLLEGE SEARCH WITH THE PSAT

When your student takes the PSAT, direct them to check "yes" on the "Student Search Service" section, which will allow colleges to see information about your student, and you'll be well on your way to starting your college search. This is a good thing, because colleges will start marketing to your student. You can find out about great colleges this way, perfect-fit colleges that you otherwise might not have considered. Yours could be the student they want! They may be looking for a homeschooled student in Oregon who wants to be a doctor, or maybe they would take any

> *Taking the PSAT is great practice, can provide estimates for your SAT score, and can help with the college search.*

student from North Dakota just so they can get another state represented at their school. The student search can tell you which colleges want you. By the end of junior year, you should know which colleges you want to apply to, and receiving mailings from interested colleges can really help.

TAKE THE PSAT FOR PROFIT

The second name of the test is NMSQT. Although people rarely refer to the test by its second name, that's the part of the test that's "for profit." This acronym stands for National Merit Scholarship Qualifying Test. If you have heard of some students becoming a "National Merit Scholar" or "National Merit Commended Student," THIS is the test that they took. It's national because everyone can take it, even homeschoolers. It measures academic merit, meaning that a good score and quality academics will get you considered for the scholarships. It's a scholarship because students who earn the National Merit Scholarship are awarded financial aid for college: $2500 per year or more. And it's a qualifying test because it's just the beginning of the scholarship process; first you take the test and then there are other hoops to jump through after that. Only juniors can take the test "for profit." Although 10th and 11th graders can take the test, only juniors in high school will have their scores count for the NMSQT function of the test. Otherwise the test is just "for fun." The sophomore year test does NOT count towards the National Merit Scholarship.

A very high score on the PSAT/NMSQT means your student will at least be a "National Merit Commended" scholar. Your children don't have to be PERFECT in order to be commended. At the same time, a very high score is not a guarantee they will get to the next level (semi-finalist) of the National Merit Scholarship competition.

Getting a very high NMSQT score means that your child is smart, but it doesn't tell you exactly how smart they are. It means colleges may give them merit scholarships, but not exactly how much scholarship money. So you can see that a very high score on the PSAT will mean that your student has a special achievement (like National Merit Commended Scholar, or National Merit Semi-Finalist). Some colleges will award merit scholarships for that. But a perfect PSAT score will also usually mean a good SAT score, so those are tied together.

The National Merit Scholarship is a very competitive scholarship. Only the top performers in the nation each year move on to become "commended" scholars or "semi-finalists." Very few become National Merit Scholarship winners. Interestingly, the scholarship for becoming a National Merit Scholar is only a few thousand dollars. Granted, that isn't chump change, but compared to the cost of tuition, it doesn't go very far. The big scholarships come directly from the colleges. Students receive more money from colleges because they are National Merit Scholars than they receive from the award itself.

Since the PSAT is a practice test for the SAT, it can be "for profit" even if you don't win the scholarship. College financial aid is often tied to SAT scores, and anything that you do to raise that score can save you thousands of dollars. Raising your score can be as easy as practice, practice, practice. Taking the PSAT is the best way to closely resemble the SAT. It has the same environment, the same kids, the same noises, sights, and smells as the real test. Using this as a practice test can really save you money on college.

> *The PSAT is tied to the National Merit Scholarship when taken in 11th grade.*

REGISTER FOR THE TEST

The PSAT is given only one week in October every year at public and private high schools. Pre-registration is mandatory. Schools sometimes register kids in June before classes end for the summer. Other schools register for the test during the first week of school. Either way, you have to be registered! It's fairly easy to access as a homeschooler. You can find schools offering the test at the College Board website (www.collegeboard.com). The College Board gives the following instructions: "If you are a home-schooled student, contact a principal or counselor at a local public or independent high school to make arrangements to take the PSAT/NMSQT at their school. Be sure to do so well in advance of the mid-October test dates, preferably during the previous June." It's often as simple as calling your local public or private school and saying, "I'm the parent of a homeschool student. How can I register for the PSAT at your school?"

LEARN ABOUT THE TEST

The PSAT is simply a measurement of reading, writing, and math skills. The test is all "fill in the bubble," and there is no handwritten essay. You can bring a calculator, and the math section includes algebra and geometry. Because of that, taking the test "for fun" may not be much fun without having some algebra and geometry under your belt. The whole test requires just over two hours, but it takes longer because of breaks between sections. Each section of the test is graded on a 20 to 80 scale. Generally speaking, a score of about 50 is average, 60 is good, 70 is great, and 80 is perfect.

I only rarely suggest that you should have your child study for the PSAT. Instead, I like to think of it as being the "starting point" for studying for the SAT. Sometimes it might make sense to study for this test. If your child has a good chance at becoming a National Merit Semifinalist or Finalist for example, then studying for the PSAT might be that little bit they need to make it. For an anxious student, some practice may help them feel comfortable with the "process" of testing. If you are interested in studying for the test, you can find PSAT test prep books on Amazon.com.

When you register for the test, you will also get one free Official Student Guide to the PSAT, which includes a sample test. Make sure that you read that guide, because there is a lot of information in there that will help you. Make sure your students fill out the student information section as well. They will be asked questions about what classes they have taken in high school. Since homeschoolers rarely talk about that sort of thing with our students, sometimes kids don't have a clue what courses they have taken or what grades they have received from their parents.

EXECUTIVE SUMMARY FOR BUSY PARENTS

PSAT PLAN
- The PSAT is offered once a year.
- Take the PSAT for fun in October of 10th grade.
- Take the PSAT for profit in October of 11th grade.
- Register very early at the local high school.

C H A P T E R   6

Why Junior Year is Critical

"All hard work brings a profit, but mere talk leads only to poverty."

Proverbs 14:23

"Look, I don't mean to be rude but this is not as easy as it looks,
so I'd appreciate it if you wouldn't distract me."

Man in Black, climbing the Cliffs of Insanity, ~ *The Princess Bride*

As you get to work on your high school planning, I want to highlight the significance of your student's junior year. The focal point of junior year should be finding some colleges where you want to apply. Although you could quickly choose by throwing darts on a map or only looking at colleges that are close by, I don't advise it. An unsuitable college, mismatched with your family values, is a very expensive mistake. Additionally, missing major deadlines and tasks can limit college choices. Plan for a successful junior year so you can check each task off your list, and be ready to submit college applications in senior year.

PLANNING IS KEY

A mother called me in May seeking advice about college applications. "It's May of my daughter's senior year, and she wants to go to college. She is very gifted, but we have never done math or foreign language, and she hasn't taken the SAT or ACT. She hasn't looked at many colleges, but I know she is smart enough to get into Harvard, and I know homeschoolers can get in there. Can you help me?"

Surprisingly, I receive these calls each year. Unfortunately, May of senior year is not the time to begin thinking about college, especially if you want to go to an Ivy League school! Getting into college requires a lot of advance planning. There's a lot of work that needs to be done, particularly during junior year, because junior year is pivotal. In fact, careful planning and conscientious effort during junior year can compensate for a lack of attention earlier in high school. If you have a junior, follow these strategies now and you can be successful at the college admission game. If your student is younger, pencil these onto your calendar now so that you are ready for junior year when it's your turn to work hard!

TAKE THE PSAT

Make sure your child takes the PSAT in October of their junior year. Taking this test will give them valuable experience in taking a standardized test in a cafeteria with hundreds of sick, unruly, unkempt teenagers. Doesn't sound like much fun, does it? But the experience can help them be more comfortable when they take the SAT later in the spring. If your child is likely to become a National Merit Scholar, you may want to study for the PSAT before taking it.

Have your child take the PSAT in October of their junior year.

As I said in the previous chapter, the PSAT is only offered on one day in October. Put that date on your calendar now. During the week before the test, make sure your child gets enough sleep. This is no time for your family vacation to Disneyland! You want your child to be rested for the early morning test. On test day, provide a wholesome breakfast before they go. These things will help them be as prepared as possible to do their best.

ATTEND A COLLEGE FAIR

Fall of junior year is the time to attend college fairs. During that time, there are scores of college fairs being held across the country. Check websites to find a college fair, locate the date for each fair near you, and put the date on your calendar. It's best to attend more than one college fair to get the most information.

VISIT COLLEGES

In the next chapter, we will go into greater depth on the importance of g...
to a college fair. Once you have gone to one or more, try to narrow down you...
college choices and focus on visiting a few colleges. You can even take virtual
tours of some colleges, and meet with graduates and representatives without
leaving home. However, there is no substitute for a real college visit. Once
you narrow your list, try to visit as many potential colleges as possible while
classes are in session.

CHOOSE COLLEGES WHERE YOU WILL APPLY

Once you have visited all the colleges you can, spring and summer of junior
year are the time to make your choices. Where should your student apply?
If you are pinched financially, don't hesitate to apply to private colleges as
well as public ones. Private colleges often have more financial aid available
than public schools do, and can sometimes be even less expensive to attend
than a state school. Choose some "safety" schools, where you are fairly
confident of admission. Some should be a good fit, where you are likely to get in.
Choose some "reach" schools, where it would be a real stretch to be admitted.
All of the colleges on your list should be acceptable to you or they don't belong on
your list.

> *Spend time searching for a college during junior year. College fairs and college visits are important.*

DO GOOD WORK

When your student applies to colleges in the fall of their senior year, what the
colleges will see first are the grades and classes from junior year. Colleges will
be looking at coursework. Did the student goof off or work hard? Remember
that planning high school courses means covering some things every year.
Other subjects only need to be covered once or twice.

Hard work involves more than just schoolwork. It also means having a job,
doing volunteer work, being involved in groups, and pursuing leadership
opportunities. These are all important aspects of your student that college
admission staff will look at.

ahead of them as they prepare their student's high school admission process. Homeschool parents need to decide ve to colleges. Will they provide just a transcript? Perhaps ng list? Should they include course descriptions? I found mprehensive records: a transcript, a reading list, course ctivities and awards, and samples of work. Because we really needed financial aid, it was worth spending the extra effort to compile all the information that might possibly be required.

DON'T DROP THE BALL!

Plan, don't panic. Planning ahead can make a huge difference in the cost of college. I remember meeting with my financial planner last year. He was so impressed that my sons got full-tuition scholarships. He said, "My daughter is going to a private school, and wasn't given any scholarship money at all, and it's incredibly expensive. I found out recently that she was actually a candidate for a full scholarship based on her SAT scores. She didn't apply in time, and didn't list that college as her first choice, so she didn't get any financial aid!" What an incredibly sad story, to go from full scholarship to NO scholarship! But she dropped the ball! So learn about the colleges, plan ahead for homeschooling, and make sure you apply on time.

EXECUTIVE SUMMARY FOR BUSY PARENTS

TASKS FOR JUNIOR YEAR

- Take the PSAT in October.
- Attend a college fair.
- Visit colleges.
- Take the SAT or ACT in spring.
- Complete high school transcripts and course descriptions.
- Decide on colleges where the student will apply.

Finding a College

CHAPTER 7

The College Hunt

you had never eve
you a tremendo
identifying th
colleges ir
many c
effor

> *"Very truly I tell you, when you were younger you dressed yourself and went where you wanted; but when you are old you will stretch out your hands, and someone else will dress you and lead you where you do not want to go."*
>
> **John 21:18**

> *"While you're at it, why don't you give me a nice paper cut and pour lemon juice on it?"*
>
> **Miracle Max,** ~ *The Princess Bride*

There are two kinds of homeschoolers in the world: those who like hanging out with huge crowds of teenagers in vast warehouse-like buildings, walking for hours on hard concrete floors, and those who don't like college fairs. College fairs are like homeschool conventions, but instead of selling products that cost $100 or less, their product is a college education that may cost $200,000 or more.

You can go to one college fair or you can go to many, but college fairs are important. In no other venue will you get more of your specific college questions answered, all in one place. You can quickly filter out colleges that had been on your "maybe-list." You might discover hidden gems that

considered. Despite the crowds, college fairs will save
us amount of time, money, and frustration when it comes to
at "perfect-fit" college for your student. With large numbers of
attendance, going to a college fair is an inexpensive way to meet
olleges in the same location. College fairs are definitely worth the

ATTEND A COLLEGE FAIR

My husband called out, "C'mon kids! We're going to the fair!!" I let my sons
pile in the minivan with images of scones, roller coasters and disturbingly
large cows dancing through their heads. I didn't tell them it was the
college fair. Thank goodness we homeschool! Because they had so many
experiences attending homeschool conventions, their first college fair was
very comfortable.

Arranged like a homeschool convention, each booth at the college fair hosts a
particular college. And like a homeschool convention, most of the booths will
have giveaways of magnets, pens, and pencils. They will try to get you to take
their college "view book" and other literature about them. Non-college
vendors are represented as well. You may see *The Princeton Review*, *The
College Board*, or other organizations talking about college admission testing.

> *Prioritize going to a college fair.
> It is a quick and easy way to start
> your college search.*

Stop by those booths if you see
them, because they will often give
you a free sample test to take home
and try. Those vendors are trying
to sell you on their review classes,
as well as talk you into taking their
tests (The SAT, PSAT, or ACT, etc.).

FINDING A COLLEGE FAIR

There are a large number of college fairs each year across the country,
some huge and some small and specific. Major national organizations like
the National Association for College Admission Counseling (NACAC, www.
nacacnet.org) host many college fairs. NACAC college fair events are free, open
to the public, and chock-full of college representatives eager to talk to college-
aspiring students. If you're looking for specifically Christian universities, the
North American Coalition for Christian Admissions Professionals (NACCAP)

hosts many college fairs, and you can find more information on their website at www.nccf.us.

In addition to these large organizations, there are also smaller organizations that host college fairs. Some small college fairs are regional, and some are even specifically for homeschoolers. Some are specific to certain majors, like the Performing & Visual Arts College Fairs. There are also colleges that group together to host college fairs, like The Exploring College Options Consortium, which represents Duke, Georgetown, Harvard, Penn, and Stanford.

BRING YOUR CHILDREN

This isn't a fair just for parents! Much of it is centered on the students. Make sure your student dresses cleanly and neatly, but not necessarily dressy. You will see some teenagers that look bored or frustrated, but in general the colleges are there to meet the students. These events can sometimes have a "job interview" feel to them. Encourage your student to ask questions of the colleges. Your student needs to learn whether the college has the classes or major that they are interested in. Not all colleges have degrees in engineering or French, for example. Beyond academics, your student will want to know if their favorite activities are on campus. It may be important to your student that the college has a pool, a sorority, or a piano in the dorm. Students want to find out about academics AND the social life. Encourage them to speak directly to the college representative themselves and not hide behind you!

It's not all about the kids, though. Parents should ask questions too! After all, we might be financing this endeavor, and the colleges know that. Parents might want to ask questions specific to homeschooling. "What records do you like to see from homeschoolers? Do you have any special requirements from homeschoolers?" You can gauge their reaction to homeschoolers, and decide if you are willing to jump through their hoops—or not. You may want to ask what kind of financial aid is available. If you know your child's SAT or ACT scores, you can find out if the college has financial aid related to specific SAT scores. If your student has a weakness, you might want to ask about their area of weakness.

Parents and students should attend the college fair together.

At the fair, pay close attention to yourself and your responses to different colleges. Which colleges do you stop to greet? Ask yourself why you skipped a particular college. Were they too close to home? Too far away? Are they an art college, and your student is science-minded? If you're interested in a college, fill out the information cards that all the colleges have, unless you have decided that you are NOT interested in that particular college. As with a homeschool convention, coming equipped with home address labels can really speed this process up!

TAKE A CLASS

Just like at homeschool conventions, there are classes you can take at a college fair. Classes typically offered include SAT preparation, financial aid, admission requirements, college life, and other topics. For example, at the Pacific Northwest College Fair, I have spoken on "How to Find a College" and "How to Get Big Scholarships." Some of the information may be helpful to you, and you can just leave the rest behind. There are counselors available to speak to your unique situation. Keep in mind that counselors have a bias (as we all do), and they don't know your child. If they recommend a particular college, check it out for yourself.

When you leave the fair, bring home the bag. Sometimes you will find some great information about colleges and financing college in those bags, so it's worth looking through it. I found some great information about scholarships. My son found some concise articles about college life that he found helpful. You can read the brochures from colleges that didn't attend the fair. The purpose of a college fair is to determine which colleges you want to visit. Whether you add colleges to your list or eliminate colleges, you are still working toward your goal of finding the right college for your student.

FIND TRUE LOVE

Finding a college that really wants your student to attend their school can be a critical step towards getting good scholarships. The college fair is the place to find the college that will love your student almost as much as you do. Colleges are pretty up front about what they are looking for in students. I have heard representatives say, "We are in Georgia. We would love to have a student from Washington." Another college from North Dakota would have given anything for students from states other than North Dakota! Ask around at the college fair. Find out if your child has that one thing that a college really, really wants, and if they are willing to award your student a scholarship for it.

There may be a college out there who thinks your student is a perfect fit for them. Some colleges will, in fact, give students higher financial aid packages if they travel farther away from home. Other colleges will give you a full-tuition scholarship if you have the one skill that they are looking for. If a college needs a skilled debater really badly, they might give such a student a full-tuition scholarship. If they already have two debate team captains and a third applies, they will be less interested. One of our family friends was given a full-tuition scholarship to a school that was quite far from home. He received the scholarship because they needed a pianist to accompany their choir. If you can find what it is that they need and your child can meet that need, then that is a school you should apply to if you're interested in it.

> *After the college fair, carefully read information about the college and their financial information.*

ALTERNATIVES TO COLLEGE FAIRS

If you can't get to a college fair, there are other "first steps" you can take. The College Board has an online search engine that will help students find a college to visit. It's like a college matchmaking service, available online. You can search for colleges at www.Fastweb.com, through *US News & World Report*, and through other online searches.

You can search for a college, but you can also have a college come looking for your student. One way to do this is to have your student take the PSAT. This test will ask your student a series of questions about who they are, what their grades are, what classes they have taken, and what major they are considering. The colleges who want your type of student will then pursue you. Be aware, however, that when you do fill out this information on the PSAT, you will receive a tsunami of information in your mailbox. Look through it carefully to help you make your choices.

You can also search on your own for colleges. *U.S. News and World Report* publishes an annual edition of great colleges. The college's ranking depends heavily on the average SAT scores of their incoming freshmen. Alternately, the *U-CAN* website (www.ucan-networking.org) does not judge colleges by SAT scores. Visit the *U-CAN* website and read snippets about a particular college, and then go to the actual college's website as well. The *U-CAN* website helps give balance to the *U.S. News and World Report* information.

As you look at college information together, parents and student should be involved in making the first cuts. There are thousands of colleges out there, and you cannot possibly know them all intimately. Therefore, you need to make a first cut to decide which ones you are going to research. By asking yourselves questions, it will become fairly obvious when you find the type of college that is appealing. Do you want something rural or urban? Religious or non-religious? Do you want a college that has engineering or music? Do you need both? In this way, you can whittle down your choices.

> *Read the college information. Make the first cut together, and narrow the list of colleges that will require research.*

As you are comparing schools, it will be helpful to have a sense of your student's SAT or ACT score. If they haven't already taken it, give your student a sample test in both the SAT and the ACT. Take the test at home, and the score will tell you where they stand in relation to most of the students on each college campus. This will also give you an idea of whether your student can handle the academic load typical of that college. It can also tell you whether the college will be a safety school (where your student is very likely to get in) or a reach school (where your student might not be admitted).

Searching for information online is easy, but it's no substitute for face-to-face exposure. A college fair will help you get to know the colleges pretty well, and since they are coming to you, it's MUCH cheaper than flying around the country visiting them. Even if you are a bit nervous, GO to a college fair! You will be amazed at the wide variety of colleges to choose from, and you'll have a good chance of finding that perfect fit for your child. Some will offer perfect-fit scholarships, some specialize in learning disabilities, some will be very similar to your homeschool, and some will have that strangely unique mix of majors your child is interested in. Most colleges have come to understand homeschoolers, and a college fair is a great opportunity to find out what the different colleges want to see in the application package.

EXECUTIVE SUMMARY FOR BUSY PARENTS

HOW TO ATTEND A COLLEGE FAIR

- Bring your high school children.
- Students ask questions first.
- Parents ask about homeschool policy.
- Take classes when available.
- Decide on colleges to research more carefully.

C H A P T E R   8

Insights Beyond Brochures

"Test them all; hold on to what is good."
1 Thessalonians 5:21

"And wuv, twu wuv, will fowow you foweva…"
The Impressive Clergyman, ~ *The Princess Bride*

After you've started researching colleges, it's time to exercise the analytical part of your brain (which may have atrophied a bit over the years). The next step in finding the "love of your life" is comparing college statistics. As you look over the college materials you've collected, keep in mind this process is similar to filtering election campaign material. All of the information will be biased, because it is written by marketing professionals who are trying to influence you. Brochures will make each college look fabulous—whether it is fabulous or not. So, in addition to getting the college's viewpoint, you must go to a source with unbiased information about the college.

COLLEGE GUIDES

College guides are a great source of unbiased information about schools. Use *U.S. News and World Report's Ultimate College Guide*, the *Fiske Guide to Colleges*, *The Princeton Review*, Barron's *Profiles of American Colleges*, and the *College Board College Handbook*. Many more can be found at www.Amazon.com.

These resources will be helpful to you after you have made your first cut of colleges, and have your list down to a smaller number of schools you are interested in.

College Guides are as big as phone books, and you should use them just like you would a phone book. Look up specific colleges you want to know more about, and disregard the rest. You don't have to read the book from cover to cover, but make sure to read every word about the colleges you're interested in. Sometimes the nuances of the college are in the fine print.

> *Read college guides like a phone book–one small section about one individual college at a time.*

Look carefully at college statistics, because they can tell you a lot. One important detail is the college's average SAT/ACT score. This will help you determine whether your student is likely to be accepted by this college and where they will fit in the student population. Also note the graduation rate for a college, which will tell you whether the average student actually graduates in four years. If the average student takes more than four years to graduate, it can make a huge difference in how much that college will ultimately cost.

The "employment rate on graduation" gives you the percentage of students who are employed upon graduation. This is important to know. If your student takes out a college loan, a higher likelihood of being employed at graduation will make a big difference in whether they can pay a loan off quickly.

The graduate school admission rate is significant regardless of whether your child is interested in graduate school. This statistic can shed light on the quality of advising. Can students who want to go to law school get in? Do the college advisors prepare students well enough to continue their education if they so choose? Similarly, the percentage of graduates who go on to graduate school will tell you about the academic preparation of the college's graduates.

College statistics can also tell you about money, and the relative cost of college. Paying for college is a lot like buying a car. Hardly anyone pays sticker price for a car. Likewise, not many people pay sticker price for college. Use the statistics to help you compare the relative value of the colleges. The reference guides may include statistics indicating the average financial aid package for incoming students or the average student loan. Compare all these factors to get a rough estimate of the overall college cost, which will be helpful when comparing colleges.

My students received full-tuition scholarships from one college. However, other private schools still offered them excellent scholarships based on things like SAT scores, grades, and intended majors. At the same time, at the publically owned University of Washington, they were offered an extremely low scholarship each quarter. When you do the math, you can see that the cost for public and private schools can ultimately be very similar. Don't ever be afraid to look at private universities, because the actual cost to attend can be very similar to public universities.

HOW MANY COLLEGES?

It is typical for most students to apply to six or seven colleges. However, if you need a big, big scholarship, you could ultimately save money if you apply to more. It's hard to know up front exactly which colleges will value your child so much that they will be willing to offer you scholarships. If you can come up with a group of colleges you think are likely to award your student a scholarship, and you have a real variety of state schools and private schools and schools far away, then consider applying to all of them. Once you receive your acceptance letters, you can compare all the scholarships each college is willing to award.

> *Most students apply to six or seven colleges. If big scholarships are necessary, consider applying to even more. Apply to a minimum of three schools.*

When you decide on the colleges your student will apply to, do not be deterred by the price of the application fee they charge, which typically ranges from $50-100. It seems like a lot, but if your "true love" is the last college you apply to, and they accept you and give you a full-tuition scholarship, which means saving $100,000, it will be worth the investment. Don't be penny-wise and pound-foolish! Some colleges will waive the application fee if you visit the school, so make sure you ask. Some colleges will waive the fee by request, so don't be afraid to ask.

As a rule of thumb, the more desperate you are for college money, the more colleges you should apply to. Under no circumstances should you apply to only one college. That college may have their fill of applicants with your child's qualifications, or they may not provide any necessary scholarship money. Avoid heartache, and always apply to a minimum of 3-4 colleges.

EXECUTIVE SUMMARY FOR BUSY PARENTS

CAREFULLY COMPARE COLLEGE DETAILS

- Read college statistics carefully.
- Compare your child's statistics to the college statistics.
- Decide on a handful of colleges and plan to apply.

C H A P T E R   9

Visiting the Colleges

"Love is patient, love is kind. It does not envy, it does not boast,
it is not proud. It does not dishonor others, it is not self-seeking,
it is not easily angered, it keeps no record of wrongs. Love does
not delight in evil but rejoices with the truth. It always protects,
always trusts, always hopes, always perseveres."

1 Corinthians 13:4-7

"Sonny, true love is the greatest thing in the world—except for
a nice MLT—mutton, lettuce and tomato sandwich, where the
mutton is so nice and lean and the tomato is ripe.
They're so perky, I love that."

Miracle Max, ~ *The Princess Bride*

Now that you've reviewed college statistics and narrowed your selection down to a few candidate schools, it's time for a visit. Keep in mind that you are trying to find the "love of your life." People would not immediately marry a person without first getting acquainted. Similarly, visiting is an important step in the college search process. Colleges can look very similar on paper. The brochures they send you will be full of sunny days and beautiful fall leaves.

Even the statistics may look exactly the same from college to college. The truth is you don't know what a college is like until you visit.

When should you visit? Early and often! Your student's freshman and sophomore year is NOT too early, although it's most common to visit during junior year. Some colleges keep records of how often each prospective student comes to visit, and if you decide a particular college may be "the one" and you've visited them four times, they will look at this very favorably and value you more because of it. While spring is the typical season to visit colleges, any time of year is fine. When you decide to visit, find out if they have special visit days that offer programs for potential students. They might also have a program for parents about financial aid, or academic preparation,

> *Visit colleges during junior year or earlier.*

etc. It can be equally important to see what a campus is like on a regular day. This will give you a more accurate picture of the school, not just what they want you to see when they know a hundred high school kids are coming.

CALL AHEAD

Whether you go on a special day, a regular day, or an overnight visit, you should sign up with the admissions department and let them know you're coming. Remember, you are trying to make them love you too, and when you tell them you are coming, they pay attention. It is very easy to register with admissions. Most college websites will have a place to contact admissions and register for a visit. All the colleges I looked at were very similar in this regard. Don't miss this opportunity to let those colleges know you're interested in them!

MEET ADMISSIONS REPRESENTATIVES

Keep in mind you're looking for a college to love, and one that will love you back. Therefore, when visiting a prospective college, your student should dress neatly and be clean, pleasant, and charming. The school will likely be watching you just as closely as you are watching them. In addition to being clean, neat, and engaging when you visit, students should make a point to talk to the college admissions staff. While it is easy for parents to take control and run the show, this is actually a mistake. This is the time your student should do most of the interaction. When you meet with admissions, they may want to sit down with you to go over the records you have brought. Many times they like to see some homeschool records, and will give you feedback, which can be very helpful to have before you apply.

TAKE A CLASS

Prospective students are usually asked if they want to go on a classroom visit. This is a great opportunity to get to know the college better, so don't miss it. Try to choose a class that interests your student. If they are thinking about engineering, take an engineering class. If they love math, take a math class. If they have no idea of their interests, then take a general freshman level class, so they can see what their first year of school will be like. Try to meet with a department head, which can be helpful if you are looking at a specific major. If your child wants to take choir, for example, arrange to meet with the head of the music department.

TAKE A TOUR

Most colleges will also provide a campus tour. Keep in mind that the tour guide will usually avoid anything under construction or run down, and will only show you the places that make the school look good. Throughout all of these activities, you and your student should be taking notes. Write down the details (names, classrooms visited, impressions, strengths, concerns, etc.). Later, I will explain how this information will be useful for your student when writing college application essays.

During college visits, use all your senses: sight, hearing, taste, touch, and smell.

USE YOUR SENSES—INTUITION!

When you are visiting, use all of your senses as you walk around. Initially, pay attention to your gut instinct about the college. Does this college seem like a positive environment? Is it a place where you can picture your child living for four years? Pay attention to the responsiveness of the staff, which can fall under the category of intuition. Not every college will have a responsive staff, or handle miscommunication well. Can you get what you need for your child?

USE YOUR SENSES—SIGHT!

Look around the campus. Do the students appear happy? Are they smiling? Is it a pleasant atmosphere? Look on the ground. Is there a lot of litter? This can indicate whether students take pride in their school. Are there cigarette butts on the floor or around buildings?   One of my friends toured a public university and found marijuana joints on the floor of a dorm. These things might be important to you, so remain alert!

You can also ask specific questions, like what happens on weekends. Amusingly, a lot of this information is posted in the bathrooms, so read the bulletin board information and see what goes on during the weekend. Does it look like fun? There were a few colleges my husband and I visited where we thought, "Why can't they have these things for adults? This is like a cruise ship!"

USE YOUR SENSES—HEARING!

Likewise, make sure you are listening. Listen to student-to-student conversations. What vocabulary do they use? Read the conversations in the student newspaper. Are they respectful? Are they laced with profanity? Get a sense about the quality of the student discussion, even in the student newspaper. You can discover amazing things by listening to the professors as well. When they talk to students, do they seem caring? Do they know them by name? Listen to professor-to-professor conversations. This may indicate the respect professors have for each other and whether or not they will be good role models for your student.

USE YOUR SENSES—TASTE!

When you go on a college visit, the school will usually give you a voucher for a meal. It is important that you eat the school's food. Your student is going to be eating there three times a day, seven days a week, for nine months out of a year. The food must be edible! I have a student with severe food allergies.

If the college couldn't feed us on our visit, then we concluded they couldn't feed my son during his college years, and that college was crossed off our list.

USE YOUR SENSES—TOUCH AND SMELL!

Another important factor is whether a school is clean. Are surfaces reasonably clean to the touch or is everything gritty and grimy? Are there unpleasant odors where they don't belong? Do your student's cleanliness habits seem to be similar to the school you are visiting? More importantly, how does it make you feel about safety and security? Sometimes you will go to a college and see a lot of safety equipment. Perhaps this will make you feel the college is safe. It may, however, make you think they have a problem with crime. Pay attention to your intuition on this as well.

TAKE NOTES

When attending a class in their area of interest, make sure your student takes notes. Write down the name of the professor, what they talked about, and specific details of the class. This information will be very helpful later when writing admission essays, especially if you decide you love this college. On one of his admissions essays, my younger son wrote, "I took a class with Dr. Reinsma in the Honors Program. I loved how he brought out words in French that I recognized, phrases in Latin that I recognized, and he tied in art with the history that we were learning." Those were class details he was able to recall from his notes. The college application essay is the love letter to the college. Taking notes on your visit will help you with the details of that letter. You want to tell them how wonderful they are, in hopes that they will think you are wonderful, too.

> *Take notes during every phase of your college visit.*

SPEND THE NIGHT

When you have narrowed down your college choices, it's time to get serious. You now get to know the college, the living situation, and the student population. While it's not possible to do this at every college you visit, it's really helpful to spend a night in the dorms, and experience what student residential life is like. Your child will spend a huge amount of time in the community of the dorm, and it will influence them just as much (if not more) than the professors in their classrooms. Most colleges provide the opportunity to experience dorm life at some kind of overnight event, so when you have your college list narrowed down to the final few, pack your student's bags and move them in for the night.

Some friends of mine had a great daytime visit with their daughter at one of her top-choice colleges, so they decided to have her spend the night in the dorms. When they picked her up the next day they asked, "How did it go?" "I'm glad we came to visit, but I'm not going to college here," she said. "Why not? Weren't the girls nice?" they wondered. "Sure. They were great, but one of them was writing a 10-page paper for her Old Testament class. The assigned topic was why wives should not have sex with their husbands during their periods! Yuck! Ten pages on that?" She was disgusted and the parents were shocked.

The student-host admitted that her professor was a feminist, and that everyone had to write a paper on that narrow topic. My friends' daughter lamented that there were so many better, richer topics to write about in the Old Testament, and felt sorry for the guys who had to spend 10 pages on that topic! It was that overnight stay in the dorm that helped them see the "true colors" of this college, and determine that it was not for them. Make sure that your student has the opportunity to check out dorm life before committing to living there for a year or more.

SAY THANKS

When you are done with your visit, make sure your student writes a thank you note to the admissions staff and to the professors with whom they spoke. This simple act may develop relationships with people who ultimately turn into long-term mentors for your student. For example, if your student took a class in economics and got to know the professor, perhaps he could email them and say something like, "I need some support in my economics studies. Do you have any resources that you could share?"

Students should write a thank you letter after each visit.

Thank them with emailed or handwritten notes. Both are useful. If you don't intend to go to the school, then emailing a thank you note is fine. If you do intend to apply, send both an email and a snail mail thank you note. Some colleges keep a record of how many times you make contacts with them. For that reason, it can actually benefit you to write a letter by hand.

Visiting the college is a critical step in the assessment process. You want to know their views. You need to know whether a college with "Christian" as its middle name will match your family values. You can tell very little by the name of a college. You can tell only a little more from their marketing materials. You don't really know the personality of the college until you encounter it in person, during a college visit. If you are unable to visit before you apply, at least make sure to visit a college before you commit your student to four years there.

EXECUTIVE SUMMARY FOR BUSY PARENTS

KEYS TO COLLEGE VISITS

- Visit colleges during junior year or earlier.
- Call or email the college to register your visit.
- Meet admission office representatives.
- Attend a class the student might enjoy.
- Take a guided campus tour.
- Student should take notes during visits.
- Student should send a thank you note.

C H A P T E R   1 0

Tale of Three Colleges

"Do not be misled: 'Bad company corrupts good character'."

1 Corinthians 15:33

"Well, I'm not saying I'd like to build a summer home here, but the trees are actually quite lovely."

Westley, discussing the Fire Swamp, ~ *The Princess Bride*

When our boys were in their junior year, our family took an entire week and visited a different local college each day. This is the tale of our week spent visiting with three of these colleges. Each school was a private, faith-based university, and they all looked very similar on paper. They all had beautiful photos in their marketing materials, and similar statistics in the books. My hope is that our experiences will underscore for you the importance of visiting colleges before making a final decision.

COLLEGE A

This college had beautiful pictures on the marketing brochures they sent us, and looked exactly the same in the statistic books as the other two colleges we visited. When we arrived, we found that the college itself looked quite lovely, but it was near a prison, and surrounded by a crime-ridden neighborhood.

When we began the tour, we found that the school was performing a sexually provocative play in the building that had formerly been the chapel (now converted into a performing arts center). On the building, the word "chapel" was almost entirely obstructed by the banner announcing this play. The symbolism was breathtaking. My students were stunned to see the name of this play in print, so large, as it was not the type of language normally associated with a chapel. We found that the student newspaper used obscenities in their discussions about this play. The words in print were shocking.

> *Colleges may look the same on paper, and be completely different in person.*

The college was having "Healthy Bodies Week," and as a nurse and believer in healthy bodies, I was thrilled. However, their "Healthy Bodies Week" included explicit demonstrations by Planned Parenthood. They offered a program called "Sex and Scones." I wasn't thrilled about the association made between food and casual sex, especially for my perpetually ravenous boys. It may have been "Healthy Bodies Week" but we noticed large numbers of students smoking on campus. I am not used to being around large crowds of smoking teenagers, and this really surprised me.

We were very surprised by the conversations we overheard on campus. While waiting for our students to come out of a classroom, we heard the religion professor say to the philosophy professor, "Let's go out and get drunk. It must be 5 PM somewhere in the world." This was spoken right in front of my husband and me, with lots of students milling about. It's pretty obvious that we are parents, as we really do not look 20. We thought it was a bad example for the students.

When we looked around, we also realized that although the kids were dressed normally, no one seemed happy. Most students were walking around with their heads down. Very few were smiling, not even our tour guide! To top off the whole experience, I actually ate spoiled ham in the cafeteria. Yuck!

College A was thereafter known to us as "Appalling."

COLLEGE B

For this college, "B" stands for "Bureaucracy." I noticed the bureaucracy immediately upon entering the admissions department. There were ceiling-high double doors that were locked, apparently to keep parents and students away from the staff. We waited in a sterile environment for our turn with the counselor. He came out to us and we sat in a small glass room in the alcove, like a fishbowl. We never saw his office or developed a rapport.

This university lost the reservation for our visit. We had applied for a reservation online, and received a confirmation. Nevertheless, they lost the information stating when we were supposed to be there. The bureaucratic rules around classroom visits prevented my students from sitting in on the class they wanted to hear. They had to settle for a class that was not interesting to them.

> *These had the same statistics, but College A was appalling, and College B had an impenetrable bureaucracy.*

When touring the engineering department, I asked a professor, "What have your students done after graduation?" He could not name a single student he had taught, or any jobs they had landed, or any projects they had done. I was amazed he knew so little about his students and didn't seem at all embarrassed about it. It was not a big college.

We noticed the staff had an agenda with visitors. When they found out that my son participated in summer swim league, they were entranced. They didn't care about his chess experiences; they didn't care about his engineering interests. They didn't seem to care about anything except his swimming. It was all they could talk about. "What strokes do you do? Did you go to the State championship?" They didn't seem to recognize that my son wasn't at all interested in swimming in college. They didn't see him as a person; they only saw him for what they wanted from him. We left that day convinced no one noticed we'd been there. We called this place "Bureaucratic College."

COLLEGE C

Like **College A**, this university also had "Healthy Bodies Week" while we visited. There was a lot of nervous laughter from my boys as we walked to the admissions department. I was wondering what inappropriate things I would be exposing my children to this time. We were not very excited about it. Surprisingly, this college's "Healthy Bodies Week" was all about nutrition, avoiding anorexia, and how to live in a healthy way with a healthy body image. What a huge relief!

I asked the engineering professor, "What have your students gone on to do?" and he was able to name many students. He told us where they were now, what their senior projects had been on, and how they acted on their first day at school. He knew where they were employed and what type of engineering projects they were working on currently. I couldn't believe that someone could remember that many details about so many students. He obviously knew some of them very well. We were very impressed. Our classroom visit was to an honors program. We noticed the professor taught the class with the sort of strategies we used in our homeschool. It seemed very familiar to all of us.

In the cafeteria, we noticed they publicized their achievement of "best cafeteria west of the Mississippi." It was true. The food was really good! My son with food allergies was gratified to see the peanut butter was sequestered to a special area, and all ingredients were clearly labeled on each dish. As we sat in the cafeteria, we looked out over the campus, and watched the students who were coming to lunch. They were all looking up, chatting and smiling. It didn't matter what they were wearing, they all looked happy! One notable couple went striding by. The gal wore heavy makeup and a mini skirt, and the guy was wearing all black with heavy chains. They were smiling and laughing, perfectly at ease with the more conservatively dressed students. They all looked happy. We felt like that said a lot about how accepting and loving as a group this college was, and we really liked that.

> *College C was filled with smiling, happy students. The last college we visited was a perfect fit for our students.*

Overall, the school felt welcoming and familiar. Hence, we dubbed College C, "Comfortable College."

NOT THE SAME

There was an amazing contrast between these three colleges. Remarkably, they all looked the same on paper. They were all faith-based institutions of a similar size. But visiting each of them clearly showed us the differences not immediately apparent in the brochures.

This experience helped us decide that some of our "maybe" colleges were actually "no way" colleges. We found the "love of our life," and they did love us as well. When we were done homeschooling, they valued what we had done. They loved my transcript even though it was a plain Word document I made myself. They appreciated that we gave our kids a homeschool diploma. They understood our homeschool to the point that they gave both of our students 4-year full-tuition scholarships. We loved them, they loved us, and our students are now graduates from a college that fitted them perfectly. And they all lived happily ever after.

EXECUTIVE SUMMARY FOR BUSY PARENTS

KEY CONCEPTS TO REMEMBER
- Colleges may appear similar on paper, yet be dramatically different in reality.
- A college visit is the only way to know if a college is a good fit.

CHAPTER 11

Ivy League Aspirations

"Be strong and courageous. Do not be afraid;
do not be discouraged, for the Lord your
God will be with you wherever you go."
Joshua 1:9

"Am I going MAD, or did the word 'think' escape your lips? You
were not hired for your brains, you hippopotamic land mass."
Vizzini, ~ The Princess Bride

Homeschoolers are admitted to all of the Ivy League schools and military academies. In fact, it often seems that being homeschooled is the easy part of Ivy admission. The hard part is everything else! It is difficult to meet the requirements that all applicants must have. There is also a certain amount of luck involved. Almost every applicant is extremely smart, and those are the people you are competing against for acceptance.

Where your child goes to college is a very big decision, with a lot of factors to weigh. Some parents are concerned about the liberal bias at Ivy League and upper echelon schools. There are other really good schools, and there are also big financial concerns as well. However, in my experience, it's the parents who know what's best for their child, because they know the full story, everything about their child's situation. Others may loudly declare what "should" be done and where your child "should" go, but usually they don't know your child's full situation, and therefore can't really make an accurate judgment.

Don't listen to other parents. They are very busy making their own choices, and they don't have time to get all the information about you and your child. Think about whether your child wants to go to an Ivy or elite school and then find the right fit. Know what's right for your student, and don't make decisions based on just because you feel like you should.

Admission to Ivy League universities and military academies requires a lot of work. Start with a gifted student with a hard work ethic. Add plenty of parental effort, particularly regarding high school records. Provide rigorous academics and extremely high test scores. Demonstrate leadership and long-term activities that are measurable. Prove student passion in something outside academics. Submit a fabulous essay and great letters of recommendation. The child must have wonderful interview skills, and be actively involved in volunteer opportunities. When you have it all and more, then you still need luck.

> *Admission to elite universities will require you to plan ahead. These schools look for very well-rounded students, and often have unique requirements.*

ADMISSION RATE

The "true" Ivies are Harvard, Yale, Columbia, Princeton, Dartmouth, Brown, Penn, and Cornell. They all have extremely low admission rates; sometimes less that 6% of the extremely smart and gifted students are admitted. Your child may have done everything perfectly and met all the requirements, and still have a 10% chance of admission.

CHECK POLICIES

Many of the Ivy colleges have specific tips and policy pages for homeschool students. For example, Princeton's website suggests that the more you can document and describe, the better. They want parents to feel free to go beyond the questions on the application forms, or skip questions that don't apply because of homeschooling.

Don't get so focused on homeschool admission that you miss the bigger picture. Read the application information for all students and make sure that you're very familiar with their requirements and suggestions, and then get the tips for homeschool students so that you can feel comfortable in putting your homeschool on paper.

LETTERS OF RECOMMENDATION

Most Ivy League institutions want letters of recommendation or references from three different adults who are not family members. They want these letter writers to comment on intellectual curiosity, academic preparation, academic promise, or extra-curricular involvement. Consider how you can encourage activities that will help provide those letters of recommendation. Some prefer to see letters of recommendation from instructors who have taught in a classroom setting. In this instance, you may want to provide what it is they prefer by utilizing dual enrolment at a community college if it will increase your chance of admission.

SECONDARY SCHOOL REPORT

Even so, Princeton clearly expects that the homeschool parent will complete the secondary school report about the student's high school academics. The secondary school report is completed by the person who is most responsible for homeschooling, which would in most cases be mom or dad, so don't be afraid. They do also like to have references from somebody who has known your child in an academic context, who can speak to the academics of the child.

COMPREHENSIVE HOMESCHOOL RECORDS

Ivy colleges want to see that a student has taken challenging courses and done rigorous study. They want a traditional transcript with course grades, and an outline of your high school curriculum with a reading list. Having comprehensive homeschool records and a normal-looking transcript is very important.

> *Provide comprehensive homeschool records and a clear transcript.*

They request a detailed accounting of the entire curriculum undertaken during the last four years of high school. They want a list of all subjects, all books, and all learning resources, so "comprehensive" is key to your homeschool records for Ivy applications.

EXTRA TESTING

All applicants are required to take the SAT or the ACT with writing, and are required to have two SAT Subject Tests. Often, homeschool applicants will provide more tests to demonstrate their academic breadth. Without grades from a traditional school, Ivy colleges often suggest that a child take more AP or SAT Subject Tests. Taking additional tests is very important, because there are so many bright, gifted, driven children who apply that it's difficult for admissions staff to make a decision without actual numbers. Tests will give them additional numbers.

Dartmouth says students can demonstrate language proficiency with an SAT 2 Subject Test or an AP exam. Read these suggestions carefully. These tips on admission policies mean they want you to demonstrate your proficiency. In this instance, don't read such things as a suggestion; carefully consider them to be an unspoken requirement.

HOLISTIC REVIEW

Many colleges, including the Ivy schools, advertise a holistic review process. This means they will read your whole application and see the whole student. It implies they won't make a decision based on the numbers alone, but will recognize that each student is unique.

COMMON APPLICATION HOMESCHOOL SUPPLEMENT

When submitting the Common Application to a college, homeschool students should complete the "Homeschool Supplement" as well. This form asks about your homeschool philosophy and why you chose homeschooling for your child. It also asks you to explain your grading scale or other methods of evaluation. The space for your answer is very small, so there is no need for a long description. There is no right or wrong answer; schools just want to know a little more about your student's education. For example, you could explain that you teach for mastery, choose literature-based or hands-on curriculum, or use cooperative classes.

The second part of the "Homeschool Supplement" is actually a transcript, which includes four blank lines for every subject. For homeschoolers, this can be frustrating, because gifted children may take more than four English, science, or history classes. When it is impossible to fit everything on these four lines, begin with the most important and academic courses. Your homeschool transcript will provide the remaining information that doesn't fit here. The school will get all your information; this form is just where you put the highlights of your own one-page homeschool transcript. (Make sure that your own comprehensive homeschool records give detailed course descriptions of everything.) The bottom of the "Homeschool Supplement" asks for the supervisor's name, which is you—the homeschool parent.

ELITE SCHOOLS

Some public universities are also very elite, and may be considered Public Ivy schools. There may be an elite public university in your own backyard, and it can be tempting to think your local school will be easy to get into. Make sure that you're familiar with the requirements of the school where your children are going to apply, even if it's in your backyard.

Beyond these universities, there are a surprising number of other elite schools. Wheaton is often called "The Christian Harvard." Other prestigious schools with low admission rates include Stanford, Notre Dame, Duke, Vanderbilt, and Massachusetts Institute of Technology. There are also really elite schools for every kind of major or specialty. And there are many other schools that are even more difficult to get into than the true Ivies.

Your local university may be considered an elite college. Do not assume admission will be easy.

MILITARY ACADEMIES

US military academies are incredibly elite, and include the Military Academy at West Point, the Naval Academy at Annapolis, the Coast Guard Academy at New London, and the Air Force Academy at Colorado Springs. If your child wants to attend a military academy, it is at least as difficult, if not more difficult, than getting into an Ivy League school. As with other elite schools, the easy part is often the academics. The difficult part is meeting the other requirements. One major difference with military academies is that they require a nomination from your member of Congress in order to be considered for admission. They also require proof of physical fitness. You can't just be physically fit; you have to prove physical fitness.

The military likes rules, and they provide plenty of rules and structure regarding their academic requirements. They require pre-calculus or calculus, chemistry with lab, physics with lab, and four years of English. They want to see two years of foreign language, and specifically state that this should include speaking, syntax, and grammar skills. For history, applicants should have one year of US history and one year of European world history. Applicants should also have taken computer keyboarding. Be sure to include these details in your course descriptions. Read all requirements carefully, and title your classes on the transcript using the same words they use on their requirements. For example, they want to see an Intro to Computer Keyboarding, so use that as your class title, rather than calling it "Computer Technology." Be specific and give details, but use their words when possible.

Course descriptions are required not only for admission, but also for nomination. Homeschooled students must provide a transcript with course title, class title, length of course, date of completion, grading scale, and GPA. Course descriptions go beyond that information, and should be very detailed.

Extra-curricular activity is extremely important. Annapolis even provides a suggested list to consider. For athletic activities, they look for extra-curricular activities and proof of physical fitness. Consider activities like track, cross country, 5K-10K races, basketball at the YMCA or the Boys' and Girls' Club, soccer through a community or club organization, lacrosse with organized matches, swim team, tennis, rowing, gymnastics at a local club or competition, and baseball summer league affiliated with Babe Ruth, Little League or American Legion.

> *Military academies have specific requirements for academics, leadership, and demonstrated physical fitness. Applicants must be nominated by a member of Congress*

For non-athletic activities, they suggest participation in leadership or church youth group, Junior Achievement, Boy Scouts, Girl Scouts, Boys State, Girls State, and music participation in a local band, orchestra, or theater. School representatives often mention Boy Scouts, Eagle Scouts, Civil Air Patrol, and similar youth organizations.

The Air Force Academy clearly indicates you need to have the whole package. They review each application carefully. Sixty percent of the application is based on academics, which is a combination of SAT, ACT, and GPA. Twenty percent is based on extra-curricular activities, either athletic or non-athletic. Twenty percent of the decision is based on an evaluation by the admission liaison officer, including the physical fitness test and the selection panel review.

APPLYING TO ELITE COLLEGES

When you plan to apply to an elite school, the most important thing to do is to start your research early. These schools are looking for very well-rounded students, but they will often have unique requirements. You need to meet the requirements, but you also need to exceed their expectations. Research the details of each school, visit if possible, and attend a college fair or an event to meet the school. Attend online and live events. Get as much information as possible.

EXCEED EXPECTATIONS

Try to exceed the written and implied expectations of each university. Find out what core classes they expect, remembering that some of the requirements are very specific and others are very broad. Find out what tests and scores are required, as well as which ones are expected, even if they aren't specifically required. As much as it is possible, find out what they want and give it to them. Keep your student's courses challenging but not overwhelming, so they can maintain an A-average. To gain admission to an elite school, your student needs a fabulous GPA, but she must also understand what she is learning in order to maintain those high grades. Particularly when it comes to classes at a community college, she must maintain an A-average. You can use AP classes, but remember that any student can take an AP test. You can teach the subject at home and take the test without having the AP class. Not all kids are suited to AP tests, so if you don't have a lot of these, consider SAT Subject Tests as an alternative. Essentially, elite schools care about numbers. They ask questions about grades and tests. They consider AP tests, SAT Subject Tests, SAT and ACT scores, and GPA. Make sure your student's numbers are superior.

CONSIDER COMMUNITY COLLEGE

Elite universities seem to prefer some community college courses. To them, such courses demonstrate proof of academics, and document how well the student functions in a classroom setting. Find out exactly what the school wants and prefers. Community college can be a "Rated R" environment, so carefully check requirements and options to make sure it is a good fit for your student.

DEMONSTRATE PASSION

Elite universities want more than activities; they want to see activities that demonstrate an actual passionate interest spanning multiple years. This can be satisfied through work experience, leadership, or volunteer work as well, but they definitely want to see activities. These outside experiences will be a great source for letters of recommendation as well.

PROVIDE POLISHED RECORDS

Homeschoolers tend to be a very private bunch and don't like to share personal information details, but universities need to know every little thing about a prospective student that might be helpful in making an admissions decision. They want to know if your homeschooler is used to a hard, rigorous education and academic experience, and whether they will fit in with the school. Polished and perfect homeschool records are really important in order to give schools all the information they might need.

> *Elite universities want students who will thrive in an intensely academic environment. They look for very challenging high school curriculum and well-rounded, successful students.*

ESSAYS AND INTERVIEWS

Parents provide perfect and polished records, but students must provide perfect and polished essays. All applicants will be interviewed, and social skills are vital. These schools require a very intense work ethic in their students, which has to come from within the child. It's not something that can be directed or forced from outside. Prospective students must convey that they are highly gifted and uniquely talented, but at the same time also genuine and humble.

BACK UP PLAN

Everybody who applies may be well-qualified to go to an elite school, but few are ultimately chosen. Preparation for an Ivy League school or a military academy will result in great preparation for admission to other universities. Not everyone will be admitted to Ivy schools, so it's important to have a back-up plan that includes "reach," "fit," and "safety" schools. Ivy Schools are a "reach" for every student, no matter how gifted. Since there's no guarantee they'll get in to those schools, make sure your child also applies to "safety" schools, where they seem overqualified and are certain of admission. Also apply to some "fit" schools, where your child's SAT score is at the 50th percentile for the school and they fit in well with the school norms.

HARVARD AND HEAVEN

Some homeschoolers are concerned about the liberal or anti-Christian environment at Ivy League schools. Others may feel that it's a mission field they are called to. My belief is that parents know best. A shipwrecked faith can happen anywhere, not just at an Ivy League school, and not just in college. It can happen to wonderful parents, even while they're still homeschooling. Harvard or Heaven is a false choice. You don't have to choose between the two, and your place in Heaven is not determined by your alma mater.

Scripture does not mention Harvard, but it is clear about going into the world. Mark 16:15 says, "Go into all the world and preach the gospel to all creation." That was spoken to all the disciples, and there are no exceptions mentioned. It does not exclude Harvard or the military. Matthew 5:13-16 says, "Let your light shine before others, that they may see your good deeds and glorify your Father in heaven." All Christian adults are missionaries in life, wherever they live and work, even at Harvard. The Bible explains that each person is different, and can expect to live and work and serve in different ways. In 1 Corinthians 12:4-6 it says, "There are different kinds of gifts, but the same Spirit distributes them. There are different kinds of service, but the same Lord. There are different kinds of working, but in all of them and in everyone it is the same God at work."

It's not our beliefs that have changed, it's our children that have changed—they have grown up. It's no longer a verse that is misused with small children; rather it's a verse that applies to our children now that they are adults. 1 Corinthians 13:11 says, "When I was a child I spoke like a child, I thought like a child, I reasoned like a child; but when I became a man, I put the ways of childhood behind me." Children do grow up. It's important to know that we make choices and decisions as adults, and yet remain firm in our faith. Even if a college is not friendly to Christianity, there may be groups of Christians on campus. Look for the fellowship of believers where your student can feel at peace wherever they attend.

PREVENT HEARTBREAK

In the end, try to prevent the heartbreak that results from rejection. Carefully plan ahead, carefully keep records, and make sure that you have detailed notes about the colleges you're interested in. Check your requirements early, exceed expectations, make sure that you apply early so that you know the results soon, and then have a backup plan. Discuss the admission rate with your teenagers so they know that ninety percent of highly qualified applicants will be rejected. And then go for it!

> *Apply to reach, fit, and safety schools to avoid disappointment.*

EXECUTIVE SUMMARY FOR BUSY PARENTS

ELITE UNIVERSITIES ACCEPT AND REJECT QUALIFIED STUDENTS
- Start your research early in high school.
- Research requirements for admission.
- Research homeschool admission expectations and policies.
- Exceed expectations.
- Provide great homeschool records.
- Develop a back-up plan, and apply to other colleges.

Applying to College

CHAPTER 12

The Senior Year Home Stretch

"My only aim is to finish the race and complete the task the Lord Jesus has given me—the task of testifying to the good news of God's grace."

Acts 20:24b

"You know, it's very strange. I have been in the revenge business so long, now that it's over, I don't know what to do with the rest of my life."

Inigo Montoya, ~ The Princess Bride

A senior in high school has one major task: complete college applications. It sounds like it should be quick and painless, because it is only three simple words, "complete college applications." However, applying to college is a process, not a moment. Applications are not difficult, but they are very time-consuming. The whole process takes a lot of time to complete. Each university will have a unique process, unique forms, and unique requirements.

START EARLY

The single most important tip to college admission and scholarships is to apply early. Begin filling out college applications by the very first day of senior year or earlier. Be sure to check admission deadlines, because some encourage students to apply in July or August. If your child is going to do dual enrollment at a community college, it is particularly important to begin college applications during the summer before senior year. A very busy student taking college classes, participating in a demanding sport or performance event, may not have the time or energy to complete applications during their busy season. Colleges may provide admission and scholarships on a "first come, first served" basis, so applying early is an important key for success.

> *College application takes time. Start in September, or during the summer before senior year.*

APPLICATION ESSAYS

College applications require multiple essays that are self-reflective and technically perfect. Homeschool parents understand that "technically perfect" is difficult. These essays take a lot of time to write, edit, revise, and rewrite. It takes time to get input from others, and allow them to read and give feedback or suggestions. For many teens, "self-reflective" is difficult, and can even be terrifying for some. It often takes a long time to consider what a self-reflective essay might be. Make sure you plan plenty of time for pre-writing. If you begin writing these essays on the first day of senior year, you can put your other English curriculum aside for a while. During the time you are writing essays, your English curriculum could be a unit study on essay writing. College application essays will be thoroughly explained in following chapters.

COMPLICATED FORMS

Colleges can have some complex application forms with many questions, sometimes worded in strange ways. They usually will require letters of recommendation about your student as well. It can be difficult to decide who should write those recommendations, and the writers must be given plenty of time to accomplish the process. Once written, you must allow time for the letters to arrive at the colleges. All these things underscore the importance of organization and preparation!

INFLEXIBLE DEADLINES

College applications are remarkably similar to April 15th and paying federal taxes. There are firm deadlines, high expectations, fine print, and words you don't understand. Avoiding the task can create huge financial consequences. Plan ahead and spend plenty of time on it, making sure to start early so everything is ready by the deadline.

> *College applications are like paying taxes. The application deadlines matter.*

COMPLETE TRANSCRIPT

By the beginning of senior year, it is absolutely critical that you have completed your high school records. Your student's high school transcript must be provided to colleges by their application deadlines. The transcript should include classes your student will take during senior year. For example, if calculus is the plan for the year, put calculus on their transcript. Do not indicate a final grade for classes that have just begun. Instead, indicate that the grade is "To Be Determined" (TBD) or "In Progress" (IP). Even without those grades, the transcript must be ready to submit to colleges very early in the fall during senior year.

COURSE DESCRIPTIONS

Most colleges will ask for additional material beyond a transcript, so most homeschool parents will need to write complete descriptions of each high school class. These are particularly important when applying to selective colleges, when the student has a strong college preference, or if scholarships are critical. Including course descriptions can strengthen all applications, however, even if you're applying to a "fit" college. Course descriptions only need to include a paragraph about what you did, a list of what you used, and an explanation of how you graded.

HOMESCHOOL RECORDS

Some universities may require additional homeschool records beyond a transcript and course descriptions. They may request a reading list, which should include books read for school and pleasure. Some may ask for samples of work, and may even request those samples in the student's handwriting. They might request an activity and awards list or a resume. Some colleges may ask for a statement from the homeschool parent, or require a counselor letter that is completed by the parent. You might find it helpful to write a cover letter as an introduction to your transcript as well. Since there are a variety of things that may be asked for, make sure to plan ahead so you have the time you need to complete anything that is required.

REPEAT TESTS

In addition to completing college applications, another big priority for senior year is to compensate for any shortcomings in college admission tests. Repeat the SAT or ACT if the tests were missed or if the scores were poor and could be improved. If tests are needed, register for the first testing opportunity so the results are promptly available. If subject tests are needed, fill those requirements as quickly as possible.

FILL GAPS

Review the recommended courses for college preparation to determine if there are any major educational gaps. Small gaps, like a one-semester economics course, can be quickly filled if discovered early in the year. Major gaps, like foreign language, may need to be filled with community college, or explained on the application.

Before senior year, evaluate high school progress and fill gaps if necessary.

WATCH DEADLINES

Keep a master calendar and watch deadlines and details for each college application. Colleges can have some pretty unusual requirements, and can ask for some pretty strange things. Be sure that you give them everything they need and want. If they ask for a lab write up from a high school biology class, submit that. If they want a transcript in a signed envelope, do it that way. Find the details they want and give the details they want. Mark all deadlines and details on your calendar.

COMPLETE THE FAFSA

Complete the Free Application for Federal Student Aid (FAFSA) on January 1st of your student's senior year, or as soon after that as possible. In November of senior year, apply for a FAFSA PIN (Personal Identification Number), which will speed up the process of application on January 1st. The FAFSA is used to determine how much money the government believes parents can afford to pay for college. This long form will need to be completed each year, from senior year of high school until senior year of college. Financial aid is first-come, first-served, so the sooner you file your FAFSA the sooner a college can give you a decision about financial aid. Parents provide a financial status estimate in January, but must update the form after completing federal income taxes in April.

WEIGH SCHOLARSHIPS

After application, expect three waves of scholarships. The first wave is almost immediate, based on SAT, ACT and GPA. The second wave of scholarships is based on the FAFSA and perceived financial need. The third wave of scholarships is based on merit or other factors. The third wave may not arrive until May of senior year, or even later. Financially, the most difficult time for parents is between March and June. During these months, the student has received notice of admission. Students get excited, and parents know where the child wants to attend, but they have absolutely no idea how they can afford to pay for it. It can be a very challenging and stressful time. Parents and students can continue a dialog with college admission representatives. Be patient until you get that final wave of scholarships somewhere in between March and June.

> *Scholarships come in waves, not all at once. Students are admitted first, but financial awards may not arrive until much later.*

DRAMATIC CHANGES

Maturity happens. Parents can expect dramatic changes over the four years of high school. Consider the changes that occur between a newborn child and when they become four years old. Similar and equally dramatic changes occur during high school. Maturity will happen. Your child will be mature enough to graduate. Eventually they must become mature enough to leave home. Huge changes take place between freshman year and senior year, so expect those changes and be prepared for anything.

BE PREPARED

Teenagers change their minds. They may vacillate back and forth between, "I'm going really far away to college," and, "I never want to leave home, what a crazy idea." They change, and their situations change as well. In order to be prepared for these changes, try to plan ahead as much as possible. A teenager may balk at the tasks required during senior year. Senior students are often 18 years old and very close to adulthood. Sometimes adults don't do what their mothers tell them to do, and some seniors don't either (surprise!). Be prepared for teenagers to make adult decisions. At the same time, recognize that they may actually be immobilized by fear. Complete as many tasks as possible a year ahead, just for practice, in order to make the transition go smoothly.

EXPERIENCE SUCCESS

The best success comes to those who begin the process early. Hit the ground running on the first day of senior year. Start to work early on college applications so they are turned in as early as possible. "Second best" success is also possible. Many parents I know are unaware of the college admission process, and recognize their weaknesses very late in senior year. It is very difficult to experience success if you have not begun work on college applications until the middle of senior year. For families who find themselves in this situation, I have developed an emergency action plan to help you salvage senior year and avoid panic.

SENIOR YEAR LAST-MINUTE 12-STEP EMERGENCY NO PANIC PLAN

1. Drop all school and outside activities and work on applications.
2. Watch "Getting the Big Scholarships" and "Finding a College" (www.TheHomeScholar.com).
3. Locate a college fair, put it on the calendar, and commit to going.
4. Register for the SAT or ACT (if missing) and put it on the calendar.
5. Determine if college requirements have been met.
6. Drop unnecessary classes and replace with missing classes if necessary.
7. Take the SAT or ACT (if not taken in junior year).

8. Apply to 2 public and 2 private universities nearby.
9. Students complete applications and essays as required.
10. Parents complete homeschool transcript and records.
11. Turn in application first; transcript and test scores may follow.
12. Return to regular homeschooling when applications are complete.

EXECUTIVE SUMMARY FOR BUSY PARENTS

COMPLETE APPLICATIONS EARLY

- Applications require many self-reflective, technically perfect essays.
- Applications require multiple forms and have firm deadlines.
- Parents must provide completed, comprehensive homeschool records.
- Fill academic or testing gaps during senior year.
- Complete the FAFSA in January of senior year.
- Decide which college the student will attend.

CHAPTER 13

Homeschool Records Provide Proof on Paper

*"For we must all appear before the judgment seat of Christ,
so that each of us may receive what is due us for the things
done while in the body, whether good or bad."*

2 Corinthians 5:10

"We are men of action. Lies do not become us."

Westley, ~ The Princess Bride

Colleges want proof of the academic preparation of all their applicants. They need information about your homeschool in order to make decisions regarding college admission and scholarships. It is important to prepare homeschool records as neatly, thoroughly, and precisely as possible. Work on homeschool records every year, to reduce the workload and stress.

TRANSCRIPTS

Transcripts are a one-page overview of your child's academic record. Many admission and scholarship decisions are based on the transcript, so it's important to make it accurate. A homeschool transcript can demonstrate your student's strengths, depth, and individuality. It can combine all the wonderful educational experiences of high school into one centralized location on paper.

The transcript should include a title, like "Official Homeschool Transcript." It should include the student's name, gender, date of birth, parents' names, and expected graduation date. It might include the address of the student and the address of the school, even though they are the same.

GRADES

The transcript should include grades and a grade point average. Colleges do care about grades from homeschoolers. Some colleges prefer letter grades (A, B, C) and some colleges prefer number grades (4.0, 3.0, 2.5), and other college don't have a preference as long as grades are included. Many colleges will tie scholarship money to grades and GPA. If you give homeschool grades, you can access that scholarship money.

Without grades, colleges may ask you to provide grades, but if they don't ask, you may simply be ineligible for financial aid. I know some homeschool parents feel uncomfortable giving grades. Colleges, however, need to be able to quantify schools, and that's how they do it. I know some parents who have chosen to create a transcript without grades. Many have written me later to say it was a mistake, and to explain how much money they lost in scholarships because they did not give grades.

> *Grade Estimate:*
>
> *A = meets high expectations or matches high test scores*
>
> *B = Pretty good, likely better than peers*
>
> *C = Not very good, but continue to the next level*

Remember that public school teachers who give grades are also subjective humans. Like you, they can only do their best to provide grades they know to be honest and true. I encourage homeschoolers to do that as well—provide grades they know to be honest and true. Let the colleges handle it from there.

CREDITS

Colleges need to know the credit value for each class. A credit is a simple measurement of how much work was involved in the class. Approximately

120-180 hours of work is a high school credit. A class lasting half a year, or a textbook that says it is a semester class, provides one half credit. A whole year of work, at least 1 hour per day, or a whole high school textbook is one whole high school credit. Providing these measurements allows colleges to understand the rigor of a homeschool environment.

The transcript is an academic record instead of a character record. Other parts of a student's character will come out in different pieces of an application. A common misconception of high school transcripts is that they encompass all areas of homeschooling. However, making a homeschool transcript is not like scrap booking. There are some things in your homeschool that are not supposed to be put on a transcript. The transcript's purpose is for high school, and in general, it is for academics only.

> **Credit Estimate:**
> **1 full book = 1 credit**
> **1 hour per day = 1 credit**
> **1 semester book = ½ credit**
> **½ hour per day = ½ credit**

COURSE DESCRIPTIONS

When you prepare your student's records, I suggest that you document their work by providing course descriptions, which form the core of your student's comprehensive record or portfolio. Some colleges require these, and others treat them as optional. The person who is not concerned about college costs may consider submitting a simple transcript. It's definitely possible to be accepted to a college with simply a transcript and SAT or ACT test scores. But for most people, it's not just about getting into college; it's about being able to afford college. Therefore, most people need more than the minimum transcript and scores. Those things are important; you do need a transcript, and the content of the transcript matters a lot. However, it is also important to provide course descriptions with grading criteria, because they give more information about your homeschool to the colleges.

When a college provides scholarships, they are investing in your child based on their confidence that your child will succeed at college. The more you can convince them that your child will succeed, the more money they're likely to give you. Providing course descriptions and grading criteria will demonstrate the rigorous quality of your homeschool.

Course descriptions are not long lists of assignments and grading rubrics, and they are not a syllabus. Course descriptions should be limited to one page per course. They should include what was used and what was done, to describe the whole experience. Some family's descriptions will simply reflect studying a textbook. Other families might include textbooks, literature, and audios. For others, their courses will be described as more experiential, and include projects, experiences, and field trips.

Keep careful records, and try to format them in the way your colleges prefer. If possible, contact the college in advance to ask their preferences. When we applied to colleges, I took an example of one course description and carried it into the college admission office during our visit. I showed them the piece of paper and asked, "I have this much information in every class in our homeschool. Is this what you want?" They answered emphatically, "Yes!" One admissions officer told me, "I wish that every public high school student had course descriptions like this, because so many kids are coming to college and can't write at a college level. I always wonder what was included in their English classes."

READING LISTS

Colleges may seem very interested in your student's high school reading list, but why do they care? A reading list gives a snapshot of the student, so colleges will know more about their reading level, interests, and extracurricular reading habits.

A reading list includes any books read during high school, both books assigned for school and books read for pleasure. Review the curriculum used in your student's high school courses, and include any literature used for academic courses. Some parents even include textbooks, although that is not common. Books may be included on the reading list as well as in a course description. The list can include books of faith and devotionals, as well as any specialized reading or magazine subscriptions. I like to encourage students to include "every great book, average book, or stupid book" they read. With prolific readers, it may not be necessary to include every book, but to simply demonstrate a breadth of reading and the impression of a well-read, voracious reader. For reluctant readers, provide one list that encompasses all four years of

A reading list includes all books read during high school, whether assigned for school or read for pleasure.

high school. Colleges want to know a student's reading level and interests. Remember that it is a reading list, not a bibliography, and that most colleges prefer just a list with title and author.

It's a good idea to include a few classics each year. Colleges care that students have a balance of classics and popular literature, and have complained that some homeschool applicants have an over-emphasis on classic literature, whereas colleges want to see reading lists that include popular literature. Including current literature shows "socialization," so it is important to include reading for pleasure on your student's list.

ACTIVITY AND AWARDS LISTS

Colleges want to see passion in your child; they want to know the interests your child has pursued over his four years of high school, or activities he is truly committed to. A commitment to an activity over the years of high school can be a predictor of success in college. If a student has pursued an activity for four years, it's likely she will be successful in completing college. Your student's activities (along with any accompanying awards) should be listed on an activity and awards page, which you can submit with your other homeschool records. Highlighting your student's ongoing activities can also fill in any gaps on their transcript. After all, not all learning can be quantified through grades and credits. The activity list presents a third dimension of your child.

Colleges don't want cookie-cutter kids, or kids who look like all the other kids. Instead, they want students who will bring unusual and different skills, interests, and abilities to their college. It's important to keep track of all activities, sports, volunteer work, community service, and employment experiences on this list. When your student is asked on college applications about their activities, they only need to refer to their list.

Often a transcript may briefly mention a student's high school activities, highlighting the most significant ones, the year they were done, and the level of mastery. For example, the activity section of a transcript might look like this: Martial Arts 9, 10, 11, 12 – Black Belt 12. Martial Arts Assistant Teacher 9, 10, 11, 12. Your separate activity and awards list would then include much more detail on each activity, and might look like this:

Highline Martial Arts Academy

Martial Arts Assistant Teacher 9, volunteer 100 hours

Martial Arts Assistant Teacher 10, volunteer 100 hours

Martial Arts Assistant Teacher 11, volunteer 100 hours

Martial Arts Assistant Teacher 12, volunteer 100 hours

As you determine how to give your student credit for their activities and experiences, be careful to avoid "credit double dipping." It's fine to give them credit for an activity, but that activity should only count towards credit in one class. For example, I took Choir in high school, and received one music credit each year I took it. However, I didn't also count my work in choir as a part of my Music Appreciation class, and neither should you!

> *It may be appropriate to count an activity as a high school credit, but avoid "double dipping." Do not count an activity hour twice, or put it in two different credits.*

COURSE SAMPLES

When visiting colleges, be sure to ask them what they want in regards to records, and be prepared to provide it. Bring a few sample course descriptions, and ask whether they'd like to see them. Sometimes colleges will ask for some very unusual things. Each college you apply to might ask for something different! Therefore, make sure to keep several representative samples from each course your student completes. Don't keep everything, just samples. These could include writing, tests, quizzes, and finished projects.

Because most people apply to more than one college, it's helpful to keep about four samples of work from each class your student completes, in case you have to send originals to four different colleges. When colleges ask you for a sample, though, it doesn't have to be from freshman year. Likewise, don't feel like you have to give them a "representative" sample either. You can give them your BEST example from each course! Some colleges may not ask you for these samples. I had everything the colleges requested—and 99.9% of it is still in my binder! The important thing is to be prepared. Assume that colleges may ask for something, and then give them the best examples from your student's high school years. If they ask you for something like a science lab write-up, make sure you have it in your records so that you can reach in, grab it, and go. I have heard of colleges who want to see graded math papers or graded English papers, so it just pays to be prepared.

ADMISSIONS STAFF

When submitting application materials, make it as easy as possible for the admissions staff. Whatever they want, give it to them. It's important to stay on their good side, especially if you need a big scholarship. Keep in mind the people who are granting you admission and scholarships are real people, just like you and me. They have real problems, they have real families, and they get real busy, just like you and me. Make it as easy as possible for them to get the information they need, get it quickly, and award your student money!

During college visits, determine how each school would like to receive your high school records. For example, when we applied, one college required a parent's signature on the flap of the envelope that held the transcripts, so we printed our homemade transcripts, folded them, put them in envelopes, and signed the flaps. Then I discovered I had switched the transcripts of my two sons. I had to rip open the envelopes, swap the transcripts and re-sign a new envelope. Signing envelopes seemed so silly! However, I have learned not to argue with people who want to give me money, and it wasn't a difficulty to provide the information they way they wanted it.

Ask how each college would like to receive high school records, and submit materials the way the college will prefer.

Submit applications their way. I encourage parents to conform to the wishes of the college, as long it does not compromise your values in any way. If they want an official school envelope, then print an envelope on your computer saying "Official Home School High School" with your home address. If they want it sealed, then seal it, and if they want it notarized, have that done as well. Read the fine print, and provide your records the way they request.

COLLEGES WANT INFORMATION

Ask colleges what they want and give it to them. Information may include:

- Transcript.
- Course descriptions.
- Reading list.
- Activity and awards list.
- Work samples.

C H A P T E R   1 4

Validation Outside the Home

"But if they will not listen, take one or two others along,
so that 'every matter may be established by the
testimony of two or three witnesses.'"

Matthew 18:16

"Are YOU a rotten liar!"

Miracle Max, ~ *The Princess Bride*

Some colleges like to see outside documentation of a homeschool student's academic abilities in the form of standardized tests or community college classes. For these colleges, outside documentation provides corroboration of your homeschool transcript grades. Typically, a transcript combined with college admission test scores will be perfectly adequate for scholarship applications, but additional documentation can help in the search for scholarships. Wherever that outside documentation comes from, it proves the student has the underlying knowledge necessary to succeed in college. Colleges value homeschool records created by parents, but sometimes they like to see more.

SAT SUBJECT TESTS

SAT Subject Tests, which measure one subject at a time, are one way to provide colleges with additional academic information about your student. These tests, sometimes called the SAT II, are primarily multiple-choice tests, measuring high school level information. Many subjects are available, including French, United States History, Chemistry, and Math, and they are one hour long. For more information on SAT Subject Tests, contact the College Board at www. CollegeBoard.com.

Colleges differ greatly in their requirements for these tests. Some will require tests of every applicant, and a small number may require additional subject tests from homeschoolers. Some very selective colleges may ask for five, while some less selective colleges may ask for three tests. Many don't require any. When looking at colleges, make sure to find out their testing requirements for admission in order to avoid any unpleasant surprises.

ADVANCED PLACEMENT (AP) TESTS

An AP exam is a wonderful way to demonstrate mastery of a subject. In one long graded exam, your child can show what they've learned on a subject. The AP test is a college level test, which means that usually a child can earn college credit for scoring well, depending on individual college policies. AP exams are often required or encouraged at highly selective colleges. There are 34 different subject exams that measure how much a student knows in one subject at a time. Each exam includes both short and long essays, as well as a couple of multiple-choice questions. Both public and private schools offer AP tests, but they are not required to let you participate in their testing. If you're looking for an AP class to take, you may sign up with a homeschool co-op or an online homeschool group, or you can get your own class approved as an independent homeschool parent. Anyone can take an AP test; you're not required to take an AP course before you take the test. For more information on AP tests, contact the College Board at www.CollegeBoard.com.

Give subject tests when each subject is complete. SAT subject tests are high school level. AP and CLEP tests are college level or honors level tests.

It's important to realize that AP exams are not always a good fit for every student. One of my clients reported that her son struggled to follow an AP course that homeschoolers commonly utilize. She said he studied each day for 4 or 5 hours, just on that single subject. Finally, exhausted, he had little emotional energy left to spend on his remaining schoolwork. Not surprisingly, he was burned out and his mother was worried. As with everything, there needs to be a balance between life and academics. An educated, well adjusted, happy student will look better on his transcript, and look better to a college, than a child who passed an AP exam at the expense of the rest of his school work.

CLEP (COLLEGE LEVEL EXAMINATION PROGRAM)

The CLEP is another great test that can provide colleges with outside documentation to support your homeschool transcript. CLEP scores give additional validation by showing colleges that your student is capable of doing college-level work. These exams result in an "official transcript" (which is sent to any colleges you designate), and give you any third-party proof you might need to validate your high school transcript.

CLEP is intended for "non-traditional learners," and is offered all year long, even in the summer, at conveniently located testing centers (often your local state college). Every test is taken on a computer, and is multiple-choice (with the exception of a few). Questions are straightforward, with little nuance, and every question is college level. CLEP is often used by adult learners returning to college after a long time, and less often by public school students, who typically can access AP classes instead. There are 34 different subject exams, and no age limit on who can test. It's not unusual to see 14 or 15 year-old kids taking (and passing) them.

CLEP test scores range from 20-80, and for most tests, a passing score is anything above 50, although individual colleges decide what score they will award college credit for. Second year foreign language tests require higher scores in order to get college credit. Most colleges publicize the scores they require for credit, so check with the schools you're interested in for their requirements.   Because so many colleges (almost 3000) give credit for a passing CLEP score, these tests can significantly reduce the amount of time and money needed for college.

> *Be certain your child will do well on all tests. Give a sample test at home before taking a test for real.*

If you decide to take any supplemental tests, whether AP, SAT, or CLEP, it's a good idea to do a practice test at home first, to be certain your child can pass. Once you are certain they can pass, you can do some additional study to increase their score. Some AP teachers suggest that students register for both the AP and the SAT Subject Test for each class. That way, if a student does poorly on the AP and chooses not to report their score to a college, they will still have the (easier) SAT test scores to show for all their hard work.

COMMUNITY COLLEGE DUAL ENROLLMENT

Dual enrollment is when high school students take classes at a community college, sometimes called a junior college. These classes will often prove that a student is capable of college level work in a college setting.

For maximum benefit, it's helpful to take a class in each major subject area: English, math, history, etc. Take classes that are required classes at the university your student hopes to attend, such as psychology. Make sure to investigate that university's policy on community college classes, because they may not accept community college credits, or consider such students a freshman applicant. Be prepared to submit all the records that homeschoolers normally provide, including transcript and course descriptions. Save the college course descriptions for classes taken, and incorporate them into your homeschool records. Be sure the student gets excellent grades, hopefully all A's, in their community college classes. The university your student ultimately applies to will evaluate their community college grades seriously, even if they don't give college credit for those classes.

Community college dual enrollment can sometimes have negative consequences, as the campus is often a "Rated R" environment. Although each community college is unique, I have heard shockingly consistent stories across the country. Make certain you research this option carefully. Even with careful control of curriculum and selection of teachers, it is still an adult situation.

Although there can be many issues in a high school environment, there are generally limits to the use of inappropriate material to sell an educational product. There are no such limits at a community college. Community colleges are meant to be an adult environment. They cater to the broad audience of adults, not the unique subset of homeschool young adults who don't want to mix education with unrelated material.

When you are considering community college, don't see it through rose-colored glasses, and think it's a perfect educational utopia. Keep your eyes open to the fact that it may be more "Rated R" than your student is ready for. Consider carefully, know your child, and trust your own judgment. If you choose to enroll your child anyway, there are strategies that can mitigate trouble. Find a support group of like-minded individuals, either homeschoolers or Christian groups that meet regularly. Utilize the "buddy system" and keep your kids in class with another homeschooler. Carefully read all online comments about the professor on www.RateMyProfessor.com. Preview the textbooks before the first day of class, so there are no surprises later on.

Community college can sometimes be a "Rated R" environment, and requires careful consideration.

RECOMMENDATION LETTERS

If you do choose to utilize community college courses, take advantage of it as a good source for recommendation letters. If you plan to do this, it's extremely important that your student gets to know his professors well. Encourage your children to sit in the front row, ask questions, participate in class, and see the professors during office hours so they become familiar with your student. A community college teacher who knows a student well can give a glowing letter of recommendation about that student's effort and work ethos, even if the student's grades are not stellar.

Letters of recommendation can come from other sources as well. Apprenticeships, internships, and work experience can all provide great letters of recommendation. More than a college requirement, a good recommendation letter can also serve as wonderful outside documentation.

EXECUTIVE SUMMARY FOR BUSY PARENTS

STRENGTHEN APPLICATION WITH OUTSIDE DOCUMENTATION
- The SAT or ACT test is often enough.
- Other test options include SAT Subject Tests, AP, and CLEP.
- Non-test options include community college and letters of recommendation.

CHAPTER 15

Surefire Letters of Recommendation

"I have much to write you, but I do not want to do so with pen and ink."

3 John 1:13

Inigo Montoya: *"You are wonderful."*
Man in Black: *"Thank you; I've worked hard to become so."*

~ The Princess Bride

Most colleges require letters of recommendation as a part of their admission process, and such letters are key to winning big scholarships. As homeschoolers, our students have the advantage with recommendation letters, because they've had the opportunity to pursue their passions and specializations. Pay attention to your child's areas of passion, and seek letters of recommendation from people who know your child well in those areas, and who can write enthusiastically about their abilities.

FIND A WRITER

When choosing a recommender, look for two major qualifications. First, the person must write well, and be prompt and trustworthy to complete the task. It is likely that neither the parent nor the student will be able to read the recommendation before it is mailed off to the dream college, so choose your writer well. While it can be challenging to evaluate another adult's writing abilities, there are several ways you can judge them. Have they written a letter to the editor? How was their Christmas letter? Do they email you occasionally? Are there typographical errors in the syllabus from the class they taught? These will give you clues to how well they write.

> *The best recommender knows your child well and writes well.*

Second, the person must be someone who knows your child well and is a big fan. Even if you got a letter of recommendation from a famous person, if they didn't know your child, the letter would be considered meaningless. Find someone who knows your child, and can enthusiastically write about them and their academic potential.

Your student is responsible for obtaining the letters of recommendation. He should be the one to make the requests. It can be helpful to provide a transcript, activity list or resume. An accepted practice, this will allow the person to fill in gaps, or refresh their memory about the student. A guidance counselor in a public school will always check the student's academic records before beginning a letter. They often ask students to provide a resume or activity list in addition. You can provide the same kind of information to the person writing a letter of recommendation.

Give the recommender clear instructions on how they should submit the letter to the college. Provide a stamped envelope if necessary. The student should follow up, and make sure the recommendation was mailed properly and was not forgotten. Once the letter safely arrives at the college, the student should write a personal thank you note for the writer's effort.

PARENT AS RECOMMENDER

Many colleges specify that they do not want a parent to write a student's recommendation, so be sure to follow instructions carefully. If so, ask someone else to do the letter. The writer doesn't have to be a teacher, just someone who knows your child is wonderful and smart.

Conversely, some colleges actually request letters of recommendation from a parent. Give colleges the letters they want, even if it means that a parent writes the letter. Do it their way, and make it easy on the college admission representative. Often they want that information so they can check off a box on the application. Don't over-think it too much; just give it to them.

How do you write a letter about your own child? Writing such a letter may cause you anxiety, but at least as a parent you know your child. Some high school guidance counselors don't have that advantage. As a parent writer, it's important to speak glowingly and in detail about your child. Be honest, but don't berate your student. When counselors write a letter of recommendation, they only say the good things, not the bad stuff. Use this opportunity to explain anything unusual, such as why your student took calculus but received a low math SAT score, or why junior year grades were the lowest.

> *Use standard recommendation formatting and carefully follow directions.*

STANDARDS AND FORMATTING

Whether the writer is a parent or another person, they should be familiar with the standard format for writing letters. The following shows a general outline for a good recommendation letter:

Recommender's name
Recommender's address
Current Date

Dear College Name (OR To Whom It May Concern),

Paragraph I: Paragraph one identifies the student, and how the writer has come to know them. Be specific if a project was completed under your supervision.

Paragraph II: Give as much evidence as possible of the student's increased knowledge, maturity, and understanding. Discuss details of their project topic or other aspects of development during the time you worked with him or her.

Paragraph III: Give as much evidence as possible for any of the following attributes or work skills:

- communication skills (written and oral)
- willingness to take initiative
- level of motivation

- planning and organizational skills
- technical knowledge or skills
- flexibility/adaptability
- interpersonal skills
- willingness to accept responsibility
- willingness to demonstrate leadership
- analytical/problem-solving ability
- group interaction and team work skills

Paragraph IV: Conclude the letter with your recommendation and accentuate the overall positive qualities you witnessed in this student. The conclusion is where the recommender should explicitly state, "I highly recommend..." or other strongly worded phrases.

Sincerely,

Recommender's signature
Recommender's typed full name
Recommender's title or position (For parents, "Home Educator")

This format is just a suggestion. Be careful to look at each college you are considering, because sometimes they have specific requirements for recommendations, such as "in a sealed, signed envelope" or "mail separately" or other instructions. Don't ruin an excellent recommendation letter by ignoring directions.

EXECUTIVE SUMMARY FOR BUSY PARENTS

KEYS TO RECOMMENDATION LETTERS
- Recommendations take time.
- The best recommender writes well.
- The best recommender knows your student well.
- Give the recommender a transcript, activity list, or resume.
- Good recommendations provide a clear conclusion.

CHAPTER 16

Paint Portraits with Application Essays

"Whatever anyone else dares to boast about—I am speaking as a fool—I also dare to boast about."

2 Corinthians 11:21b

"This cause is noble, sir. His wife, crippled. His children, on the brink of starvation."

Inigo Montoya, ~ *The Princess Bride*

Colleges don't want much, just a self-reflective, technically perfect, very compelling 500-word essay. This essay is a key part of your student's application. It should be a well-written partial answer to the question, "Who are you?"

> *The application includes one or more self-reflective, technically perfect descriptive essays written by the high school student.*

The essay is a love letter to the college. It's where the student reveals in a "love letter" the height, depth, width, and breadth of their feelings for the college. This is their opportunity to answer two things most colleges want to know about students—who they are and how well they communicate. A college may see 4 years of "English" on a transcript, but that doesn't mean the student can write well. They may see 4 years of choir on an activity list, but they won't know if choir was an "easy A" or a true passionate interest. Through the essay, colleges learn who students are, or who they think they are, and determine their true writing skills.

COLLECT TOPICS

The first step in producing stellar application essays is to collect the essay prompts from each college where your student plans to apply. College websites will usually list the application essay topics, and they usually don't change from year to year. Some colleges will ask for just one essay, and others will ask for several. Collect the topics and make a master list that includes all of them.

Make sure that you and your student read the topics together, to truly understand the questions. College essay topics are written by adults, but read by teenagers. If you think about the communication issues parents sometimes have with teenagers, it's easy to see why this might pose a problem. My teenagers were faced with this essay topic: "Tell us about your experiences with diversity." My teens truly believed that they were incapable of writing an essay on diversity because they were white males. They were convinced they had never had a diverse experience in their lives.

But as adults, we saw things differently enough to help them. To one son we said, "You've been teaching chess to inner city youth, and you've been teaching chess at the Chinese academy. These are very different, very diverse, situations. Why don't you write about that?" My son was dumbfounded. It had never occurred to him that working with these wonderful children, who adored him and hugged him all the time, could be used in an essay on diversity.

BRAINSTORM TOGETHER

Brainstorming is an idea-generating technique where a group calls out spontaneous ideas, without evaluating them. Nothing is too silly or far-fetched to be suggested. It's a great way to think outside the box, and it's an activity that parents and teens can do together to generate good essay ideas. Begin by helping your teen spend some time reviewing their life. Look at scrapbooks, calendars, photo albums and activity lists. Parents might look at their checkbook to remember expensive or meaningful events over the years.

Consider and make notes about summer camp, projects, hospitalizations, difficulties, or any surprising events, both good and bad.

ESSAY AS PORTRAIT

As you brainstorm, remember that each college admission essay is like a portrait of the student. If a college asks for three essays, they want three different portraits. Each essay should be a completely different perspective on your child. For visual thinkers, three portraits means three costume changes, three background choices, and three different props! Think about professional photographers creating senior portraits. They often suggest bringing in props, like a guitar,

> *Each college admission essay is like a unique portrait of the student, each one written from a different perspective and topic.*

chess set, or football. A portrait of a teenager playing baseball will give a different perspective than a picture of the same student playing piano or studying economics. Each portrait should show a different aspect of the student's personality.

SELF-REFLECTIVE PERSONAL ESSAYS

Once you've collected the essay topics, discussed them, and brainstormed ideas, it's time to begin writing. Try to think about a picture of the student in action. This picture might have a student rappelling from a cliff. Think about the details behind the picture: the size of the mountain, the training required to rappel, the feeling of falling backwards while not really falling, the fear and exhilaration. That's what a self-reflective personal essay is like—telling a first-person singular short story about yourself that is true. And yes, the student can use the word "I" in this essay!

This style of writing is easier if you start with one specific moment in mind. Try to think of a moment that created a gasp, a sigh, or a thrill. Recently, I talked with a mom and daughter who had been wilderness hiking in the middle of a tremendous thunderstorm. She told me how scared her daughter had been, how they had crouched in their lightning strike position so that they wouldn't be hit, and how they stayed in that position for hours. That's a great moment to write a personal essay about!

My younger son loved writing about government, so he wrote an application essay called "The Voice of Dissent," which described what it was like to be the only Republican in the Seattle delegation to a state-wide mock legislature. In another essay entitled "Determined Never to Be Idle," he wrote about a hospital stay that left him in bed for six hours, waiting for an allergic reaction to resolve. In a third essay, he wrote about his decision to CLEP out of psychology, because he was impatient with the secular aspects of psychology textbooks.

My older son wrote one essay about his experiences teaching chess at the Chinese Academy. Next, he wrote an essay about how he struggled in his faith to not be overly aggressive as a soccer player, and how he found balance in that area. Then he wrote about his experiences with Youth in Government.

Each child wrote three different essays that reflected three unique aspects of their lives, and subsequently gave the colleges a very well-rounded picture of themselves. Remember, each application essay is an opportunity to give the college a different snapshot of your student's life, so the school will see a great, 3-dimensional image of your student as an individual.

Although your student's job is to tell the college all about themselves, they must do this in a way that endears them to the college rather than offends them. A good essay should avoid portraying the writer as a narcissist, which is difficult when teens are asked to write glowingly about themselves. The antidote to this dilemma is to include honest self-reflection in the essay, with perhaps a dash of self-deprecating humor. The colleges know students aren't perfect. It's not necessary to pretend to be perfect.

Never repeat any facts or details in admission essays. Use a story, activity or event in only one essay.

NEVER REPEAT ANYTHING

It bears repeating: never repeat anything in college admissions essays. If you mention the word "chess" in one essay, never use that word in another essay to the same college. If you refer to "Thomas Jefferson" in one essay, don't use the name again in another essay. Each essay is unique, and nothing should be repeated between essays.

Don't repeat anything found in another place on your college application either. Don't mention your grades, course titles, grade point average, or test scores. Don't list all the activities on the activity list, or count volunteer hours. Those things are found on the application already.

The essay is an opportunity for your student to demonstrate her passion, explain her values, and show her true personality. It's not meant to be a list or transcript. Never repeat anything, but make the most of each opportunity to express something new.

TAILOR ESSAYS

Once your student has written an essay, it can easily be modified for use in another college application, although it's important to tailor the essay specifically to each different college. When visiting colleges, have your student take notes. The essay provides the opportunity to use those notes. Incorporating information from college visits into the application essays shows how much a student cares about that college.

When using one essay for multiple college applications, edit each version carefully. Remove identifying statements about the first college, and change them to be specific to the next college. Before submitting the essays, make sure to include the right college details on the right college essay. Do not mention Dartmouth or express interest in Harvard in an application to Yale. That would be like sending a love letter to two different people, and getting their names reversed. It would not help the relationship!

As your student tailors each essay, he should include as many details specific to the school as possible. He could write, "From the first time I met you at the college fair in the Seattle Event Center in 2010…" or, "I visited in March of 2011, and I've always felt that you are the friendliest of people." My son included information about the specific class he took when he visited campus, how

Include specific details about each college using information from the college visit.

they talked about art and literature and Latin, and how cool he thought it was to blend subjects. These are the kinds of details that you want to include, so the college knows how much you love them, and will want to love you right back!

Some essay questions actually ask for a very specific answer, such as "...and how did that change your way of thinking?" When writing these essays, make certain that your student answers the question. Be very clear, and make sure that the question is completely answered.

SEEK PERFECTION

While the admission essay helps a college get to know your student, it's also used to evaluate how well your child writes. Therefore, the essay must be technically perfect. It is sometimes difficult for teens to accept feedback, but in this case it's extremely important. Parents and other adults should help the child edit their paper. Remove redundancies, cut down the fluff, and keep the meat.

While the essay must be perfect in terms of spelling, punctuation, verb tense, and grammar, it also needs to have the "voice" of a student. Point out any errors, but allow the student to correct those errors. This will help the essay to retain the student's voice, or style, which is how the college will get to know them. Because it is a portrait of your student, it has to have their voice. This is what makes their writing unique, and conveys their attitude, personality, values, and character. The voice of the essay will show whether it was written by the student or a parent. Believe it or not, teens don't write like adults. For those who live in the world of application essays, this distinction is <u>very</u> easy to detect.

A well-written essay uses active words. It will not merely say what happened, but will describe what happened. Use vivid details in the essay, including specific facts. Avoid using a passive voice, such as the words "were" or "was," and focus on action words. Instead of saying "it was horrible," describe the situation: "The stormy weather caused thirteen lightning strikes. I could feel the fear in my bones." At first, consider the simple edit technique. Circle each time you see "was" and "were" used as verbs. Sometimes these words are appropriate, but much of the time the use of an active verb will improve your student's writing.

A technically perfect essay will comply with the school's written instructions. After editing, consider again the parameters of the essay. How many words are expected? Is there a word or character limit? How many pages? Some essays are very short, only 250 words. Sometimes the requirement is 500 to 1000 words, or more. Whatever it is, make certain that your student follows the directions.

If possible, have the paper edited by a second person. That might be a teacher, pastor, close friend, or community college instructor. An English teacher or tutor may be a good resource, and could provide a valuable second opinion.

When the essay is in its final draft, make certain you review it once more for spelling, grammar, and college-specific details. An effective way to do this is to enlarge the font, print it out, and read it much more slowly than you normally would, which will help you spot things that may not be picked up at all by a spelling and grammar check. Then complete a spell check again.

REDUCE, REUSE, AND RECYCLE ESSAYS

Each college will require one to four essays. On average, students apply to six colleges. That means they could be required to submit twenty-four essays, which would be completely overwhelming to anyone. Fortunately, essay topics often overlap significantly from college to college. If you carefully choose which topics to answer, you can reuse the same essay for multiple colleges, and significantly reduce the number of essays the student needs to write.

Each essay may be used for many colleges, with slight modification.

EXAMPLE COLLEGE 1

As an example of how to combine essay topics into fewer papers, let's consider four actual colleges and their essay requirements. The first college is a conservative college that is not religious in nature, with a 30-50% homeschooled student population. Their essay question is, "Tell us about yourself and your interests. Indicate your strengths and weaknesses. Describe your educational and career goals, the kind of person you wish to become, and how [our college] can help you reach these goals." This kind of essay topic is called a personal statement, and even though it includes a lot of words, this topic is very common to most colleges. In fact, the colleges that don't require many essays will often say, "Send us your personal statement."

This same college then requires a second essay. The student is allowed to choose one of the following topics:

"What is good character and why is it important?"

"What are the goals of a liberal arts education?"

"Discuss how an event, novel, or experience has changed your life."

"Respond to the college's mission statement."

EXAMPLE COLLEGE 2

The second college is a Christian college, also with a significant homeschool population. This college requires two essays. The first is a faith essay: "Describe your Christian faith." The second essay is a purpose essay: "Describe what book, person, or event has had the biggest influence on your vocational goals, and the role that you believe [college] can play in those goals." Notice how that last question is very similar to the question from the first college, which asks about an event, novel, or experience.

EXAMPLE COLLEGE 3

The third college is an extremely competitive Christian college. Their first essay is "Your personal story of faith in Christ." Their second essay allows a choice from these topics:

"Have you ever had the experience of having a strong opinion about something and then changing your mind? What was that like?"

"Given your desired major, what draws you to that area of study?"

"Discuss a local, national, or international issue and why you're passionate about it."

"G.K. Chesterton once wrote, 'An inconvenience is only an adventure wrongly considered. An adventure is an inconvenience rightly considered.' Describe an experience that illustrates this idea."

"Describe a time when you have made a whole-hearted commitment to something bigger than yourself like a church, small group, family, or team. What were the challenges you've faced, the sacrifices you made, and how did that commitment help you grow more whole?"

EXAMPLE COLLEGE 4

The fourth college requires students to use the Common Application (www. commonapp.org). Over 400 colleges nationally use this format instead of a separate college-specific application, which is supposed to cut down on the amount of work required for multiple college applications. The Common Application offers a variety of essay topics to choose from:

"Discuss an issue of local, national, or international concern, and its importance to you." (Note that this is very similar to college number two's topic about a local, national, or international issue, and why you're passionate about it.)

"Evaluate a significant experience, achievement, risk you have taken, or ethical dilemma you have faced, and its impact on you."

"Indicate a person who has had a significant influence on you, and describe that influence."

"Describe a character in fiction, an historical figure, or a creative work like art, music, and science that has had a big influence on you, and explain that influence."

"A range of academic interests, personal perspectives, and life experiences add much to the educational mix. Given your personal background, describe an experience that illustrates what you would bring to the diversity in a college community, or an encounter that demonstrates the importance of diversity to you."

FIND COMMON GROUND

As you consider these questions from four different schools, notice what they all have in common. Each of them requires some sort of personal statement. Both the first college and the Common Application ask, "Give us your personal statement." Both the second and third colleges ask for a statement of faith, which is fairly common among Christian schools. The first and second colleges and the Common Application each ask a question about an event, book, person,

Careful planning can reduce the number of essays needed. Look for similar topics from each university.

or experience. They use different words, but are basically asking the same thing. College three and the Common Application ask what issues the student is concerned about, what they're passionate about, and why. With careful planning, you may only need to write four essays to cover all four of these colleges' requirements.

PLAN AHEAD

Essay writing, editing, and rewriting takes an enormous amount of time, so make sure to start the process early. Practice essays before senior year, if possible. Collect essay questions, and use them as writing practice for English. After a college fair, bring home some application packages and look at their essay topics. Incorporate them into your writing assignments for the year. By the time your student is a senior, you'll have plenty of written essays. In case of an emergency (like writer's block), you may be able to use some of those essay ideas from a previous year.

During my sons' junior year, we made college essay-writing our English course. My sons wrote essays all year long, not only for applications, but also for private scholarships. College applications alone involve lots of questions, require lots of thinking, and take a lot of time to complete. Use the year prior to senior year, and give your students a head-start on this process.

Practice essay writing skills in junior year.

KEEP IT REAL

Colleges are looking for real students, people who are authentic. From their perspective, even a diamond in the rough is more valuable than a rhinestone. Sometimes being honest and real translates into "being a character." In this regard, homeschoolers have a distinct advantage over their public school peers. Homeschoolers have tremendous freedom in the high school years to seek outlets for their areas of interest. This, by definition, will make your child stand out from the crowd. As a parent, your job is to help them first discover and then communicate their uniqueness to the world.

EXECUTIVE SUMMARY FOR BUSY PARENTS

KEYS TO QUALITY ESSAYS

- Self-reflective, technically perfect essays take time.
- Each essay is a unique self-portrait written by your child.
- Never repeat anything between essays or transcript.
- Reuse essays for many colleges when possible.
- Tailor and personalize the essay to each college.
- Check to be sure the essay answers the question or topic.
- Practice writing application essays during junior year.

CHAPTER 17

Review Admission Policies Carefully

"I have told you these things, so that in me you may have peace. In this world you will have trouble. But take heart! I have overcome the world."

John 16:33

Buttercup: *"We'll never succeed. We may as well die here."*
Westley: *"No, no. We have already succeeded."*

~ The Princess Bride

When you look at a college website to see what their admission requirements are for homeschoolers, it can feel intimidating. Sometimes it's just downright scary! They use big words, acronyms, and bold font. But if you cut through the fear, you will often find a college policy that is actually fairly reasonable.

Voice quivering at first, a client recently asked me about the homeschool admission policy at the university her child wanted to attend, so we looked at it together. Together we decided, "Hey! That's not so bad!" Using this college policy as an example, let's see what that scary-looking website really means to homeschool parents. Let's take those big words, scary phrases, and ridiculous acronyms, and break them down to see what is truly behind all that edu-speak.

SCARY! "COLLEGE ACADEMIC DISTRIBUTION REQUIREMENTS (CADR)."

This simple phrase is more intimidating because of the acronym. At first glance, you might think you should already know what "CADR" means. That phrase is not part of a normal parent's vocabulary! It's not at all like "CPR," which most people understand the meaning of, and it's OK that you don't understand when you see it the first time. Even if you don't understand the simple phrase, when you look at the policy, it becomes clear. CADR means "core classes." These are the classes they want students to take before applying to college. Whew! I'll bet you are already teaching those classes.

INTIMIDATING! "HOMESCHOOLED COURSEWORK REQUIRES VALIDATING TEST SCORES."

Uh oh! Reading that phrase for the first time, you might immediately think we are being treated unfairly, and given additional testing. And what about the word "validating?" Does that mean that without a test score, you are not a valid homeschool? No! They are looking for some outside documentation, that what you say on the transcript is true. And actually, their outside documentation is pretty easy to get!

> *College Admission Policies may appear scary or intimidating at first glance.*

EASY! "EXAMINATION OPTIONS: SAT REASONING TEST OR ACT WITH WRITING."

Those intimidating "validating test scores" may look pretty scary, but take away the extra words and the answer is simple. SAT or ACT. Your child just needs to take the regular SAT or ACT that all students take. Virtually all children who apply to a university will take those tests and have those scores. It looks like a unique requirement for homeschoolers, but it's really pretty run-of-the-mill ordinary. Now, if you are a non-tester, or someone who might balk at a nationally standardized test, this may be frustrating, I'll admit. Still, it's not really unusual.

SUGGESTION! "SCIENCE EXAMINATION OPTIONS: ACT WITH WRITING OR SAT SUBJECT TEST OR ADVANCED PLACEMENT (AP)."

Read the details on each subject area, and which test will cover each area. Do you notice anything? The ACT test will only work if you take the test with the optional essay. But that test still has an advantage–it validates science. Read the details carefully. In this instance, these details can save a lot of trouble! Your child would only have to take the ACT with Writing to meet almost all their validation requirements. This is like an un-spoken suggestion. That's particularly interesting, because this college is on the West Coast, where most high school kids take the SAT test, not the ACT. So read those details; they can help you work smarter, not harder.

OPTIONAL! "SUBJECTS COMPLETED AT A HIGH SCHOOL OR REGIONALLY ACCREDITED COLLEGE DO NOT REQUIRE TEST SCORE VALIDATION."

This sentence may contain two of my most-hated words in the English language: accredited and validation. But I'm willing to look past my prejudices against these two words, and actually read the sentence. Lo and behold, I find out this is actually good news! Not all homeschool kids get sky-high test scores. Some kids simply aren't good test takers. Like the proverbial square peg in the round hole, standardized tests don't fit them. But within this scary-sounding sentence is an option for poor test-takers. Without having SAT or ACT test scores, students can still achieve that frustrating, required validation through community college. Not required or even encouraged, the community college option is for kids who don't have or can't provide SAT or ACT test scores.

INTERESTING! "FOREIGN LANGUAGE PROFICIENCY EXAMINATION OR SAT SUBJECT TEST OR ADVANCED PLACEMENT (AP)."

Read options and suggestions carefully, and choose what works for your child. "Optional" is not the same as "required."

Proficiency means competence. Apparently this particular university cares about one subject that is not covered by the ACT with writing. They would like to see competence in foreign language. When a child is admitted to a university, they will often provide proficiency exams in different subjects; they are pretty common. However, those tests are often in reading, writing, and math. Did you know that almost one third of students admitted to college are remedial in those subjects? Colleges give exams to help direct those remedial students to additional resources before they flunk out of college. However, at this school, they seem to have a proficiency exam before the child is even admitted. Before you panic, though, notice how all they really need is an ordinary, run-of-the-mill subject test. They can take either an SAT or AP subject test in foreign language. The school will even provide a foreign language exam of their own!

CHANGE! POLICY DIFFERENT FROM PREVIOUS YEAR

What I found particularly interesting about this college's foreign language policy is how it has changed over time. When our sons applied to this school, the school required homeschoolers to jump through even more hoops regarding foreign language. I was unable to meet their requirements in my homeschool, so I wrote to them and explained our situation, and provided thorough course descriptions of our foreign language, instead of test scores. My students were admitted and were given great scholarships. Still, it was interesting to see how their policy has changed. Always assume that admission policies can change over time, so check each year, and especially the year you begin applications.

SPECIFIC! "LAB SCIENCE: VALIDATION IS REQUIRED FOR AT LEAST ONE OF THE FOLLOWING: BIOLOGY, CHEMISTRY, OR PHYSICS. EXAMINATION OPTIONS INCLUDE ACT WITH WRITING OR SAT SUBJECT TEST OR ADVANCED PLACEMENT (AP)."

Homeschoolers are a diverse bunch, and colleges are each unique too. For that reason, when a university gets this specific, it helps to pay attention. Notice how this long, boring sentence with lots of capital letters gives us a clue about the unique requirements from this particular college. This school really wants students to take biology, or chemistry, or physics. And then they want you to prove that you have taken one of them.

College policies may change from year to year. Read what each admission policy says, and does not say, prior to application.

Although this is specific, it's helpful to pay attention to what this list does not say. It does not say that you have to take biology plus chemistry plus physics. It does not say you have to take physics at all! It doesn't say you are not allowed to take another science, or that other sciences don't count. It doesn't even go into detail about what must be included in the "lab" part of your lab science. It just wants to see a valid test at the end. It's very specific. Just make sure that at least one of your sciences is biology with lab, chemistry with lab, or physics with lab.

Because it is so specific, if this is one of the colleges your child might apply to, I suggest you make your transcript match this specific request. Put the word "lab" by your science classes that include a lab.

HOLISTIC! "ALL APPLICANTS ARE ASSESSED HOLISTICALLY IN THE CONTEXT OF THE SCHOOL'S COMPREHENSIVE REVIEW PROCESS."

I say it all the time: nobody is perfect. It's possible to get admission and scholarships even if you don't have a perfect application packet. That's why I like this reassuring admission policy. When a college says they review applicants "holistically," they usually mean they look beyond test scores or GPA. Yes, they do look at those things, but they also look beyond those numbers. "In addition to grade-point average (GPA) and test scores, the university takes into account many aspects of an applicant's achievements and personal history." They look at academic preparation, like your homeschool course descriptions, which provide documentation about the academic rigor of each class. They look at performance in ways not measured by tests, like letters of recommendation. They look at personal achievements listed in the activity and award lists. And they look at personal characteristics, often by carefully reading between the lines on the application essays. So yes, the test scores and GPA count, but the school is also looking beyond numbers. And that's encouraging!

ENCOURAGING! "STUFF WE LIKE: FRESHMAN FROM 50 STATES & 90 COUNTRIES."

This tiny phrase was way off in the corner, almost hiding, really. And yet, it can be one of the most encouraging tidbits on any college website. Do you see how they highlight that information? If you are a military or missionary family, and you can represent the 91st country on that campus, you might have an advantage. In fact, think about this in terms of other colleges as well. They all want to claim that statistic, of having students from all 50 states. What if they only have students in 49 states? What if you live in that one last state they need to claim all 50? Consider looking for a college that needs someone to represent your state or country. It could mean more scholarship money. Colleges want students from all over. If you are from "all over," that means they want you!

UNIVERSAL! "ALL FRESHMAN APPLICANTS ARE REQUIRED TO MEET MINIMUM ACADEMIC DISTRIBUTION REQUIREMENTS."

Don't get bogged down in the homeschool policy, but remember to read the fine print on the general admission policy as well. Even if you meet the listed homeschool requirements, you must also meet the admission requirements in general. This university provides an excellent example of this universal truth: you are not just a homeschooler. You are also a regular applicant. For example, even if you have great SAT scores in math that prove "validation" in math, but you don't have math during senior year, you aren't meeting the minimum requirements for admission. You are a homeschool family, but meet the universal application requirements, too.

OFFICIAL! "AN OFFICIAL HOMESCHOOL TRANSCRIPT IS REQUIRED FOR ALL HOMESCHOOLED COURSEWORK."

Virtually all colleges will require a homeschool transcript. Did you know your homeschool transcript is official? Sure, the word "official" can sound intimidating. I think that's because some people get the word confused. "Official" does not mean "accredited" or "validated by the state." It only means you, as the homeschool parent, have determined this to be the official transcript for your homeschool. So instead of getting all freaked out by the word "Official," let me give you some simple steps for making your transcript official enough for this college. Step one: create a homeschool transcript with the title "Official Homeschool Transcript." Step two: submit the transcript and say it is official. Whew! That was easy! Your transcript is now official.

> *Your parent-made transcript is the Official Homeschool Transcript.*

THOROUGH! "THE TRANSCRIPT MUST INCLUDE: COURSE TITLE, DURATION OF STUDY, SHORT DESCRIPTION OF COURSE CONTENT, GRADE FOR PERFORMANCE, AND TEACHER SIGNATURE."

While this college says it wants a transcript, it's actually asking for more than that. What they really want to see are course descriptions along with the transcript. They are looking for thorough documentation of each class. A course description can be difficult to whip up at a moment's notice, so I strongly recommend that everyone keep course descriptions each year. A common request, there are many colleges that will ask for this detail. So whatever they request, whatever they want, and whatever they call it, give it to them.

Each college is unique, and they may ask for things in a strange language or have unusual requests. As a homeschool parent, do your best to figure out exactly what they want so you can give it to them. I actually like what they wrote here, because it's in English, not edu-speak. But what they are specifically requesting is actually a bit unusual. They want to see "duration of study." You rarely see that. It's unusual, and a unique aspect of this college. It wouldn't be hard to provide, it's just different. Having a teacher signature is also an unusual request. Not all colleges ask for that. But you need to know what they want, in order to give them what they want, so read the fine print and be thorough.

MOMMY-MADE! "THE HOMESCHOOL TRANSCRIPT MUST BE SIGNED BY THE TEACHER OF RECORD; THIS MAY BE A PARENT."

It can be pretty scary to see the words "official transcript" and not know you can create your own. It can also be scary to see the words "teacher of record" and think it means someone else. This is not saying you need to have a certified teacher sign the transcript, and it is not saying you need to have a teaching certificate in order to be the teacher of record. It's saying that the person who taught the child should sign the transcript, and they know it will probably be the parent. You are the teacher of record. So when you break this down, you see what they really want.

A college may say they require a transcript, when they actually want a comprehensive record with complete course descriptions. Be prepared with thorough records updated each year.

They want a Mommy-made or Daddy-made transcript. Give them what they want. Now, the signature request is a little unusual, but so what? Just know what they want and give it to them. Sign your own transcript as the parent (I mean teacher!) of record.

EMBARRASSING! "ALL OFFICIAL TRANSCRIPTS, INCLUDING COLLEGE TRANSCRIPTS, MUST BE SUBMITTED BY THE APPLICATION DEADLINE."

Turn the transcript and course descriptions in on time. It's kind of embarrassing that they need to include this on the homeschool admission policy. I wonder if they have to say that to public schools as well? I don't know! But I do know that we are not immune to deadlines, just because we homeschool. The rules do apply to us. Follow the deadlines. They are usually completely inflexible. In fact, if you turn in your materials early, long before the deadlines, sometimes they will be so thankful they end up liking you more, and viewing your application more favorably. It's not just deadlines; try not to be embarrassing in other ways either. Create a transcript that looks neat and official, and turn it in on time, and you won't be embarrassed.

SCORES! "WE DO NOT HAVE AN ESTABLISHED LIST OF PREDETERMINED MINIMUM SCORES BUT REVIEW EACH HOMESCHOOLED APPLICANT IN LIGHT OF THEIR UNIQUE EDUCATIONAL HISTORY."

This university does not have a minimum requirement for test scores, but they don't really need minimum requirements. This school has so many applicants; they have plenty with great test scores. While this statement may be true, it will still help to compare statistics about each college. For example, their "quick facts" page provides statistics that describe the average student admitted to the school. Here is what you might learn: they admit only 56-59% of people who apply, the average high school GPA is 3.63-3.92; most admitted students get these test scores: SAT Critical Reading 520-650, Math 580-710, Writing 450-650, and the ACT Composite 24-30. For a good chance of success, your child should have scores in the middle range for their college. To feel more confident of admission, you need to have scores in the high end of the range. To achieve scholarships, you may need to have scores above the range. Scores matter, even when they say they don't matter. You can use scores to figure out how successful your child may be with college admission and scholarships for a particular school.

CORE! "ENGLISH 4 CREDITS, MATH 3, SOCIAL STUDIES 3, WORLD LANGUAGES 2, LAB SCIENCE 2, SENIOR YEAR MATH-BASED QUANTITATIVE COURSE 1, FINE ARTS 0.5, ACADEMIC ELECTIVE 0.5."

While I can provide guidance about what colleges are looking for in general, each college may have unique requirements from students. The only way to tell what a specific college wants from core classes is to find out their unique policy. Policies vary widely, and nobody can tell you exactly what each college in the nation might like. That research is up to the student and parent. My best advice is to cover the common classes colleges tend to require, and then do your research during junior year. That way, if you find something unusual in their policy, you will still have time to modify your homeschool plan and include an unusual core class in senior year.

Check admission test scores and core class requirements during junior year to improve test scores or fill gaps if necessary.

What I found particularly interesting in this school policy is that they say they want 3 math classes, but they also say they want a "quantitative" course taken in senior year. Most quantitative classes are math classes, like statistics. Essentially, they are saying they want a fourth math class, but it can be "math-like" as well as a regular math class. It also demonstrates how senior year is important. They want their applicants to have the ability to think mathematically during senior year – not wallow in senioritis. Read the details, and give them what they want.

GRADING! "PASS/NOT PASS GRADES ARE PERMISSIBLE, BUT WE RECOMMEND THAT COURSES HAVE A LETTER OR NUMERICAL GRADE."

Many parents feel uncomfortable providing homeschool grades because they worry that we can't be objective about our own child. What they don't realize is that public and private school grades aren't objective either, and colleges know that. Colleges prefer a grade–any grade–over a pass/fail indication. Give them what they want. If they want you to give number grades (4.0, 3.0, 2.0) or they want you to give letter grades (A, B+, C-), then be like Burger King, and make it their way! By providing number or letter grades, the GPA calculation will often be high enough to earn scholarships. With only pass or fail grades, colleges may not give your student GPA-based financial aid. Be honest about your grades, but don't stress too much about being objective. Honest, yes. Objective, give it up. No teacher is completely objective. The goal is to be honest and true with your homeschool grades.

FUNNY! "YOU MUST ATTAIN AT MINIMUM A PASSING GRADE (INCLUDING D)."

As homeschoolers, we worry so much about academics, and learning, and the love of learning. I hear concerns about lack of motivation, or poor performance or attitude. But really, is a D your definition of passing? It's important to remember that during the college application process, your children are not being compared to "perfect homeschoolers" that all have test scores in the 87th percentile. They will be compared to the great unwashed masses of college applicants. And some of them may have some D's on their transcript.

> *Colleges value the diverse experiences of homeschoolers.*

Whether you are confident about your objective grades or not, I doubt your child has done so poorly that you have been tempted to give a grade of D.

THANKS! "HOMESCHOOLED STUDENTS BRING UNIQUE QUALITIES TO OUR CAMPUS AND WE WELCOME THEIR INTEREST IN OUR UNIVERSITY."

It was nice to have this example of a homeschool policy. I liked seeing their introduction, expressing their value of home education. I'm usually very glad to see a college with a homeschool admission policy. It's important to recognize, however, that these policies may change over time. They don't stay the same from year to year. The college admission representatives may not be familiar with the homeschool policy, or notice a yearly change. They are often reasonable people, however, so speak to them kindly if you have a concern, and they are usually glad to help. At the same time, be flexible, and continue your research on interesting colleges each year, to notice any changes that may occur.

BOTTOM LINE FOR THIS UNIQUE SCHOOL

Now what does this scary policy actually mean to a homeschooler? After all the scary looking words and phrases, capital letters and acronyms, the bottom line for this school was not scary at all. One college admission test was better than the other. Regular college prep classes were required. They asked for a homeschool transcript and course descriptions. The only thing really unusual for this college was a subject test for foreign language. See? That wasn't so bad!

EXECUTIVE SUMMARY FOR BUSY PARENTS

KEYS TO COLLEGE ADMISSION POLICIES

- Each college is unique.
- When requirements seem scary or intimidating, read the words carefully.
- Policies change over time, so stay current on the schools you're interested in.
- Read the fine print and make sure to follow instructions for all students.
- Comprehensive records can give your student the edge in college applications.

CHAPTER 18

Cross the Application Finish Line

"I have fought the good fight, I have finished the race,
I have kept the faith."

2 Timothy 4:7

"You've been chasing me your whole life only to fail now?
I think that's about the worst thing I've ever heard...
How marvelous."

Count Rugen, ~ *The Princess Bride*

I have encountered two schools of thought about the college application process. First is the laissez-faire method for parents who take a hands-off approach. The teen is responsible for every aspect of the college application experience, from initial college search to the final result. These parents may only become involved during the final selection. Not surprisingly, their concern increases dramatically when the student has been admitted to college and the conversation changes to college costs. They first become involved when they exclaim, "You have got to be kidding! How much?"

Laissez-faire parents may be shocked by the college environment if they are not part of the process with their children. Some college policies include co-ed rooms and gender-neutral housing. If you don't want your child sharing a bedroom or bathroom with a stranger of the opposite gender, you need to be involved in the process. Colleges that offer substance-free dorms may not be the perfect solution if the statistics show that most residents still consume drugs, alcohol and cigarettes. While hands-off parenting can lead to shocking situations, there is a solution. You can become involved with the college admission process, and proceed with caution. Don't be paralyzed with fear; participate and become involved.

While I'm a strong proponent of natural consequences and allowing teens to take increased responsibility for college plans as they mature, detached indifference may not result in a positive outcome. There are three reasons for this: teenagers, parents, and colleges.

TEENAGERS

In addition to deciding about marriage and career, teens are often ill-equipped to rationally consider all of the subtle implications associated with selecting a college. Short-term, emotion-based thinkers don't naturally focus on their five-year plan, or consider the 20-year ramifications of their decisions. While the hands-off approach has some merit, the reality can be devastating. Teenagers may not turn everything in before the due date, may not understand the consequences of delaying their application, and may not understand how much time and effort is required to recover from each misstep.

> *Be hands-on about college applications. College is a big decision, and teens require parental guidance along the way.*

PARENTS

Unless parents completely divorce themselves from financial responsibility for college, they will have a vested interest in the outcome of their teen's behavior. Four years of college is a huge investment with a potentially great reward. Most people do not have a hands-off attitude in other areas of financial planning. I've never met an adult who handed a briefcase full of money to a financial advisor and told them to handle the details. Even if the financial advisor has a long and successful track record, grown-ups usually care enough to ask how the advisor will invest the money.

Teenagers, by definition, don't have a long track record of wisely handling money. In fact, the time span between their foolish money choices might be measured in hours or days, rather than years. Most parents will retain some responsibility for the investment of college money, and they want to know that their investment will have a good return. Failure of due diligence can only lead to frustration.

COLLEGES

College admission is a very involved, time-sensitive process, and each college has a unique formula for admission and scholarship. Competition between students can be fierce, and each applicant and application requires close attention. The rewards for following the unique procedure for each college can be great; the risks of failure can seem disastrous. Sometimes it is the disappointment a child feels when they don't gain admission to the college of their dreams. Other times it is the terror a parent feels when they fully comprehend the total cost of tuition, books, room and board without financial aid. I have known average students who were meticulous about college admissions and were rewarded with full scholarships to their perfect-match college. I have also known extraordinarily gifted students who took a casual approach, but received no scholarships whatsoever. This can be a huge stress and hardship on parents and students alike, but fortunately, it can be avoided.

PARENT AS PROJECT MANAGER

The second approach to college applications is more successful. I suggest parents take a project management role in college applications. A project manager is not a general contractor. The student must do the work, while the parent organizes and provides structure with encouragement. Parents should not complete the applications, write the essays, or decide on the college major. Doing too much can lead to resentment and strife. At the

The student must do the work, but the parent is the project manager, providing organization and encouragement.

same time, colleges are intuitive and will know when the parent is filling out an application. They may reject students if they sense parents have done the application rather than the teen.

Most teens are not known for insightful self-knowledge. Without parental guidance, the college search may only mean looking at the schools where their friends attend. Parents can guide and shape their steps, helping them identify and articulate personal likes and dislikes. Children need help making decisions about colleges, and discerning which ones might be a good fit.

Deep personal reflection is also important during the college application essays. Before preparing a personal statement for application, brainstorm together. Help children recall different events that help them answer the essay questions. Teens may only remember the most recent experiences, or might not recognize the significance of some past incidents that seem mundane to a young person.

The most important project management role of a parent is helping students meet important deadlines. The financial implications of missing a due date can be significant. A missed deadline can cost many thousands of dollars in college expenses. Teenagers may not appreciate the difference in financial aid, but it is critically important for parents. It is appropriate for parents to supervise deadlines, and encourage timely submissions. Other aspects of the process may also require encouragement from the parents. Few teenagers would spontaneously write a thank you note after college visits and interviews, for example. While thoughtlessness isn't a mortal sin, it can make a difference in the world of college admissions.

PARENT AS GUIDANCE COUNSELOR

Closely related to a parent's project management role is their role as the high school guidance counselor. When it comes to helping our students, parents are GREAT guidance counselors. Our love for our children can ensure success, and our careful consideration will help prevent any major slips. The student does the applying (filling out the forms, asking for the recommendation letters, and writing essays, for example). The parent (guidance counselor) guides the student (provides opportunities for college fairs and visits, giving timely reminders each step of the way).

During the application process, when a response is required from the "high school," it is the parent's responsibility to respond. When a response is required from the "parent," then it is (of course) your responsibility as well. However, when a response is required from the "student," then it is your child's responsibility to follow up. For example, questions about scholarships, financing, course descriptions, and school records usually require parental involvement. If your student has a question about the application or college life, then your student should pursue that question. If you feel confused at any point, ask yourself what would happen in a public school situation. Would this interaction or question be the responsibility of the public school, or the responsibility of the student attending the public school?

The best approach is for parents to assume their role as guidance counselor, and students to assume their role as pro-active applicants. When necessary, call the admissions office directly and ask questions. Asking questions will show genuine interest in the college. In order to get colleges interested in you, you have to show you are interested in them. Ask clarifying questions to demonstrate interest. Colleges pay attention to families who are asking application and admissions questions. When possible, have the student call when there is a question. Later, the school might recognize your student's name when they see their application

> *The student is the pro-active applicant. The parent is the guidance counselor and school.*

The parental guidance counselor encourages and provides college visits. Without a car, permission to drive long distances, a credit card, or control over the home calendar, teens must rely on their parents. While the student should arrange each visit with the college, scheduling will require help from the parent. The guidance counselor encourages teenagers to dig deeply into the subtle points of choosing a college. Without prompting, the worldviews of likely professors may seem less significant than whether pizza is served in the cafeteria. Not all teens emphasize superficial aspects of college, but having a balance of perspectives is important when making any significant decision.

The college application process is like teaching your kids how to ride a bike. You can run as fast as possible to prevent them from crashing, but eventually you will need to let go. When you do, they may sail successfully off into the future, or they might fall a time or two. As a parent, project manager, and guidance counselor, you will be there to celebrate with them or help them dust off and try again.

DIVISION OF RESPONSIBILITY

- Parent and student brainstorm topics together.
- Student writes and completes the essay.
- Parent may provide feedback on the essay.
- Student completes the application.
- Parent completes the academic records required of a school.

Getting
Scholarships

CHAPTER 19

Keys to Merit Scholarships

"Now to him who is able to do immeasurably more than all we ask or imagine, according to his power that is at work within us, to him be glory!"

Ephesians 3:20-21a

"That day, she was amazed to discover that when he was saying 'As you wish,' what he meant was, 'I love you.'"

Grandpa, ~ *The Princess Bride*

Now is the time to return to the money question: how on earth can college become affordable? This chapter will focus on merit-based scholarships, which are not related to financial need. Merit scholarships may be academic, athletic, or related to something else, but all merit scholarships require something to be completed or accomplished. These are different from need-based scholarships, which are awarded based on the information you complete on the Free Application for Federal Student Aid (FAFSA).

HOW TO WIN A MERIT SCHOLARSHIP

Merit scholarships are given for many reasons. Students may be awarded one based on what they have done in the past or may do in the future. Scholarships for military service are one example. Scholarships can be given because a student has a particular skill or ability the college currently needs. An academic skill might lead to a scholarship, but scholarships are also awarded for sports or musical ability.

Some scholarships don't require any action, just specific qualities that fulfill the giver's criteria. When we looked for private scholarships, we found one for Italian-Americans. Being Italian was all they required! There are also degree-related merit scholarships. If your child wants to be a teacher, nurse, or engineer, for example, there are specific scholarships for students entering those fields.

AIM LOW

Merit scholarships are often awarded to the most outstanding students a college sees in a year. For that reason, one strategy in seeking the big scholarships is to "aim low." This seems contradictory. As homeschoolers, we usually hear the message, "go forth into the world and achieve." That's good advice, and is great when you can afford it. When you can't afford college, and might not be able to go without a scholarship, then a different strategy is better.

If you need a big scholarship, aim at a school where your child is the best-qualified applicant the school will see that year. This will make your child really shine and be fabulous in comparison to everybody else. You can do this by comparing your student's SAT or ACT scores to the college's average SAT or ACT scores. Make sure that the college realizes that your student is a very well-qualified applicant.

> *For the best scholarship, be the best-qualified applicant the school will see that year.*

AIM HIGH

For some merit scholarships, the best strategy is to aim high. A child who is good at math or science might get better scholarships by aiming high for a demanding degree in engineering. Some rigorous degrees will offer better merit scholarships than liberal arts degrees. In some instances, applying for science, technology, engineering, math or medical fields can increase financial aid considerably.

NATIONAL MERIT SCHOLARSHIP

Have you seen billboards and newspaper articles announcing that a student is a National Merit Scholar? Those students entered the competition by taking the PSAT. The National Merit Scholarship is the best known high school scholarship in the nation, and the only way to win is to start with the PSAT test. Therefore, the single most important thing you can do to win that scholarship is to make sure your children take the PSAT in October of 11th grade, as I discussed in chapter 5.

MONETARY AMOUNT VARIES

The National Merit Scholarship is a non-renewable, one-time award of up to $2500. Not everyone gets the whole prize amount, and some will get far less. When you compare the award to the cost of colleges, it doesn't seem like much. But the National Merit Scholarship can be a stepping-stone to other scholarships.

Corporate-sponsored Merit Scholarship awards can provide additional money for some students. College-sponsored Merit Scholarship awards usually provide the most money. Colleges love to publicize how many National Merit Scholars they have on campus. College-sponsored merit scholarships can be very large, even full scholarships. Some colleges will only give their largest monetary award to a student who names that college as their first choice university, and will provide lesser scholarships to other National Merit Scholars. On the other end of the spectrum are colleges that provide special scholarships to any National Merit participants, not just winners, including commended students and semi-finalists.

NATIONAL MERIT SCHOLARSHIP PROCESS

The National Merit Scholarship competition is a long, drawn-out process, lasting over a year. The competition is based on the Selection Index score of high school juniors. The Selection Index is the sum of all three sections of the test: reading, writing, and math. Although you can clearly see the Selection Index on the PSAT score report, you can't tell how your student did in comparison to the other students across your state, so you won't immediately know yet whether they will advance in the scholarship competition. Scholarship participants are chosen by state, so students are only compared to other high school juniors within their state.

Although you receive PSAT test scores during junior year, it's not until the following August or September of senior year that Commended Students are notified, and for them the competition has ended. Later, some students will be notified they are semi-finalists, and for them the competition continues. Semi-finalists must complete a detailed scholarship application demonstrating the academic rigor of their education. They must take the SAT test, which will confirm the validity of their PSAT performance, and their SAT score must be reported to the National Merit Corporation. Homeschoolers have become National Merit Scholars, and parents must play the role of school administrator, providing documentation of a rigorous education through well-documented record keeping.

> *The National Merit Scholarship competition is a long process, lasting over a year, requiring tremendous parental involvement.*

Fine print details abound. The PSAT only counts toward the National Merit Scholarships Competition during the third year of a four-year high school, which is usually junior year. However, the administrators do understand that bright and gifted kids sometimes graduate early. There is even a way to enter the competition if a student missed the PSAT due to an emergency situation.

PLANNING FOR SUCCESS

If your child tends to score in the 90th percentile or higher on standardized tests, there is the possibility of winning these awards. There are also things that might increase your child's chances of winning. Have your child take the PSAT in 10th grade for practice, so they are comfortable with the test-taking environment. During 10th grade, have your children study for the PSAT regularly, teaching the skills of reading, writing, and math in the context of test preparation. Familiarity with the test can increase test scores. Plan to complete geometry before sophomore year or earlier, if possible, to maximize the score on the math section. Carefully notice the deadlines at your testing site to register for the PSAT, so you don't miss it. Make

> *Children that tend to score above the 90th percentile on standardized tests are more likely to qualify for these awards. Make sure they do not miss the PSAT.*

sure that your homeschool records and course descriptions are up to date, so you can demonstrate academic rigor if your child advances to the semi-finalist stage.

The complete process of winning a National Merit Scholarship can be a bit complicated, so the information here can only provide an overview. If you are notified that your child is a semi-finalist, immediately spend time doing research. For general information on the PSAT, go to www.collegeboard.com. For detailed information on the PSAT, search www.professionals.collegeboard.com and read the PSAT/NMSQT Supervisor's Manual. For general information on the National Merit Scholarship, go to their website, www.nationalmerit.org and read their information about entering the competitions.

EXECUTIVE SUMMARY FOR BUSY PARENTS

NATIONAL MERIT SCHOLARSHIP PLANNING CALENDAR

Sophomore year

- October 10th grade – Take the PSAT for fun and practice.

Junior year

- September or earlier – Register for the PSAT.
- October – Take the PSAT for the National Merit Scholarship.
- December – Review PSAT scores available.
- Spring – Take the SAT.

Senior year

- September – Commended and Semi-Finalists are notified.
- October – Parents act as the school, and must complete the application.
- December – SAT scores must be sent to National Merit Corporation.
- February – National Merit finalists are notified.
- March – National Merit Scholarship announced.
- April – Corporate-sponsored scholarships awarded.
- May – National Merit Scholars are notified.
- Summer – Scholarship awards are announced to the media.

CHAPTER 20

Finding Private Scholarships

"Ask and it will be given to you; seek and you will find; knock and the door will be opened to you. For everyone who asks receives; the one who seeks finds; and to the one who knocks, the door will be opened."

Matthew 7:7-8

Inigo: *"Who are you?"*
Man in Black: *"No one of consequence."*
Inigo: *"I must know."*

~ The Princess Bride

Our family wasn't able to save much money for college. Like many others, we were a single income family when we homeschooled. Returning to work was not an option, so I did research instead. I spent hours learning the basics of scholarships, and discovered that I could use scholarship applications to supplement my homeschool while also supplementing our college savings.

Most private scholarship applications require an essay. In our homeschool, I required essays too. By combining these two ideas, I found that I could use college scholarships for high school credit. During junior year, I searched for scholarships that matched my students. While private scholarships may yield less money than scholarships from colleges, I noticed that small scholarships led to much bigger

cholarship was listed on our sons' college applications,
e scholarships they had been awarded—even the small
lined to award them larger scholarships.

buy one, get one free" is my favorite phrase. Using
as the English curriculum for the school year is like
a buy one, get one free sale. First, there is no cost for the English curriculum.
Second, a student may be "paid" to write the essays through the resulting
scholarship awards! If your child finds writing particularly difficult, focus on the artistic and hands-on scholarships instead. Your child's work on those scholarships could be applied to other high school classes, such as fine arts rather than English.

> *Apply for private scholarships, and count the number of hours worked. Those hours may count toward high school credits.*

STEPS TO PRIVATE SCHOLARSHIPS

There are five steps to searching for private scholarships: find, filter, format, follow through, and file. Following the steps one at a time will make the process as simple as possible.

FIND SCHOLARSHIPS

An online search for "college scholarships" might return 53 million hits. It's tempting to imagine receiving 53 million scholarships, but in reality, it's not humanly possible to apply for 53 million scholarships, even over four years of college, and certainly not during one year of high school. The big online searches do not help. Instead, use a search engine that is specific to scholarships. Here are some common search engines that are most suited to college scholarships:

www.fastweb.com
www.collegenet.com
www.finaid.org
www.edfinancial.com
www.scholarships.com

In addition to these general sites, there are also sites that are unique to different states. These research sites are effective because the search is tailored to the student. When searching on these sites, first supply information about your student. The more details provided about the student, the more specific and targeted the results will be. Generating specific results will save you time wading through scholarships that may not apply. It would be impossible to apply for thousands of scholarships, just as it is impossible to apply to millions, so allow the search engine to cut out as many as possible. Providing specific information about your student will help you focus on the scholarships most likely to result in a match.

Frankly, scholarship searches take a long time. Allow at least two hours, or even half a day, just to input your student's personal information. Either the parent or the child can do this step. Your student does not need to be with you, because you will know most of the information needed. While you're putting in this preliminary information, take notes as you go. During the process, each time you see something potentially helpful, write it down separately, because it will be helpful later.

After you input your student's personal information, the scholarship possibilities will shrink from 53 million hits to a few hundred. Hundreds of scholarships are, unfortunately, still too many. If each scholarship takes a week of work, and there are 36 weeks of school, it isn't possible to finish 36 within a school year. Even working year round would only result in about a hundred scholarship applications at most. Narrow down the list to 30 or 40 scholarships if possible.

Look beyond search engines as well. Although they are particularly helpful for large national scholarships, search engines are not as useful for finding smaller, local ones. Look at scholarships won by family members and friends. Note scholarships which local students have won, and search at local businesses. I was really surprised by the number of scholarships I saw advertised on the walls of neighborhood stores!

Another scholarship resource is your local high school. Many school districts have a webpage devoted to scholarships. Lastly, use the notes you took when you input your student information in the search engine. Those notes indicate a student's areas of specialization or unique activities. Search for those words plus "scholarships" to locate any potential opportunities.

FILTER SCHOLARSHIPS

Filtering scholarships can be a long and arduous process unless you remember one key concept. Remember the phrase, "one strike and you're out." Your first search may return hundreds of results, which must then be quickly whittled down to a reasonable number. You don't have to understand every nuance of each scholarship opportunity; you just need to give each one a quick "thumbs up" or "thumbs down." Unless otherwise stated, assume that each scholarship will accept applications from homeschoolers. As you search, at the first negative strike, delete the scholarship without a second thought. With the first detail that implies this scholarship is a misfit for your student, eliminate it and move on. A scholarship that is only for girls is a waste of time for boys, regardless of the large award. Essays specifically for public school children will not be won by a homeschool student, no matter how unfair that may seem. With hundreds of scholarships to weed through, there isn't time to argue with people about their scholarships. Eliminate scholarships at the very first strike.

> *Keep the number of scholarship options to a reasonable amount using the "one strike and you're out" rule.*

Remove scholarships that are school-specific. Some scholarships may be used only at a specific university. If a child is not planning to attend there, don't bother—move on! Eliminate scholarships that require skills your child does not have. For example, my son applied for several scholarships dealing with economics, but did not apply for any scholarships that required making a video about economics. If your student does not already have the ability to complete an application's requirements, it's a waste of time.

After using these scholarship-filtering directions, read the fine print for each potential scholarship. Pay attention to the details. See if homeschoolers are specifically excluded. This rarely happens, but if it does, find out before you waste any time on the application. Some scholarships require videos, art, or photography, and others are simple applications. Some will be based on chance, not skill, and may be tied to advertising.

The next step in filtering is to do a cost-benefit analysis. A small essay with a small cash award may be easier to win, and might be a better choice for your student than a really long essay. Local scholarships may be easier to win because there are fewer applicants. Compare how much work an application will entail with how much money it might provide. If a scholarship requires a 3,000-word essay on a topic your child doesn't love, and the award is only $50, that scholarship may not be worth the work. On the other hand, if the scholarship requires a 150-word poem and you have a poetry-loving child, and the money reward is $2000, that might be a great opportunity. Weigh the cost to your child, in terms of time and effort, against the potential payoff.

Consider the interests and delights of your student. It is important to determine if your student is interested in a topic, or whether only the parent is interested. For example, my son was very interested in politics and economics, but did not want to write about Democrats and Republicans. He snubbed essays based on politics, but loved applications involving economics, even though they seemed very similar to me.

Is it worth applying? Consider the financial reward, the chance of winning, the amount of work, and the interest level of the student.

Consider the stress of follow-through as well. It is easy for a student to complete an assignment they love for the possibility of financial reward. It is much more difficult for them to complete an assignment they dislike, regardless of the potential award. It often boils down to the "fight factor." Is this scholarship worth the effort required to convince your child to do the work?

FORMAT SCHOLARSHIPS

Once scholarships are found and filtered, they must be arranged, or formatted. This next step is to keep track of each scholarship and the date it is due. To do this, keep a notebook or file folder for each application.

I used a notebook and printed out each scholarship. I copied the descriptive paragraphs from the website and printed them, along with the application itself. Sometimes I printed previous winners' essays for comparison. I arranged them in order of due date, with the most immediate due date first.

It may help to estimate the time it will take to complete each assignment. Think about how long it will take your child to write the essay or complete the project. For example, I estimated that my children could produce a pretty good 1,000-word paper in a single week. Time estimates can help you prioritize upcoming scholarships based on due dates. In addition to writing essays or completing projects, the student must also have enough time to fill out the application and complete any other details. Some scholarships require letters of recommendation or other time-consuming additions that take planning.

Set clear expectations of what is required from your child, but also allow enough time for the tasks to be completed.

FOLLOW THROUGH

Follow through is the most difficult part of the scholarship process. Parents may have control as they find, filter, and format scholarships, but they have little control over the follow through! This is because the student has to do the work, not the parent. The parent can supervise and direct, but students are sometimes the weakest link in the process. The student must read each application thoroughly, and pay attention to the specific details. If a letter of recommendation is necessary, the student must obtain it. It's also important to apply in a timely and accurate manner. One year I was on the scholarship committee for my state's homeschool organization. As the first applications came in, I found myself wanting to reward those who turned their applications in early. Apply on time, as early as possible, because it can make all the difference.

Create a unique submission. First prepare the initial draft, and then check previous winners to see what the judges might prefer.

Review previous winners. Good essays include editing and rewriting a first draft. After the student has written a draft, have them look at essays from previous winners. Writing the first draft before looking at winning essays can help ensure their own creative, unique product. Look at previous winners afterwards to determine if your student's tone, content, and format are comparable to the winners. Just as you might seek to model college papers after the preferred style of the professor, model your scholarship application after the preferred style of the scholarship committee. If past winning essays have typically been written in the first person, then change your essay to the first person. If past winning essays used an extremely youthful tone, that may be what reviewers will be looking for in a winner. Did past winning essays use 12 point Times New Roman? Did they justify the documents on both sides or simply on the left? Imitate the winners.

Although the format should be similar to previous winning essays, the content should be unique, and should set your student apart from their competitors. If your student looks at winning essays <u>before</u> they write their first draft, they might be biased or swayed to match their content to the winners, and thus lose their uniqueness. Match the format, but let your student's own winning uniqueness shine through in content! It's best to edit essays multiple times, just as you might edit a regular English paper in your own homeschool. Don't write the paper for your student, but provide them with feedback that they can incorporate into their final version.

Completing the application form is an activity best done together with your child. This is an opportunity to teach children how to quickly complete application forms of every kind. It is surprising to learn what child know and don't know on these forms. Each application is a teaching opportunity for you and for them. Read the details carefully, knowing every detail is very important. Submit applications early, and keep your focus on the actual learning process, not just winning scholarships. After all, the learning process is more important than earning the scholarship award.

A student may write a beautiful essay, follow through perfectly, and submit early, but still may not win the scholarship, even if the scholarship seemed like a perfect fit. Scholarship review committees can't choose everyone. Often there are several perfect-fit applicants. If they can only choose one winner, then several wonderful candidates will not win. Once a scholarship application is completed and sent, try to put it out of your mind and move on to the next one. Keep trying!

FILE CREDITS

Scholarship application work can be included in your student's homeschool records. Whether it included essays or something else, the work can be added to their homeschool classes. Save the essays or other work, as many essays can be used again for future purposes, such as scholarship applications or college admission.

> *Include the number of hours worked on scholarship applications in determining high school credits.*
> *75-90 hours = ½ credit*
> *120-180 hours = 1 credit*

If you use scholarship applications for high school

classes, determine a class title, a credit value, and a grade. You can award one high school credit for the completion of 120-180 hours of work. For instance, if your student is writing and researching for an hour a day, they could earn a full credit of English over the course of a year. Of course, English is not the only subject that may apply. If your student completes most of their applications based on a specific topic, such as economics, they could then earn a whole credit of economics. If most of the scholarships they worked on required photography, artwork, or videos, then they might earn a credit in art. Determine grades for writing scholarship essays in the same manner in which you determine their other grades. In addition, if a student wins an award, their grade for that project should be an "A." Winning an award is a clear indication that a third party highly values their work.

WINNING BENEFITS

Winning means more than getting money. Of course, the goal is financial reward, and the student might win money for college or gift certificates. If your student wins or is recognized for something, include that on their activity and awards list. Include all scholarship results in the awards list for college applications. Even work that is "commended" or given an "honorable mention" can be included on those lists. But there are also non-monetary benefits to winning. Sometimes, even if an award doesn't have a lot of monetary benefit, it can lead to even bigger awards. For example, when my child received a $25 award from the Veterans of Foreign Wars, he became eligible for the next step up, a larger monetary award. That small award was a stepping-stone to winning a bigger award.

Non-monetary benefits might include publication. If an organization chooses to publish your child's winning essay, include that on their awards list. One of my sons had an essay published in a children's book. My other son wrote an essay on economics, which was published in a trade journal. This publication led to a monetary award, and further publication in *Liberty* magazine. Non-monetary benefits are sometimes just as valuable as monetary ones.

NON-WINNING BENEFITS

Even when students don't win, there are still benefits. My favorite "non-winning benefit" is the opportunity to use and re-use the written essays. My sons used their scholarship essays for college application essays the following year. One common scholarship essay topic is, "What are your goals in life?" A similar topic is often used for college application essays. Other portions of the application may also be useful again.

One of my sons experienced an interesting non-winning benefit during his high school years. He applied for a scholarship at a local bookstore, and following the instructions, he wrote a story for children. After reading some of the previous winning essays, he realized that they didn't really want a children's story. All of the previous winners had written poems, and most of them rhymed. Clearly what the scholarship committee really wanted was poems.

My older son didn't want to be bothered with writing a poem, so he went back to his computer files and found a poem he had written in 5th grade. He submitted his 5th grade poem, and he won. The award for this competition was a $50 gift certificate to a bookstore, not a college scholarship. However, the winning essays were compiled and published in a hardback children's book. We received copies of the book, and sent one copy to each of the colleges where he applied. Being a published author is priceless! The non-winning benefit turned out to be a real benefit after all.

EXECUTIVE SUMMARY FOR BUSY PARENTS

HOW TO FIND PRIVATE SCHOLARSHIPS

- Find scholarships with scholarship search websites like FastWeb.com.
- Filter irrelevant suggestions with "one strike and you're out!"
- Format scholarship by due date.
- Follow through is required by the student.
- File credits and awards on high school transcript.
- Reuse essays for other scholarships.
- Reuse essays for college applications.

C H A P T E R   2 1

Test Prep Payoff

*"The plans of the diligent lead to profit as surely
as haste leads to poverty."*

Proverbs 21:5

Vizzini: *"Inconceivable."*

Inigo Montoya: *"You keep using that word. I do not think it
means what you think it means."*

~ The Princess Bride

Most college admission decisions depend on SAT or ACT scores. Most big scholarships come from colleges based on these test scores. Therefore, for college admission and scholarships, it's important to study for the SAT or ACT. In fact, some colleges specify the amount of scholarship money they will award for a specific test score. One score may qualify for a $3000 scholarship, another score will earn $8000, and a higher score could earn $12,000 or much more. The amount of each scholarship will vary from college to college, depending on a number of factors, including the college's level of endowment. But most colleges will give you more money for higher test scores. Some colleges will give a huge scholarship for the test scores they want. If a student studies for the SAT or ACT and earns a scholarships worth $10,000 per year of college, that is $40,000 in savings, $40,000 in real money. It would be wonderful to have an extra $40,000 in the family! Study hard for the SAT or ACT. It really makes a difference in scholarship awards.

BUSINESS FIRST

Remember, colleges are a business. Although they must like educating young adults, this can seem almost like an aside. Colleges are assessed and evaluated by college rankings in different magazines and websites. Colleges care about those rankings, because that is how prospective customers (parents) evaluate them. Each year, many of the rating journals (for example, *US News and World Report*) will rank colleges based on a number of different criteria, one of which is the school's average SAT/ACT scores. A student with a high test score will raise the ranking of a college. In raising your student's score, you can potentially raise the value of a college's business. This is one thing that motivates colleges to offer scholarship money to high scoring students.

> *College rankings are established by well-known magazines and websites. Colleges are often evaluated by their SAT and ACT scores.*

STUDY FOR THE SAT

Studying for the SAT and ACT is not a waste of time. Research has shown that preparation can increase SAT scores by 100 points. Higher SAT scores can increase your chance for college admission and academic scholarships. Making test preparation a regular part of your high school experience will make it much easier for your student to succeed. Public school students may have trouble finding time to prepare for the test, but homeschoolers can make studying a part of their total educational experience. Homeschoolers have an advantage in test preparation.

Like many homeschool parents, I understood that studying for the SAT test was necessary for college admissions and financial aid, but I was frustrated that I had to "teach to the test." My teenagers were also resistant. But the tests measured basic skills in reading, writing, and math. And of all the things you want for your children, good skills in reading, writing, and math are pretty high on the priority list. There are many benefits of college test preparation:

- Earn great scholarships with higher scores
- Learn important essay writing skills
- Master math concepts from basic to advanced
- Gain confidence in test-taking abilities

SAT BASICS

The SAT is a standardized college entrance exam with three sections that measure reading, writing, and math skills. Each section is graded on a 200-800 scale. For each section, a grade of 500 is average, 600 is good, 700 is great, and 800 is perfect. Because there are 3 sections, a perfect score on the SAT is 2400. The test takes about 4 hours and is offered at most local high schools and some colleges.

ACT BASICS

The ACT is also a standardized college entrance exam. It covers reading, writing, and math like the SAT, but also includes a science section. Unlike the SAT, the essay section of the ACT is optional. While the SAT penalizes a student □ a point for incorrect multiple-choice answers, the ACT does not deduct any points for incorrect answers, so there is no penalty for guessing.

CHOOSE THE RIGHT TEST

Colleges are familiar with both tests, and usually either test will be acceptable. Statistically, one-third of students will do better on one test and one-third will do better on the other, and it's not always the test you think is the best. Try a sample of both tests at home first, without pressure, and see which test makes your child look like a genius. Then decide which test to take for college admission.

Use the test that makes your child look smarter. Give a sample SAT and a sample ACT at home first. Then decide which test is best for your child.

Sample tests are available online, at www.collegeboard. com and www.act.org. Sample tests are available at most local libraries, and you can check out SAT and ACT preparation books there too.

The daughter of one of my clients earned a full academic scholarship, plus room and board, plus books and expenses, plus a monthly living stipend, to attend her first choice college. The parent said she was thankful for my help, so I asked her what information was the most helpful to her. She credited my advice on sampling both tests. She said she would have NEVER guessed that her daughter would do better on the ACT, and it totally didn't make sense to her. However, she tried my advice and pre-tested her daughter, and based on the results, had her take the ACT instead of the SAT. Even if your child doesn't test well in general, most will do better on one test than the other. You won't know until you try!

HOW TO STUDY

Homeschooling parents have the advantage on the SAT test when they provide a quality, well-rounded education for their child. Before high school begins, you can prepare for the SAT by providing a quality education that includes "reading, writing, and arithmetic." Penmanship is important as well, since part of the SAT includes a hand-written essay. Perfectionists, please remember that penmanship may be important, but that does NOT mean it has to be perfect. It only needs to be legible. Penmanship preparation means you teach your child how to write quickly and legibly—not perfectly.

> *To study, use a study guide with real tests. Give one section of one test each day, timed. Review the answers to questions marked wrong.*

Struggling math students will benefit by refreshing their skills through regular math review prior to taking the tests. Review will also help advanced students who may not have seen beginning concepts for many years. The reading sections have a lot of vocabulary that students need to know in order to succeed in college. Instead of buying a vocabulary curriculum, you can use test preparation for your vocabulary studies. I have to confess that the writing section with the essay is my favorite part of the test, because essay writing is crucial to success in college. My youngest son actually thanked me later in college for teaching him to write a quick essay.

During high school, the best way to study for the test is using high quality test preparation books. There are some great test prep books, but I prefer the ones from Princeton Review. They have a youthful, conversational style that appeals to teenagers more than the dry "business only" approach of other books.

I suggest using the books *Cracking the SAT/ACT* and *11 Real Practice Tests* by Princeton Review. Each book has a short, easy to understand explanation of the test, and includes many complete exams for practice. All the answers have clear explanations. Test preparation books are relatively inexpensive, and can be used at home with your child working independently. I suggest using one practice test at a time. Each day, have your child take one section of one test. Each section is 25 minutes long. Use a timer so that it simulates the real testing environment.

I remember my dawdler son's surprise when I began timing the test. Our conversation went something like this:

Me: *You have 25 minutes. I'm setting the timer.*

Son: *Why do you have to set the timer? I'll know when to stop, and I don't think that timing is important anyway, and I can't possibly get it all done with the timer on, so I might as well not use a timer since I won't finish anyway, but if you really wanted me to learn then you wouldn't time it at all....*

Me: *You have 24 minutes, and the timer is still going.*

For the record, my son has grown up to be a wonderful young man, he is grateful we homeschooled, and no serious damage was done to his self-esteem, even though I timed his practice sessions! Plus, it was wonderful preparation for the timed tests of real college courses.

After completing a section of the review book, my children corrected their tests by themselves, and looked over the explanations for each incorrect answer. If they had further questions, my husband would go over the explanations with them.

Some students may need more practice with essay writing. The Institute for Excellence in Writing has some excellent resources: *High School Essay Intensive* and *Advanced Communication Series*. For students who need practice instead of instruction, a gentle way to start might be the book *501 Writing Prompt Questions* by Learning Express. It has simple essay topics that you can use regularly, as well as a great section for parents about how to evaluate the essays.

Other kinds of test preparation can also increase scores and yield great dividends. For those students who learn better without textbooks, prepare them for the reading and writing sections of the tests using a "real books" approach. Reading lots of quality literature is the best preparation for these students. Some test prep companies offer classic literature that highlights SAT Vocabulary words. Kaplan has a series of books called *SAT Score-Raising Classics*. Books such as *Frankenstein, Wuthering Heights*, and *The Scarlet Letter* have text on one side with vocabulary words in bold print. On the opposite page each word in bold is defined in simple terms. I used these books to read aloud as part of our regular curriculum, and they doubled as SAT preparation. Other auditory learners might prefer *Verbal Advantage* for vocabulary development.

You can enroll in a formal SAT or ACT class using a variety of online courses through test preparation companies. This may be a good option for a student who is a visual or auditory learner. Classes may be available through a homeschool co-op (usually inexpensive) or a private course (usually pricey).

> *Free practice tests may be offered in your area. Check your local library or community center for SAT or ACT practice exams.*

Our local library offered a practice test twice a year through Princeton Review. It was the most realistic practice we found, because it was an actual test in actual test situations, graded so that we had an objective score for each child. The SAT is such a very long test that we were thankful we could try it in a safe environment before our sons took it for real.

Studying for the SAT can benefit children, but it's possible to go overboard. Studying for hours a day, for weeks on end, may cause burnout. Do not frustrate your teenager so they hate homeschooling. Learn test-taking skills, and reinforce basic skills, but do it with a light touch. Know your student, and trust your own judgment.

Beginning in their freshman year, and using these techniques, my two sons were both able to get above 2300 on the SAT, including a perfect 800 on one section! By studying for the SAT, they were both able to raise their scores approximately 200 points per section – a huge gain. Even though "actual results may vary," you can be confident that preparing for the SAT is worth it!

Don't stick your head in the sand, ignoring test preparation. It is tempting to hope the tests will simply go away. They won't. Just spend a few minutes learning about the tests. Educate yourself. You'll be glad you did, and you may save thousands of dollars. Peace of mind. Money. It's worth the effort to learn about high school testing.

EXECUTIVE SUMMARY FOR BUSY PARENTS

TEST PREPARATION BENEFITS

- Test scores affect admission.
- Good scores can earn big scholarships.
- Choose the test that is right for your child.
- Study for the test regularly each week during junior year.

CHAPTER 22

Scholarship Competition and Interview Tips

*"And my God will meet all your needs according to
the riches of his glory in Christ Jesus."*
Philippians 4:19

"Humiliations galore!"
Inigo Montoya, ~ *The Princess Bride*

Imagine you've done a great job educating your kids. They are bright, intelligent, well socialized, and have an area of passionate interest. They've received great grades and SAT scores. In addition, assume you have kept a complete set of homeschool records that have impressed the colleges. Your children have wowed the colleges during visits, and have followed up with charming thank you notes, including details from those visits. If this is true, then they might have a good chance of getting invited to an interview or scholarship competition at that school. Now what?

BE PREPARED

During an on-site scholarship competition and interview, colleges are looking for students with great social skills. Do they look you in the eye and have a firm handshake? Can they talk with anyone of any age? Are they polite, yet confident? One of the reasons why homeschoolers do so well in such competitions is that they often have these skills in spades! So relax; most of your preparation for the competition has already been done! Schools are looking for someone who's warm and friendly. They understand kids will sound like kids and not like adults. At the same time, they are trying to decide if "the lights are on" inside. For example, if they mention a current cultural issue, can the student give an educated opinion?

SEVEN WAYS TO PREPARE

1. Follow instructions indicating what they should bring.
2. Read the college brochures.
3. Read the college catalog.
4. Read information on their intended major.
5. Review their college essays.
6. Keep up with big news in current events.
7. Consider bringing a resume or activity list.

PRACTICE INTERVIEWING

Similar to a job interview, colleges will likely ask general questions like, "Tell me something about yourself." For that reason, it is good to brainstorm some possible answers with your student beforehand. Colleges may ask specific questions about a student's area of specialization. Think for a moment about some possible topics and stories your student could mention. Help your child also think of questions they could ask the college about

Brainstorm questions and answers at home with your student beforehand.

their intended major, or the campus living situation. They might ask how many classes are taught by part-time faculty, or how difficult it is to get into classes they need.

Because college interviews are very much like job interviews, it's a good idea to practice answering some questions that admissions staff might ask. You don't need to like the questions, but you will have to answer them as best you can, so be prepared.

PRACTICE INTERVIEW QUESTIONS

- Tell me about yourself.
- What are your strengths?
- What are your weaknesses?
- What has been your biggest success?
- Describe a time when you failed.
- What is the most important thing you learned in high school?
- What do you want to do ten years from now?
- How do you define success?
- What have you liked or disliked about your school?
- How would you describe yourself to a stranger?
- What is your proudest accomplishment so far?
- If you could talk to anyone living or dead, who would it be?
- What events have been crucial in your life?
- What mark do you feel you've left on your school?
- What do you want to get out of your college experience?
- What about you is unique?
- What could you contribute to our college community?
- What do you want to do after you leave college?
- What do you wish you could change about your high school?
- What question do you want me to ask you?

PLAN AHEAD

Before they actually meet with the admissions staff, discuss with your student appropriate behavior for interviews. This is a great opportunity to learn important skills that will help your child with future job applications. There are certain "Do's" and "Don'ts" that are common to any interviewing situation. Talk about these with your student, and discuss why they are important.

IMPORTANT "DO'S"

Discuss the "Do's" and "Don'ts" common to all interviews.

- Look people in the eye.
- Give a firm handshake.
- Speak loudly enough to be heard.
- Dress cleanly and neatly, conservatively and professionally.
- Bring 4 or 5 ideas to discuss.

- Bring 4 or 5 questions to ask that are not answered in brochures.
- Brainstorm answers to common questions.

IMPORTANT "DON'TS"

- Don't be late—not even a little bit.
- Don't bring your parents.
- Don't bring your phone—keep it turned off completely.
- Don't be rude to anyone, especially receptionists and staff.
- Don't lie or stretch the truth.
- Don't respond with "yes" or "no" when you can elaborate.
- Don't chew gum.
- Don't wear perfume, cologne or aftershave.
- Don't swear, even a little bit.
- Keep tattoos and piercings covered.
- Avoid excessive jewelry.
- Don't use excessive slang.
- Don't give a memorized speech.
- Don't be arrogant or boasting, just confident.
- Don't say or imply "this is my safety school."
- Don't ask questions that are answered in the college catalog.

My students experienced this interview process when they participated in an all-day competition for a full-tuition scholarship at their first-choice university. Each of the students was asked to bring something that represented them. My younger son brought a charcoal drawing he had made of the French economist, Jean Baptiste Say. My older son brought a chess demonstration board that he used to teach chess in inner city classrooms.

All applicants that day had fabulous academic records, great test scores, and an interesting passion. All of them were able to talk intelligently. There were some "Survivor" moments, when students would try to out-answer, out-talk, and out-volunteer others. My younger son was surprised that other kids would actually speak up more than he did!

I remember when they came home from the competition. They both told me, "It was so much fun!" They loved getting to know new people, really smart kids with lots of interests. They met kids who talked about interesting things all day, and had a blast! The university invited 108 students to participate in this competition, and only 10 were awarded full-tuition scholarships. Two of the students selected that day were homeschoolers—and both were my children! Boy, did we have a party the day we got the amazing news that they had won!

THE HOMESCHOOL ADVANTAGE

Ultimately, we learned that our students weren't chosen solely on their performance that day. They were also chosen for intangible reasons. How did they interact with the other students? How did they handle the competitiveness? How did they behave when they thought nobody was looking? In reality, the selection boiled down to socialization and character. Talk about a homeschooling advantage! Ultimately, I think they won because of how much fun they had. They went in with the right attitude, and their authenticity and enthusiasm were apparent to all. Even my "quiet" son did well, thus proving it's not as much about being outgoing as it is about being genuine.

> *A key assessment in these competitions is how the student behaves when he thinks no one is looking.*

A WORD TO STUDENTS

Relax. After you have practiced, the best thing you can do to prepare for an important college event is to get plenty of rest and relax during the event. You have been well prepared for this moment. Think about a few ideas you can use for the general "who are you?" questions. This is an opportunity to meet some great new friends and share your opinions on a wide range of topics. You can do this! Just let your light shine and have fun!

AFTER THE COMPETITION

If there was ever a time that called for a heartfelt thank you note, it's after being hosted for a scholarship competition. I recommend a very nice card with a heartfelt note. Below is the message my son sent after his all-day competition. Note how specific he is, recalling details of the day. Notice also how he is complimentary to the university, to

> *Be sure to write a heart-felt, specific thank you letter (not an email).*

the professor of the class he attended, to the professor who interviewed him and to the other students.

Dear Mike,

Thank you so much for both the scholarship competition and our interview on Monday. The competition in general was exceptionally well-organized for the candidates. The group discussion was excellent, fast-paced and quite insightful. I also thoroughly enjoyed my visit to the "Capstone: Political Economy" class, taught by Professor Smith. It was fascinating to listen and participate as the class worked their way through current political issues using economic principles.

I also wanted to thank you for our interview and time together. You may not realize it, but the questions you asked, and even the visual feedback, really helped as I was formulating my thoughts. This was my first experience in an interview where I was able to talk about my motivation— not just what I'm passionate about, but also why. The beauty in fine arts is generally understood, but I am equally fascinated by the aesthetic of society and nature. I want to thank you for asking great questions.

Good luck in choosing the finalists from the exceptional candidates I met yesterday; you have quite a job ahead of you!

Au revoir,

Alex

EXECUTIVE SUMMARY FOR BUSY PARENTS

KEYS TO SUCCESSFUL COLLEGE INTERVIEWS

Student should:

- Dress cleanly and neatly.
- Be confident and polite.
- Look people in the eye.
- Shake hands firmly.
- Engage in the conversation.
- Relax and have fun.
- Send a note of thanks.

Facing Reality

CHAPTER 23

Cut College Costs

"All the believers were one in heart and mind. No one claimed that any of their possessions was their own, but they shared everything they had."

Acts 4:32

"I've never worked for so little. Except once, and that was a very noble cause..."

Miracle Max, ~ *The Princess Bride*

We all know we should be saving for college. However, intentions don't always match reality. Fortunately, college tuition is similar to buying a car. Hardly anyone pays the sticker price, so don't be afraid and give up when you look at the list price of a school, especially a private school. Private schools sometimes provide considerably better financial aid than public schools, and usually their costs are ultimately comparable. Although many students take out some student loans, it's possible to go to college without using them. Effective strategies to cut down on college costs include saving money along the way, preparing your child well so they earn scholarships, and making sure they are presented in a positive way to the colleges. If a college degree is your student's goal, there are multiple ways to get one!

DECIDE BETWEEN COLLEGES

If cost is a significant factor in your student's choice of colleges, there are several steps to help you determine which school to enroll in. First, develop a chart and compare all the colleges you're interested in to each other. Make sure the financial comparison only includes "dollars out of pocket each year." There are too many variables present to use any other numbers. The dollar amount of scholarship money may not be relevant since the tuition at each college is different. Instead, look at how much you will need to spend. This step underscores how important it is to apply to several colleges, in order to choose the best financial offer.

Second, consider the livability test. Where does your student want to live for the next four years? It's not quite like choosing a spouse, but it's still a pretty significant decision. Would your student like to live there for four years?

Compare college costs by reviewing the out-of-pocket cost before loans for each university.

It's important to note that the parent isn't living there, but the student. Although parents can determine what college to financially support, it is the student who ultimately lives on campus.

Third, consider a support system. Determine if your child will have an adequate support structure in place at college. This might be a solid church home near campus, extended family members nearby, close friends attending the same school, or the ability to drive or fly home in case of emergency. It may just mean the presence of some good and trusted friends near campus. College students can sometimes face challenges that require support. Make sure to factor this into your decision.

HOMESCHOOLING COLLEGE

Another method of saving money on college is to homeschool college through AP, CLEP, and community college. This can reduce the number of classes a student needs to take, and can shorten the actual time spent in college. Homeschooling one year of college can save an enormous amount of money. Some families have success with AP Exams, which when carefully utilized, can save a tremendous amount on college costs, as each passing exam eliminates one college class.

We homeschooled one year of college by using CLEP testing (College Level Examination Program). Our children also went to community college for one year through dual enrollment, saving yet another year of college costs. When we began the college application process, we knew that even if we didn't get a penny of scholarship money, we still would only have to pay for two years of college, because we had already homeschooled two years of college. This is good to consider when evaluating the cost of college.

ASSESS KNOWLEDGE

The first step to homeschooling college is to assess your student's knowledge. The book we found most helpful in this process was *The CLEP Official Study Guide*. My sons looked at the table of contents in this study guide, and decided which of the tests they thought they might be able to pass. Then they took that particular sample test, and if they got 50 or more correct, we knew it was worth studying for the official test. A score of 50 (slightly higher for advanced foreign language) is a passing score on the CLEP, because all of the questions are hard.

STUDY THE SUBJECT

After assessing my students' knowledge, we bought a study guide for the subject area they were going to take a test in. For example, my youngest son's highest score was in American History, so I bought a REA study guide for CLEP American History, and he took one week to look over it at his leisure. He read his study guides during swim meets. It wasn't hard, and it didn't bother him at all. Other people might do a little bit of study for half an hour to an hour a day for a while, just to see if they can get the best possible score.

TAKE THE TEST

After your student has studied and prepared to take a CLEP test, it's time to actually take them to the testing area. You must make an appointment to take an exam, and you can do so by visiting the College Board website (www.collegeboard.org). Select the CLEP section at the bottom of

Passing college level exams is a great way to save money on tuition. Find out whether your college choice will provide credit by examination.

the page, and find the locations closest to you where tests are offered. Tests are scored right after your student completes the test (with a few exceptions), so you will know before you leave what their final score is. Different colleges award credit for CLEP scores in different ways. For example, one college might give your student 5 college credits for a score of 50, while another might award only 3 credits for the same score. Check with the colleges you're interested in to learn their policies and score requirements. There are a few colleges who do not give any credit for CLEP tests, so it's a good idea to find out whether the colleges you're interested in will give you credit before you invest the time and money.

REPORT SCORE

Although you can if you want to, you don't have to report your test scores to a college immediately. During the summer when we homeschooled college, we only reported scores to my sons' number-one college. We did this because I felt very confident that this college would be happy that I was keeping in touch with them, but we didn't report scores to all the other colleges that they applied to.

SAVE MONEY

Homeschooling college can save a lot of money at a university. Eventually, you will want to report your student's CLEP scores to the colleges she's interested in applying to. The College Board allows you to choose which scores you send where. There is a slight fee for this service, which was always worth it to me for my mental health. If you wait until the end of the summer to send your scores, it may result in $100 in fees, but because these scores ultimately translate into thousands of dollars in college credits, we didn't mind the small cost of this.

REMAIN CALM

If you're experiencing the "desperate parent" feeling, I want to assure you that it is completely normal! Winter and spring of senior year are the absolute worst times of year for this feeling. Most students have already chosen a college by this time, have already been accepted, and are eager to leave home. Yet most parents are still looking at the sticker price of the college and feeling completely overwhelmed, because they haven't received much financial aid yet. This is the time to remember that virtually no one pays the sticker price for a college. In fact, the average financial aid package covers 43% of tuition, fees, and room and board for one year at the average four-year college, public or private.

EXECUTIVE SUMMARY FOR BUSY PARENTS

COMPARE COLLEGE COSTS

- Do not compare scholarship awards between colleges.
- Compare cost out of pocket, excluding loans.
- Consider livability at each college.
- Consider the support system available at each college.
- Homeschooling college classes can save money.

C H A P T E R 2 4

College Opposition and the GED

"There is no fear in love. But perfect love drives out fear,
because fear has to do with punishment. The one who
fears is not made perfect in love."

1 John 4:18

Buttercup: *"We'll never survive."*
Westley: *"Nonsense. You're only saying*
that because no one ever has."

~ The Princess Bride

Once upon a time, colleges sometimes required a GED from homeschoolers before providing financial aid. GED stands for General Educational Development, meaning equivalent to a high school diploma. Since 1998, however, Congress has provided a better way for homeschoolers to demonstrate their "ability to benefit" from federal financial aid. The law states that students who have "completed a secondary school education in a home school setting that is treated as a home school or a private school under state law" can receive federal financial aid. When you fill out the FAFSA, the government will decide how much financial aid you should receive. You can receive financial aid as a homeschool student, and you do NOT have to take a GED.

The U.S. Department of Education's regulations explain that a student is eligible for financial aid if he was homeschooled, and either (1) obtained a secondary school completion credential as provided by state law, or (2) has completed a secondary school education in a homeschool setting under state law. What does that mean? If you are homeschooling within your state homeschool law, then your student is eligible for federal financial aid. There is no need to take the GED.

I saw a movie the other day about a high school dropout. She wanted to get a good job, but wasn't able to without a high school diploma. She studied hard, and finally got her GED, proving that she had a high school education. It was a heart-warming story, but it illustrates one thing: a GED can have the stigma of "high school dropout." Many homeschoolers prefer to avoid that stigma. Homeschoolers are NOT high school dropouts! Homeschoolers are recognized under the law, as shown above. Our homeschool transcript is a real transcript. Our homeschool diploma is official. Our students can receive federal financial aid, just like private and public school students. In the working world, when an application asks if you are a high school graduate, the answer is YES. If the application asks if you have a high school diploma, the answer is YES.

> *Homeschoolers are not high school dropouts, and a GED should not be required.*

GED REQUIREMENT IS NOT HOMESCHOOL FRIENDLY

When you begin to contact colleges, ask them about their policy regarding homeschool students. They do not need a GED from your student. If they require a GED, you can bet they are not a homeschool friendly college. There are some colleges that accept a GED from homeschool students who do not provide either a transcript or portfolio. This is an option that colleges use to provide flexibility in their homeschool admission policy. However, allowing a GED as an option is different than requiring a GED as part of their policy.

Get to know the college admission policy to determine if the school is homeschool friendly. Few colleges these days will require a GED. Most colleges see and admit homeschoolers regularly, and are unfazed by homeschool transcripts. If you run across one that doesn't understand independent homeschooling, you should likely shop for another college, one that is more homeschool friendly. More and more colleges are learning that policies requiring a GED from homeschoolers are counter-productive, and they are changing their policies to be more accepting of homeschoolers. As homeschoolers in college become more and more common, colleges will feel growing pressure to take down barriers that discourage homeschool families. This is good news for families considering homeschooling high school.

SOCIALLY ACTIVE HOMESCHOOLERS CHANGE COLLEGE ADMISSION POLICY

Not all colleges appear homeschool-friendly at first glance. The college website may include an out-dated policy discriminating against homeschool applicants. During college fairs, an admission representative may state an unfavorable policy for homeschooled applicants. Not all schools are homeschool friendly, and not all representatives understand home education. Be prepared to intervene if necessary, and create change. Be proactive, be assertive and ask for change. Simply asking with kindness can change college policy, and may make a better situation for your child and for other homeschoolers as well.

POLICY DISCOURAGES HOMESCHOOL APPLICANTS

College policies change overtime, and information you read on the website may not be accurate. Information from one college representative may not be up-to-date. Don't be shy. Speak up, and contact the Director of Admission to ask for clarifications. If their policy has not already changed, you could be the change agent, encouraging a reassessment of policy.

Be proactive and assertive. Ask for homeschool-friendly admission policies.

A college website provided an example of a poor homeschool policy. I wrote to them and received a favorable reply. This is the email I sent to the admission department.

To: Admissions

Subject: Homeschool Policy Discourages Homeschool Applicants

Dear University Admissions,

A homeschooler has contacted me for help regarding your university homeschool admission policy. You school is not a homeschool friendly college, as it has unique requirements just for homeschoolers seeking admission. A homeschool friendly college is one that treats a homeschool applicant the same as a public or private school applicant.

Your homeschool admission policy requires an accredited home school program and successful completion of the GED (see attached.) Your policy is mystifying for homeschoolers, which is why I have been contacted. Most homeschoolers do not use accredited programs, as you require. Instead, most homeschoolers are independent, like a private school, and are not required by law to provide accreditation by their state. In Washington State, for example, we homeschool legally under the law, and our state does not provide a homeschool accreditation program. An ordinary homeschooler from my state would not be able to provide records from an accredited program.

Admission policies that require a GED are frustrating to homeschoolers. Often a GED is used for high school dropouts. Our students have not dropped out. Homeschoolers are willing to provide the SAT or ACT that other high school students must submit, but the GED should not be required. Since 1998, homeschool students can receive federal financial aid without having a GED, so it should not be required for admission.

There are public and private high schools that are not accredited. I suggest that you treat homeschoolers the way you would an unknown public or private school, which may not be accredited either.

Can you please respond to these concerns, and let me know how I can advise students that have been homeschooled independently by their parents? I am eager to hear your response.

Thank you,

Lee Binz, The HomeScholar

I was pleased to receive this reply from the college:

Hello Lee,

There seems to be some confusion with our policy that is stated below, as I thought it was updated when I began at WWU. I appreciate you bringing to my attention the language provided about a GED and an accredited home school program.

Home schooled students must meet the same requirements any other student would meet attending a public or private high school: 2.5 GPA, a 19 on the ACT or 900 on the SAT Reading and Math are our standard admission requirements. Please let me know if you have any additional concerns, but we will get this updated soon.

Dean of University Admissions

When I received the response, it became clear the college website did not accurately reflect the current admission policy. It's also clear that a college admission department is staffed with real human beings who are reasonable and willing to listen and discuss each situation. They aren't scary or intimidating automatons. I encourage parents to contact colleges directly when concerned about admission policies. You can be a positive change agent for homeschoolers in the future. One week later, the college had a new policy for homeschoolers on their website. Brief and encouraging, it now says:

> *A college admission department is staffed with real human beings. They are usually reasonable and willing to listen and discuss each situation.*

HOME-SCHOOLED APPLICANTS

Our University has experienced a dramatic increase in enrollment from the home-schooling population, and has found that prospective and current home-schooled students offer strong academics and a positive contribution to student life.

This University seeks students qualified to benefit from a university education, and who will actively contribute to student life. Every aspect of an applicant's credentials, such as classes taken, grades, performance on the ACT or SAT, and community involvement are taken into consideration. The University operates on a rolling admissions process.

As usually happens, this Dean of Admissions was friendly and helpful. Don't be shy when dealing with colleges, just be kind. Here is how one mother took matters in her own hands, and became socially active to defend the rights of her own child, helping other homeschoolers in the process. She told me, "I wrote to the president of the college a couple of weeks ago, telling him that my son would not consider his college because of the GED requirement unfairly imposed on homeschoolers. The president sent me an email today! Quick answer: GED, be gone! Here is his letter."

Dear Ms. Jones,

Thank you for your recent letter. I have been in touch with the Dean of Admission and Financial Aid, and am pleased to report that she has reviewed our policy that requires the GED of homeschooled applicants without an official high school diploma, and has removed that requirement effective immediately.

Homeschooled students will, however, need to complete the Common Application Home School Supplement to the Secondary School Report form. Our website and catalog are currently being updated to reflect these changes.

I appreciate your communication, and the Dean of Admission and I both hope your son will keep our college on his list of colleges to which he may apply.

Sincerely,

President of Connecticut College

This homeschool mother was thrilled with the response from the college, and said, "I definitely commend the college for responding quickly and intelligently to my letter questioning the wisdom of requiring the GED of homeschooled applicants."

Her expression of concern changed homeschool policy quickly and easily with one simple assertive letter spoken in kindness. College admission policies are constantly changing, and you can influence change in the positive direction! Be a positive force for homeschooling. Ask the question and state the obvious, because colleges will listen to you.

EXECUTIVE SUMMARY FOR BUSY PARENTS

GED DETAILS
- The GED indicates high school completion.
- The GED may have the stigma of "high school dropout."
- Colleges that are not homeschool-friendly may require a GED.
- Asking with kindness can change a college policy about the GED.

CHAPTER 25

Gap Year: Time Off for Good Behavior

"Therefore be as shrewd as snakes, and as innocent as doves."
Matthew 10:16b

Man in Black: *"You've done nothing but study sword-play?"*
Inigo Montoya: *"More pursue than study lately."*
~ The Princess Bride

Take time off between high school and college? In my day, such a thing was almost unheard of, unless the student joined the military or the Peace Corps, or ran away to "find themselves." These days, taking a year off between high school graduation and college is becoming more common, is viewed more favorably, and is even seen as a benefit by some colleges. Children can do amazing things before college, so a gap year is a legitimate option to consider.

WHAT IS A GAP YEAR?

A "gap year" usually lasts between 6 months and a year, during which time a high school graduate takes a job or does some volunteer work to gain experience before beginning their college career. Students are still considered freshmen when they subsequently enroll in college, unless they take a college course of any kind during their gap. Gap year policies vary widely between colleges. Some defer enrollment, which means the student is accepted and then waits a year to actually attend, while others do not defer enrollment, but require application again the following year.   Some colleges consider students as transfers if they take a gap year, and others (including Ivy League colleges) will admit you, give you great scholarships, encourage you to take a gap year, and still allow you to have your scholarships and freshman status when you return!

CHECK YOUR COLLEGE POLICY

To make sure that your student doesn't get penalized for taking a gap year, contact three or four colleges that your child would most like to go to, and ask them specifically for gap year information. Keep in mind that their policies can change from year to year, so try to get assurance that the policy they quote you is "grandfathered" and won't change while your student is away!

Contact each college to determine their gap year policy if that is appropriate for your student.

In general, I advise all students considering a gap year to still submit their college applications during their senior year. Provide a transcript, reading list, and course descriptions just as though you were intending to go directly from high school to college. Some colleges will consider a student a transfer student after they've been out of high school a year, which causes those students to miss out on any freshman scholarships. If you have your student apply while they are still in high school, you can avoid this problem.   Encourage your student to focus on their gap year plans in one of their application essays, and discuss what they will specifically do and what they hope to accomplish.

While your student completes the applications and essays, you can call the colleges to research their policies. Make sure you visit each college, and have your student talk face to face with the admissions department. That's as good as an "interview," and can go a long way towards proving that your student is really taking a gap year and not just goofing off. Fill out the FAFSA too. Colleges base their financial aid on the FAFSA, and (with luck) that financial aid decision will carry over once your student begins college. You don't want your child to return to a situation where they've been accepted to college but are unable to afford attending.

Gap year is usually not affected by "dual enrollment" college courses. These are college level classes that are taken at a community college or online while the student is officially a high school student. When your student has dual enrollment credits, you should include the information from the community college courses on their high school transcript, to show that it is "dual enrollment" and not a post high school college class. Only college classes taken <u>after</u> high school graduation might complicate your gap year. Your student can take anything before graduation, but nothing after graduation (no college classes during the gap year), and still retain their status as an incoming freshman.

GAP YEAR EXPERIENCES

Gap year is more common in other countries than it is in the United States. Dorothy, who lives in the United Kingdom, says it's quite common there. She says, "There are hundreds of organizations which offer gap year experiences, mostly abroad. Christian kids tend to do missions work with people like Youth With a Mission (YWAM). Rich kids will sometimes just go traveling. Some will go working through another country. We have two different young friends in Queensland at the moment, one working in Brisbane to see the country, another with YWAM. The way it works is you apply to university, and once accepted, you simply "defer" your place for a year. Talking about what you plan to do in your Gap Year or putting it in your application gives very useful insight into your personality to the university. It's all automatic."

WHO TAKES A GAP YEAR?

Taking a gap year can work out nicely for two types of students. One student might still need a bit of seasoning or maturing before attending to the challenges of university life. Another may have a passionate interest in a subject and would like to acquire some real-world experience in it. Both types of students need to be self-motivated, and have a plan, or the year might end up being a waste. You don't want a "gap year" turning into a "couch potato year." If you think it could fit your family, discuss gap year options with your student first. If there is any interest in a gap year, then pursue the possibilities with the colleges.

> *A successful gap year requires a plan. You don't want a "gap year" turning into a "couch potato year."*

GAP YEAR BEFORE COLLEGE

- Check college policy carefully.
- Each university will have unique rules.
- Even one college class after high school graduation may change scholarships.

C H A P T E R 2 6

College for Struggling Learners

"My grace is sufficient for you, for my power is made perfect in weakness."

2 Corinthians 12:9a

"Life <u>is</u> pain, Highness. Anyone who says differently is selling something."

Man in Black, ~ *The Princess Bride*

Dealing with learning challenges is difficult, but in high school, it can become seriously concerning. You don't have to be afraid, though. With the great student to teacher ratio of homeschooling, and the love for your child, you have what it takes to succeed. It can feel like a lonely path, but others have successfully navigated from serious learning struggles to college achievement. These parents have given me permission to share their stories.

LEARNING TO COMPENSATE

Debbie was at her lowest point when she realized her 12-year-old son, Dan, could not read or write in his Sunday school classes. She had to carefully shield him from the judgment of others. Her homeschool friends were very understanding, but she worked hard to keep him away from situations where he would have to read aloud. She was distraught. Again and again, they changed curriculum, hoping each time that a new curriculum would change everything. It seemed like nothing would ever work. He struggled with learning all the way through high school. She never had him officially tested, because she didn't want him to be labeled as an adult. Dan has achieved wonderful things since graduating homeschool!

When Dan turned 18, he started working at a coffee shop. An excellent worker, he received nothing but positive feedback, which motivated him to continue his education. He decided to attend college. He didn't score well on the SAT, so they did not report his scores to colleges. He entered college "through the back door" his mother said, by attending community college first. His excellent work ethic and love of learning helped him thrive where others felt adrift. Dan transferred from community college to a university with a 3.89 grade point average. There were 300 applicants to the business school that year, and Dan was one of only 100 admitted. Debbie said, "He finally realized he can do it!"

Debbie has some great advice for other parents: Don't push children before they are ready. She was glad she kept her son at home, so he could avoid the negative feedback of a public school setting. She read aloud to Dan constantly—even high school textbooks, when necessary. She used verbal assessments in all his classes, and didn't introduce essay writing until much later.

> *Don't push children before they are ready. They will learn to compensate as they get older.*

She recommends books by Dr. Raymond Moore, including *Better Late Than Early: A New Approach to Your Child's Education*, Grace Llewellyn's *The Teenage Liberation Handbook: How to Quit School and Get a Real Life and Education* and Cynthia Tobias's book, *The Way They Learn*. She says, "You feel like you're failing—like you didn't do something right." Don't be deterred, though. It takes a lot of one-on-one time, but that's the benefit of homeschooling. Read to them their textbooks and the classics, and use audio books if possible. Even in college, they can be allowed help with reading.

In her lowest moments, Debbie remembered her own grandfather. He also could not read. His wife would read blueprints to him each night so he was prepared for work the next day. Even so, her grandfather was a successful businessman. He was able to compensate. Young adults can learn to compensate as well.

Debbie's biggest surprise was realizing that Dan wanted a college degree. She had never thought he would go to college, and only vaguely considered a technical school. But while working at the coffee shop, he identified his gift in business. "Even if you think they won't go to college, they may—so always be prepared!" Debbie suggests.

Dan is thankful he was homeschooled, and he plans to homeschool his own children. Nurturing is critical, and homeschooling can provide vital ingredients. Debbie says, "I remember the hopelessness. They CAN succeed and excel—just give them the tools."

LEARNING TO TEACH

JoAnn homeschooled her two daughters, feeling extremely unsure of her abilities, until her girls were officially diagnosed with learning disabilities. Once she had the diagnosis, she realized that homeschooling was the best option. She didn't want her girls ostracized and placed in a special group that would have a negative effect on their socialization skills. Even her mother became increasingly supportive of homeschooling after the diagnosis was made.

Her two girls could not read until halfway through 5th grade. They struggled in reading, writing, and spelling. JoAnn's advice is, "Never despair! The timing of brain growth is on your child's timetable, not yours. Accept it, because you certainly can't change it!" She wishes she had dropped more academic subjects when they were in elementary school. Still, she is so glad she homeschooled. "Homeschooling is better for dyslexic kids for the positive encouragement and socialization."

> *Homeschooling provides encouragement and positive socialization for children with learning challenges.*

She taught with multi-sensory input and multi-sensory output. In every subject, she worked to provide lessons with audio, visual, AND tactile input. She supplemented courses with drama, hands on projects, and verbal assessments all the way through school. Her daughters were especially helped by the use of color. Her daughter color-coded college lecture notes to improve retention even when she entered college.

JoAnn's older daughter went directly into university, and majored in Biology with a minor in Chemistry. She graduated with an advanced degree as a

Veterinarian Technician. JoAnn's younger daughter also went directly into university, and graduated with a degree in Interior Design. Both girls were very successful in college. Both were struggling learners through high school.

LEARNING TO COPE

Jill was hesitant about labeling her daughter in any way, but knew she faced some unique challenges even without a formal diagnosis. Her daughter recently became a National Merit Scholarship Semi-Finalist. Here is what Jill says about her daughter's struggles: "She worked hard and I'm very proud of her. She is the daughter that would fit into the statement, 'I could never homeschool my child because....' She is very active, intense, dramatic and a joy to be around. I am convinced that if she were in a public school, we would have been 'encouraged' to put her on medications. The standard line around here, when she is getting jumpy, is to 'run up to the mailbox and get the mail,' which is a mile round-trip. She has forced me to think outside of the box, and it is an adventure I'm sorry to see come to a close."

Like the other mothers, Jill was able to find a way to harness strengths and weaknesses, and teach her child to compensate for difficulties. With close attention, unique coping mechanisms can develop. A homeschooling parent can see small successes, and learn to shape and mold new ways of coping with each new challenge.

KEEPING FAITH

Joelle is still homeschooling her child. She emphasizes that coping comes from faith, and gives expert advice as an experienced homeschool parent.

"A learning 'disability' isn't something you can just make go away if you have a clinic and a handful of web links. A learning challenge is best addressed with being sensitive to learning style and interests, which, as you know, vary from child to child.

"A learning challenge is also a mindset, a lifestyle, and sore knees from prayer. A learning challenge means you'll come face to face with your pessimism and lack of faith, through tears of mourning for the child you don't have. But lest anyone abandon hope, a learning challenge also means seeing God answer those tears by turning them to tears of what is, hands down, absolutely the most incredible joy when you see the triumphs. You will see those victories sooner or later on Earth or in Heaven.

"A learning challenge leads to personal growth in the siblings of the challenged child. A learning challenge is a worldview, a lens, and a perspective. It's the fierce mother-bear love you have when you whisper to your child, 'Don't listen to the naysayers. I love you no matter what, and I'm still your teacher.'"

LEARNING TO GROW

During a college fair, college admissions representatives are quite open about learning challenges. Be proactive in your college search process. Students should not hesitate to ask a college about their policies. Ask if the college will offer support for people with learning disabilities, and what that support entails. Many colleges understand the unique learning styles of the students that attend, and understand that people learn in different ways.

> *Many colleges provide extra support for students with learning difficulties. A college fair can be encouraging.*

Some colleges have an extremely supportive environment for children with learning disabilities, and may offer special programs. At some schools, students may become part of small study groups. Other colleges provide extra support such as note taking, accommodated examinations, and material in alternate formats.

When I go to college fairs, I notice how many colleges truly specialize in students with learning struggles. They want your students to enter and succeed in college. They are ready, willing, and able to teach them. There are colleges that specialize in dyslexia, and market to students with dyslexia. You should be able to find a college that is a perfect fit for your student, even if your student has difficulty, even when he is a senior.

LEARNING TO SUCCEED

During the college preparation process, parents can request accommodation for the SAT and ACT if necessary. Don't feel like your student will necessarily score poorly on the test. Both college admissions tests allow special accommodation, usually by allowing extra time for the test, but there may be other accommodations as well. This kind of accommodation requires a recent diagnosis by a medical doctor. It will take a lot of effort on your part, but it may be worthwhile.

If you do not want or require accommodation for college admissions tests, then an official diagnosis may not be necessary. Many parents are comfortable with homeschooling methods, and don't need additional help or direction. Perhaps a specialist will not impact or change the daily homeschool routine, and may not be worth the time and effort. On the other hand, if you are completely baffled about how to teach your student in a way that makes sense, and the input of a specialist will help you and change what you are doing, then evaluation may be useful. If you think a diagnosis will help you, then it will likely help your child. In that situation, testing might be worthwhile, even if it's inconvenient. If testing will not help you, then it may not be necessary.

What happens when REAL homeschoolers grow up? You know, the kids who have to actually work to learn? I'll tell you what happens—they succeed! This is a letter I recently received from a friend willing to share the ups and downs of her journey, and their ultimate success!

Emily shared that her son won the National Guard Outstanding Achievement Award for having the highest GPA in Automotive Technology. She shared her joy with me: "What makes this so amazing is that this child has ADHD, and a serious reading comprehension issue for which there is no cure. This is the student that the public school told me was unable to succeed because of his reading problems. I've been ridiculed and degraded for choosing to homeschool my children, and this feels like a sort of vindication to me! I'm so proud of him and of all he's accomplished. God is so good!" She asked me to share her message with other parents: "Never, ever, ever believe what someone else tells you about your child's abilities. God gave your child to you. Our children will live up to our expectations, so set the bar high and be there to help them reach above and beyond. Believe in your child and his dreams, and do everything in your power to make sure he can achieve them."

> *Real students with real challenges can grow up to become successful in college and career.*

Keep in mind your long-terms goals. You want your child to grow up and have his own home. You want her to succeed and thrive in anything she chooses. There are colleges that specialize in learning disabilities. There is a great college out there for your child, and there are colleges that understand learning issues without hesitation. If college is the plan, search until you find the right situation.

EXECUTIVE SUMMARY FOR BUSY PARENTS

COLLEGE IS POSSIBLE FOR STRUGGLING LEARNERS

- Teach your children to become lifelong learners.
- Help your students to compensate for weaknesses.
- Some colleges specialize in students with learning challenges.
- Real students with real challenges can really succeed.

CHAPTER 27

Overwork Causes Turmoil and Strife

"So do not fear, for I am with you; do not be dismayed, for I am your God. I will strengthen you and help you; I will uphold you with my righteous right hand."

Isaiah 41:10

"I've got my country's 500th anniversary to plan, my wedding to arrange, my wife to murder and Guilder to frame for it; I'm swamped."

Prince Humperdinck, ~ *The Princess Bride*

I've noticed an odd pattern among homeschool parents who are stressed about high school. In freshman year, they tend to do too much, because they aren't sure what high school looks like, or how much they need to accomplish. In sophomore and junior year, they pile on more work as they start to panic about college. In senior year, they hit the accelerator again to compensate for perceived weaknesses from the prior years.

Are you trying to do twice as much homeschooling this year? If this describes you, take a step back and look at what you are expecting. Are you doing too much? Remember the saying, if your only tool is a hammer, every problem looks like a nail. Are you beating your children over the head with more work? Is that how you are addressing every homeschool concern?

OVERWORK CAUSES TURMOIL AND STRIFE

Parents who panic about high school will sometimes try to allay their fears by piling on the work. That won't help. Trying to do too much causes turmoil and strife. Expecting too much can only cause problems, so only require a reasonable amount from your student. Add up how many hours you expect them to work each day, and make sure it's reasonable.

> *Choose peace. Children learn more when they aren't stressed. Make sure you expect a manageable amount of work.*

Math or English may take a couple of hours, but every subject shouldn't take more than an hour. Some classes can be easier than others. It's important to allow some down time, so that your home has peace and tranquility. It's hard to learn in a tumultuous home. Strive for a peaceful homeschool, so your kids have the ability to learn MORE because they aren't stressed. High school isn't a time to panic and pile on the schoolwork. Add it up, and make sure it's not too much.

CHARACTER FLAW CONFESSION

I know what it's like to pile it on. I really do. I consider it a character flaw in myself. Here is what I initially tried to do for freshman year of high school. You can see why I failed. I defy you to try to speak this list out loud without taking a breath: Jacob's Geometry, Patty Paper geometry supplement, Latin Road to English Grammar 3, Power Glide French 1, Apologia Chemistry, Sonlight American History, Teaching Company history supplement, current events, Spelling Power, dictation, analogies, Learn to Write the Novel Way, Sonlight Language Arts writing assignments, journal writing, Piano, composer and poet and artist each month with reports, timeline, mapping, read-aloud, Sonlight literature with literary analysis, scripture memorization, Bible study workbook and personal devotions.

I still can't read that without my heart racing. It took about a month until we did what homeschoolers call a "crash and burn." No matter how fast and how hard we worked, we couldn't seem to get it all done. When you look at this list, notice how all those ideas are just wonderful. My plan was simply filled to the brim with great educational opportunities! It was just too much good stuff to actually be achievable.

DO NOT SUPPLEMENT THE SUPPLEMENTS

Look at my plan and see if you can spot all the supplements. What if you eliminate supplements? I could eliminate Patty Paper Geometry. Teaching Company courses and current events were history supplements. English was supplemented with spelling, dictation, analogies, and journal writing. Bible study was supplemented with memorization and a workbook. Composers and artists were supplementing the piano lessons. Poet study was supplementing English. I had a talk about this with another parent, and we discovered that she actually had supplements to her supplements. That is how she knew she'd gone completely over the top!

Finding boundaries in English is very important. For some reason, this is the subject I usually see over-supplemented, particularly since most homeschoolers will mix and match curriculum within this area. It can be hard to figure out how much time to spend reading and writing—particularly with struggling readers and writers who may suffer and struggle through the process. I suggest nice soft boundaries that you can modify to fit your own students. In general, spend about one hour on activities to make writing better. That might include writing, worksheets, vocabulary workbooks, writing in a journal, spelling, grammar, or whatever a child might need. In high school, some children are finished with skill building activities, and this portion of the day will be spent on writing. In general, spend about one hour on reading. The number of books is less important than the time spent reading. Within that boundary, a reluctant reader might read six books, and a prolific reading might read sixty. Reading includes pleasure reading, classical literature, popular novels, research, and trade magazines.

AVOID DUPLICATING SUBJECTS

My biggest "ah ha!" moment came when I recognized my duplicate subjects. I was using two complete foreign language programs: Latin and French.

> *Avoid duplicated subjects. List your curriculum or expectations and remove duplicates.*

I knew in advance that I was doing that, actually. My children WANTED to do both, and we talked about how difficult it might be, but my children were motivated. What truly surprised me was English. I was using two complete English programs: Learn to Write the Novel Way, and Sonlight Language Arts writing. Not only was I using two complete English programs, I was supplementing English more than any other subject!

Once I identified all the duplicates, all the supplements, and all the unnecessary stuff, I started to prioritize. I had to put the most important stuff into our homeschool first. Once the big stuff was working, then I could supplement with the smaller things. My pastor gave a sermon called "Put in the Big Rocks First." Suppose you want to put some sand and rocks in a glass. If you have a glass that is half full of sand, you can't add another glass full of rocks; they just won't fit. But if you put the rocks in the glass first, and then pour in the sand on top, you will be able to fit them both. In the same way with your homeschool, put the big subjects in first. Then sprinkle the wonderful supplemental fluff on top, and eliminate any of the "sand" that doesn't fit.

SAY NO TO GOOD THINGS

At the beginning of the year, I was concerned about my children's attitudes. I wondered if they were lazy or unmotivated. Why did they work so slowly? My husband and I talked about all the problems we were having. I told him about the duplication, the supplements, and the fluff stuff. We took a marker, and started cutting down the list. We cut some wonderful curriculum and great activities. It was heart-breaking, but you know, there isn't enough time in a day to do ALL the good stuff. Something just had to go.

REVISE YOUR PLAN

Review and revise your homeschool plan. Look at your plan with a fresh eye. Is it still too much? Add up the hours you are expecting from your child now. Is it more reasonable? Are you back in balance? Your goal is to keep students challenged, but not overwhelmed.

Once things improve, there is a tendency to slip into old habits, and start expecting more and more again. It's like when you are very hungry and you pile mashed potatoes on your plate. After a while, you realize that your eyes were bigger than your stomach. We homeschool because we love to educate our children—it's fun! But that can cause us to attempt too much. Watch for the return of the "Do More Blues" later in the year, because it can come back again.

HOMESCHOOL LESSON FROM HUMMINGBIRDS

I love birds. Whenever I see a hummingbird out my kitchen window I scream like a little girl. The excitement I feel when I see these beautiful creatures is overwhelming. But have you noticed that hummingbirds seem to flap the fastest when they are hovering?

> *Attempting too much can cause children to fail. If you feel frustrated, check to see if you are doing too much.*

Homeschoolers are like that too. Sometimes they'll try to work so hard and so fast that they actually get less work done instead of more. Make sure you have enough time in your day to actually get the homeschooling done. If you try to get too much done, you'll end up going even slower through your year. In other words, don't try to do too much; you'll just end up standing still.

Another thing about hummingbirds you should know: although they look sweet, according to the books, they are actually pretty violent and aggressive. Could that be because all that hard flapping is stressing them out? I'm not naming names or anything, but if you feel like you're flapping your wings as fast as you can, and not getting anywhere, and if that frustrates you, maybe you're a hummingbird.

Are you angry, frustrated, burned out, and snapping at your kids? Attempting too much can cause them to fail. And their failure will just make you angrier. But they can't do it all; no one can. If you feel frustrated, check to see if you are doing too much.

I was watching a bald eagle fly the other day. Unlike a hummingbird, they really don't flap much at all. And yet, they really get a LOT done. As you homeschool high school, consider not flapping so much, but soaring a little more. Relax, and let the delights of your children provide the lift you need for your homeschool.

EXECUTIVE SUMMARY FOR BUSY PARENTS

KEEP CHILDREN CHALLENGED, BUT NOT OVERWHELMED

- Attempting too much can cause strife and reduce learning.
- Evaluate your homeschool and eliminate duplication.
- Say "no" to some great opportunities.
- Adjust and adapt regularly.

C H A P T E R   2 8

Restart After a Crisis Year

"Trust in the LORD with all your heart and lean not on your own understanding; in all your ways submit to him, and he will make your paths straight."

Proverbs 3:5-6

"I always think everything could be a trap... which is why I'm still alive."

Prince Humperdinck, ~ *The Princess Bride*

What will happen if your family situation changes and you feel the need to put your child into public school in the middle of high school? In some states, it's easy to take kids out of public high school, but much more difficult to put them back in. This combination of concerns leads some parents to consider abandoning homeschooling altogether during the later grades, and to put their kids into public or private high school in 9th grade. For others, the fear leads them to consider accredited programs. It's not because they don't like homeschooling, or because homeschooling isn't working for their family. They do these things because they're afraid of the "what if" situations:

- "What if" there is a family trauma, and we have to put our kids into school?
- "What if" the high school doesn't accept credits earned at home.
- "What if" my child is put back into 9th grade, and made to start high school all over?

The good news is that you don't need to put your kids into school because you are afraid! There are other options!

YOU CAN'T PREVENT LEARNING

You can't PREVENT a child from learning. Even when there is major life change, major trauma or major illness, you can still allow your child to learn at home. They will learn, whether you're paying close attention or not. And if there was a major family emergency, how much would your student learn in a public school anyway? Wouldn't your child still be concerned and traumatized? School isn't a panacea or a balm, after all. It doesn't solve the family problems. The challenge of educating a traumatized child will exist whether that child is learning at home or at school.

> *Even when there is major life change, major trauma or major illness, you can still allow your child to learn at home. It will not prevent a child from learning.*

FORCED UN-SCHOOLING

One time I heard a speaker who had faced years of family trauma. The homeschool parent faced repeated serious health issues, which caused serious financial issues, which led to near homelessness. Her state required yearly testing. Each year, she would "fail" at homeschooling, leaving her kids to learn on their own as she dealt with the struggles she faced. Essentially it was a forced, against-your-will un-schooling situation. And yet, each year, her children's test scores remained right where they should be, or even went up! They kept learning and kept succeeding, even without mom's help. Although I didn't un-school my own children, I have always thought that it was a worthwhile homeschool choice. Did it matter that this mom was forced to un-school? No, her children were still successful and making progress. Her story was so motivating to me!

DON'T GIVE UP!

Listen to what I read today in the Bible: "Let us not become weary in doing good, for at the proper time we will reap a harvest if we do not give up." (Galatians 6: 9) Or, as we say in our family, "Be brave, Little Piglet!"

Don't give up! Don't quit homeschooling because of fear. You don't have to second-guess yourself. Just stand firm, and don't panic. It's working, and you're doing a good job. You're experiencing what many parents experience: a moment of normal homeschooling-high-school panic. It will pass. Do not give up!

Homeschoolers are resilient, even in the midst of extreme difficulty. Everything is not always peaches and cream, and sometimes trauma happens. Sometimes LOTS of trauma. If you are having an extremely difficult time, with situations far beyond control, please read this mother's story, below, and be encouraged. She has wonderful 20/20 hindsight about what works when dealing with family trauma.

Dear Lee,

You helped me out a couple of years ago, and assisted me with a high school transcript for my son. I was just beginning to deal with some brain tumors and several surgeries, and I so appreciated your help. Things are still not as easy for me as they used to be, and I did very little homeschooling with my then 13-year-old that school year.

We really have had our share of trauma these past almost 6 years. That was the year our 19-year-old son died in a tragic accident. The grief made it nearly impossible for me to concentrate on teaching my other children, or for them to concentrate on learning. It was nearly a year of just spending time together, and not putting any pressure on them to accomplish much in the way of schoolwork.

> *"Homeschooling gave us the flexibility to just stop and take a break, and resume when the time was right."*

I really do not see that this set them back in any way. I cannot imagine them having to attend public school during such a traumatic time in their/our lives. Homeschooling gave us the flexibility to just stop and take a break, and resume when the time was right.

I thought I would give you an update on my older son. In June, he graduated with honors from Eastern with a degree in Business Administration and Economics. He did get two scholarships of $2000. We didn't really have the time and energy to pursue more, because these past 2 1/2 years have been filled with doctors, hospitals, surgeries etc. He now lives in Spokane, and in January of this year started a business buying and restoring foreclosed homes. He bought a home for himself too, remodeled it, and moved in the month of December. He is our 5th child homeschooled, and another success story. One to go! Actually, our final child is 15, and just took the Compass test [for community college] and passed. In a year, he will begin dual enrollment. He is interested in taking a computer class there, so he will probably do that this September.

Thanks again,

Linda in Washington

BRITTANY'S STORY

I want to share another very important story about success, perseverance, and planning ahead in case of a crisis year. Let me share with you the success story of Brittany, a 20-year-old young woman. Before I begin, I have a suggestion so that you don't panic: To prevent major upheaval, work conscientiously on your homeschooling each year. When things are going well, cover the core subjects each year, right from the beginning of high school. Try to avoid dropping classes unless it is a true emergency. Plan ahead like this, so that nothing will ever deter you in your success of homeschooling.

PROBLEMS WITHOUT REGRETS

Brittany contacted me to share the struggles of her family. They faced huge family difficulties, and handled them without regrets, but it left her feeling hopeless about her goals.

Dear Mrs. Binz,

I happened upon your website today, and I'm hoping you can help me. I'm not sure I'm your traditional candidate, or that my situation is common. But you seem like someone who knows a lot about homeschooling, and I'm hoping you can give me some advice. My name is Brittany. I'm 20 years old and I was homeschooled by my mother starting in the second grade. I was homeschooled through the rest of elementary school, middle school, and through most of my senior year. Here's where things get complicated.

In my senior year my grandmother became very ill, and I was greatly needed to help care for her, so for all practical purposes I dropped out of school to do so. I kept saying I'd start back, but my grandmother stayed sick for over a year and a half, and things just didn't work out for me. I do not regret taking care of her though. I just wanted to make that clear, because I don't want to sound like I begrudge that time away from school. Family took precedence over school. I knew I'd have my entire life for school.

So last year I was going to finish what I had left of high school and start pursuing college, like I've always dreamed of. But then family health tragedy struck even closer to home. My mother had a massive stroke and has suffered severe effects from that. Her ability to speak is very limited, and her mobility was also altered. She is now wheelchair bound. Right now I am her primary care giver, so obviously I still haven't completed what I have left of high school. But enough back-story, I know you're probably busy, so here are my questions/problems.

I have no transcripts. My mother, God bless her, did not make them, so I'm doing my very best to assemble them now. Do I fill them out through the part of my senior year where I had to stop, and then submit them that way, along with my college applications when I'm ready to start applying? I don't want to lose those credits, because I was a very good student. I took a lot of electives and things that I'd really like for colleges to see. So how do I do that?

> "My mother had a massive stroke. I still haven't completed what I have left of high school. I have no transcripts.

My plan was to get my GED this month or the next, take the SAT in March, register at the local community college for the summer semester, and then transfer to Western University (if they'll have me) as an art major. (Yes, I realize these are lofty goals.)

I know this is a long email and that my situation is really complicated, but please, if you have any advice or tips for me, I'd greatly appreciate them. Because I'm simply lost right now, and I hoped you might be able to guide me.

Sincerely, Brittany

A COMPELLING ADVANTAGE

When Brittany and I spoke, I told her she had one very real advantage: a very compelling personal story. Colleges love to provide admission and scholarships to students with unusual life situations, and to students who have overcome obstacles. With a compelling admission essay, transcripts and SAT scores, she should be able to achieve her dreams. As we spoke, it soon became obvious that Brittany was anything but a drop out. She was well spoken, well educated, and an excellent writer. Her parents must have worked conscientiously during her early high school years. Working together, her transcript looked remarkably complete for a young girl with a complicated family situation. Though her transcript only showed three years of high school, she had met the requirements for college admission within those three years. We talked about how she could apply to a university immediately, rather than attending a community college first. This alternative plan could bring more scholarship money, as she would be considered a freshman. Her original plan included obtaining a GED, but I thought that might not be necessary.

I suggested she pursue both options, college admission immediately and community college as a backup plan, in case financial aid didn't materialize. In discussing her homeschool classes, she had enough credits to graduate, and enough to get admitted to college. We discussed how it might be less expensive to start at the university with scholarships rather than beginning in community college without scholarships. For college admission, the SAT carries more significance than the GED. I suggested she take that test as soon as possible. It's easy to delay the GED if necessary, and it is rarely a college admission requirement for homeschoolers.

THE "HAIL MARY" PLAY

In January, I explained how to proceed. "Your best chances of admission will happen if you apply as soon as possible this week. Instead of waiting, take the SAT or ACT as quickly as possible, the very next time it is offered. Write the application essay using the tips I gave you. In a few months we will find the results, hopefully admission and scholarships. If you aren't happy with the scholarships, then go back to your original

> *Colleges love to provide admission and scholarships to students who have overcome obstacles.*

plan of community college, GED, and later college entry. Immediately after applying to college, fill out the FAFSA. The FAFSA is like the federal income tax forms for college scholarship, and much of the financial aid money will come from that form."

This strategy is like a "Hail Mary" play in football, when players throw the ball just to see if someone catches it. I explained to Brittany, "We're hoping that your application will be caught. If it's not, you have a good, solid back up plan. While I don't think you should cram for the test, I do think that if you take one sample test of the ACT or SAT at home it could help. Try to get a letter of recommendation from someone that is well educated, like a pastor, doctor, or other homeschool friend that is a professional."

The Hail Mary Play can solve the biggest fear that some parents have: "What if I fail?" What happens if you really do fail? You can try the Hail Mary Play, and apply for college anyway. Failing in homeschool can look significantly better than failing in public school. Without the "Fs" and rock-bottom GPA, colleges may see a well-educated child with a willingness to learn. Reading, writing, and a work ethic can compensate for a lot.

CREATE A NEW BEGINNING

Brittany's transcript included plenty of English and history. She had completed Algebra 2 and Geometry, plus two years of Latin, before the family crisis occurred. In fact, there were 30 credits on her transcript, demonstrating her interests in delight-directed learning.

In February she found out she was admitted!

> Dear Lee,
>
> I just wanted to email you and tell you that I GOT INTO WESTERN! I literally just found out. I don't have my financial aid packet yet or anything, but I do know for sure that I got accepted. Thank you so much for all your help with everything so far. Now all I can do is hope for the loans, grants, and scholarships I need and I'm golden. So yeah, thank you so much for everything. Without all of your help, I would be nowhere near where I am right now.
>
> Sincerely,
>
> Brittany

I explained that she would receive the "first wave" of scholarships within a week or two of application, although they may take longer because they are based on SAT or ACT scores. I told her, "Keep your backup plan in your pocket, but remember that scholarships come in waves, and you haven't even gotten the first wave yet." I explained that the first wave of scholarships is based on test scores. The second wave of scholarships is dependent on the FAFSA that is filed. Sometimes there is also a third wave of scholarships. That wave will be dependent on additional factors other than scholastic achievement or financial need. It may be associated with a specific talent (football) or interest (engineering major) or skill (piano), or it may be the result of special consideration or competition.

In April, Brittany was still working hard on the details of financial aid. She asked me how to find more scholarships, and I suggested she pursue private scholarships as described in earlier chapters. I told her to consider herself a high school senior and a college freshman during those applications. Since she had been notified that she was admitted, she could say she was enrolled in college. I encouraged her to work on these applications through the spring and summer. I also told her to speak directly to the college about her concerns. When they recognize the seriousness of the situation, they may provide additional scholarships as well.

> *Plan for a possible crisis year.*
> *Keep homeschool records current.*
> *Cover all high school subjects each year.*

SUCCESSFUL RESULT

In June, Brittany provided a follow up report, thrilled to tell me she had achieved her goals.

Hi Lee,

I hope you're doing well. It's been quite a while since I've talked to you. Everything is still a go for attending Western in the fall. I got $15,000 in aid and scholarships. I'm going to get a student loan for the remaining $20,000 for my degree. $20,000 was my goal, so I'm more than happy with it, and I'm still waiting to hear back on a few private scholarships. I'm just getting my student loan set up, and saving money at this point. I'm going to be taking math, English, Art, French and possibly Sociology if the course load isn't too heavy. My moving date is August 27th. It'll be here in no time. But anyway, I just wanted to thank you for all of your help with everything. Without you, there is NO WAY I'd be where I am right now. I'm so thankful that I found your website. I'll probably still email you one or two more times before I move, and then maybe after I'm situated and in class, just to tell you how things are and keep you posted. I think YOU are awesome and thank you again. God bless you.

Sincerely,

Brittany

TAKE-AWAY LESSON

This story is a lesson in encouragement. From the beginning, we could see how Brittany's family did things right. They educated their daughter from the beginning, creating a strong, independent young woman capable of learning, reading, writing, and thinking. She didn't shirk academics during the beginning of high school, but pressed forward until stymied by trauma.

The lesson of this story is also a purposeful warning for homeschool families. I encourage homeschoolers to plan for a possible crisis year. Don't assume that something horrible will happen, of course. But planning for a crisis year can make success achievable through that difficulty. Plan your high school courses. Make sure that you cover all subjects from the beginning. Don't wait until senior year to cover your core subjects, but begin with challenging classes from the beginning. Plan high school courses for success.

EXECUTIVE SUMMARY FOR BUSY PARENTS

BAD THINGS CAN HAPPEN TO GOOD HOMESCHOOLERS
- Do not panic for fear of trauma.
- Plan ahead to prevent heartache from trauma.
- Plan high school courses and subjects.
- Keep transcripts and records updated regularly.

CHAPTER 29

Difficult Times and Dangerous Situations

"Start children off on the way they should go, and even when they are old they will not turn from it."

Proverbs 22:6

"And YOU: friendless, brainless, helpless, hopeless! Do you want me to send you back to where you were? Unemployed, in Greenland?"

Vizzini, ~ *The Princess Bride*

It can happen overnight. One day your child is pleasant, cooperative, and enthusiastic about learning. The next day, not so much. It happens to boys and girls, but not to all children. It's not a universal problem, and parents are usually hesitant to discuss it in public, fearing their friends will not understand. This frustrating change is common, but that doesn't make it easier for parents to deal with. What do you do with a child who will only complete the bare minimum, and who really isn't interested in learning?

Some teenagers will remain pleasant and generally cooperative, but will do everything in a uniquely slow-as-molasses way. Other teens are more aggressive in their discontent, but are demonstrating the same lack of motivation. That's when parents look heavenward, asking the age-old question, "Now what?"

Sometimes it is just a phase, as if the kids are checking just to see who really is the boss, and what really matters to Mom and Dad. If it's a phase, the solution is to hang on, stand your ground, and wait until the phase is over. Waiting for this strange season to end is difficult, and feels like nails on the chalkboard all day, every day. Sometimes it will last just a couple of weeks, while the child or parent figures out what adjustments must be made. Other times the lack of motivation lasts for months, or even a year, until the child finds something that really sparks an interest.

MISERY LOVES COMPANY

One parent I know was devastated when her daughter started acting this way at age 14. Her daughter had always been a driven, perfectionist person. But suddenly her daughter wasn't interested in piano or flute any more, and had no activities that she enjoyed. This parent was very worried about her daughter sitting around on the couch all day. Finally, the daughter picked up a guitar for the first time. A few months later, she was helping the worship leader at church. When I spoke to the mom recently, she hardly remembered those difficult times.

Another parent had a very similar concern. Her son had no interests but the couch and video games, and she was beside herself. When I saw this parent some time later, her son had completely turned the corner. She forced him to take a class for school, and he suddenly discovered politics and debate. Suddenly he was going full speed ahead, on fire, having fun, and learning with reckless abandon.

Is it a passing phase? Wait two weeks and it may resolve.

When I was homeschooling, I was concerned about my oldest son. For a time, we thought he was wasting his life, doing nothing but playing chess. He sat on the couch reading books about chess, and playing chess with himself for hours on end. At the time, I thought I would go nuts. Now I realize he was working on his area of specialization, but at the time, it was just horrible.

Other parents have experienced these problems and survived. It doesn't make it easier, but perhaps it can make it more tolerable. Beyond knowing that misery loves company, here are some considerations and solutions. Take what will work for your family.

ASSESS YOUR EXPECTATIONS

Assess the expectations you have in your homeschool. Sometimes when I consult with parents about this issue, I find that the child is actually overworked. If

> *Are you expecting too much? Adjust expectations and work load as necessary.*

you are giving your child a classical education, particularly at a classical homeschool co-op, you may be at greater risk of having expectations that are too high. Regardless of your curriculum choice, look at the schoolwork you are expecting.

Is the level of work too high? Are you expecting too much, beyond what your child can do? Is the number of hours too great? How many hours would it take a normal child to work at normal speed to get that amount of work done? How long would it take you to complete all the assignments, if you were doing them at a normal speed? Is your child expected to work longer at school than your spouse spends at work?

The opposite may also be true, when the expectations are too low. When kids are bored, it's hard to get them motivated to do anything. If you child works with younger siblings, if your child is gifted, or if you are using curriculum meant for younger grades, then you may be at greater risk for this. Working with siblings and friends will often encourage academics, but not always. It can backfire sometimes. Homeschool co-ops and multi-age curricula are wonderful things that are great for homeschoolers much of the time, but parents still need to assess even wonderful things. If something isn't working, you have to find out what is wrong before you can fix it.

RAISING BOYS OR RAISING MEN

The teenage transition to adulthood may cause stress. If you have a son, this stage may be their unique attempt at becoming a man. It's difficult to grow from boy to man without meaningful work. One of the benefits of homeschooling is having the flexibility to incorporate employment into your school day. My sons each obtained a meaningful job when they were about 14 years old. We did our regular homeschooling four days a week, allowing the 5th day for them to spend working. Is there something that your son has been saying he wants to do? Can you find a situation, a mentor, or employment that can help him do that?

Parents may be concerned that their schedule will not allow time for employment. The opposite may actually be true. However, without meaningful work, they may work on school even more slowly, because they are bored and frustrated. Avoiding opportunities can add to the problem. Therefore, one possible solution might be to search for some meaningful, real adult work. Some parents work from home, and could start to include their son in their work activities. Others could allow work-related activities or mentors.

SPECIALIZATION SOLUTION

Boredom may have something to do with a lack of specialization. Young people need to have something they can do well. Adults often say to each other, "where do you work?" or "what do you do?" Children want their own "thing," so they can grow up. They want to be known as "the kid who..." The problem is that young adults don't have very much exposure to the world, and sometimes they haven't stumbled upon a special interest yet.

The solution to a lack of specialization is to expose children to a wide variety of experiences and subjects through a liberal arts education, and give them plenty of time to do new things. I confess that it can take a long time before something "clicks." Many people suggest speech and debate, or political organizations as your first attempt at something new. For young people, these activities can give them an opportunity to speak their mind and argue (without arguing with their parents), and it can improve their sense of self.

Are they bored or frustrated? Allow time for socialization and meaningful activities.

Look carefully at a lack of specialization as a possible cause of boredom or frustration. When I see parents with this problem, they often miss important clues about their child's interests. One way to identify specialization is to pay attention to what annoys you. Use your "annoy-o-meter" to recognize specialization that may be hidden just below the surface.

Give your child more input with their activities and involvements. Perhaps they should quit Boy Scouts—or not! Instead, they may want to quit the sport club. Would your child prefer acting or computer programming instead of the activities you have provided?

CAUSE AND EFFECT

When I had toddlers, I spent a lot of time thinking about natural consequences. I wanted to provide real-world, cause and effect reasons for my children to behave. Using that same strategy, try to brainstorm ideas that will have a direct cause and effect result in your teenage children. The key is a simple if-then statement, presented in a matter-of-fact way. Here are some effective suggestions. "IF you text while driving, THEN you are not mature enough to use my car." "IF you are too tired to do school, THEN you are too tired to have friends over." This example is an ineffective statement that may have been used in my home from time to time: "IF you don't do your work, THEN Mom will throw a fit."

HIGH QUALITY PROBLEMS

Motivation problems can occur even in wonderful children with great attitudes. My older son was like that, always pleasant and cooperative. I remember when he was two years old and didn't want to be in the shopping mall. He simply sat down and said, "No thank you, Mommy." He was so obedient and sweet! He was the same way at 14 years old. "No thank you, Mommy" doesn't work as well when you are trying to teach a math lesson, though. In high school, teenagers are too big to pick up and remove from a situation when they are being disobedient.

For some parents, this lighter version of teenage angst may present easier problems, on a completely different plane from the problems that many other parents face. Knowing that our problems are good problems rather than bad problems will only help a little. At the core, it is still a problem that causes stress and anxiety. Knowing you have a good problem isn't a solution, but perhaps it might be encouraging to know that it could be significantly worse.

WHEN IT GETS REALLY BAD

If teens make bizarre or unsafe decisions, look closely for signs of serious problems.

Not everything is perfect in homeschool families. Sometimes our problems are huge and horrible. Teenagers can make their own decisions. Sometimes they make the biggest, most horrendous decisions. Worse still, sometimes the consequences of their actions are life-altering.

If you teen is making ridiculously bizarre or unsafe decisions, look closely for signs of serious problems. Consult your family physician, counselor, or pastor. It may be, however, that you need to place the blame squarely where it resides: with the teen. God designed us to have free will. Sometimes children will act on their free will earlier than others. Evaluate their behavior and step in if they are at risk of hurting themselves or others. Watch for devastating issues that are common in our society. Look for very serious problems, like depression, drug or alcohol use, pornography, gambling, bullying, or excessive gaming. Depression is very serious, and when parents are concerned about the possibility, I strongly encourage them to seek counseling. A licensed counselor, perhaps recommended by a pastor or close friend, can help determine if there is a serious issue. They are unlikely to recommend medication because they can't prescribe, so they are often a good place to start looking for help.

It used to be that parents were concerned about our children receiving accidental exposure to pornography, or wasting time with video games. Now the issues are much bigger. Internet, technology, and computer game companies try to make their products addictive to young people, to increase their sales. But Internet usage and digital media is now shown to cause depression and psychological distress. Internet addiction, which is becoming more common nowadays, causes brain changes similar to alcohol and drugs. Henrietta B. Jones, a psychiatrist at Imperial College (London) said, "I have seen people who stopped attending university lectures, failed their degrees, or their marriages broke down because they were unable to emotionally connect with anything outside the game. When someone comes to you and says they did not sleep last night because they spent 14 hours playing games, and it was the same the previous night, and they tried to stop but they couldn't, you know they have a problem." In such cases, it's important to seek professional help.

To avoid these issues, take steps to minimize Internet usage. Reconsider the percentage of classes your children take online. Carefully weigh curriculum options, and consider non-computer curriculum when possible. Teach your children to monitor their own behavior on computers and online. Recognize the signs and symptoms of Internet addiction. Limit "wasting time" on digital media of all kinds. Balance the need for technology education with time spent on the computer.

TRUE SUCCESS

Right now, your teen may seem to be making a horrendous waste of their God-given potential, destined to live the loveless life of a vagabond. In truth, this is most likely a phase that will pass, not a terminal problem. Regardless, though, success in homeschooling is not dependent on how your children turn out. Parents can't measure success or failure based on the behavior of others. Success is when you try like a champion, and "leave it all on the field" as they do in sports. True success means you did your best, tried your hardest, and worked to prepare your children for the future. Parents cannot be perfect, but they can give their best effort. Success means giving your children the best possible education and character you can provide. After their education is complete, their choices are up to them. Your measurement of success cannot depend on your children's behavior, because you can't control their behavior. It can only depend on you.

EXECUTIVE SUMMARY FOR BUSY PARENTS

PARENTING TEENAGERS CAN BE DIFFICULT

- Difficult times may be a stage that is best handled with firm patience.
- Assess expectations and workload.
- The teenage transition to adulthood may cause stress.
- Allow teenagers to specialize in their own interests.
- Bizarre or unsafe decisions require careful assessment.
- Watch for serious issues common in our culture.

CHAPTER 30

Should Christians Go to College?

"No temptation has overtaken you except what is common to mankind. And God is faithful; he will not let you be tempted beyond what you can bear. But when you are tempted, he will also provide a way out so that you can endure it."

1 Corinthians 10:13

"I wasn't nervous. Maybe I was a little bit 'concerned' but that's not the same thing."

The Grandson, ~ *The Princess Bride*

"Should Christians even go to college?" The mom who asked me this isn't alone. I have heard this question at more than one homeschool convention over the years. After all, the question goes on, college is filled with faulty humans. As parents, we may hear horror stories from neighbors and friends who send their kids off to college, only to have them emerge four years later with no job, huge debt, and worst of all, a shipwrecked faith. It's enough to give any Christian parent cause for pause.

While some homeschool leaders vociferously disapprove of homeschoolers attending college of any kind, I disagree. For many people and for many reasons, college is the next step after high school. There are risks inherent in every life choice, but attending college, even a Christian college, is not uniquely risky. Consider 1 Corinthians 13:11, which says, "When I was a child, I talked like a child, I thought like a child, I reasoned like a child. When I became a man, I put the ways of childhood behind me." Letting your child go to college can be compared to the first time your child rode his bike without training wheels. For both parent and child, that probably was very scary. Even with a helmet, a child could get seriously hurt or hit by a car. Likewise, even with careful care and selection, it is still possible for a child to get hurt by a college experience.

FIRM IN FAITH

As parents, we spend a lot of our homeschool years explaining to others the reasons we keep our children safe at home. Those reasons don't change when our children grow up; it's our children that change. In fact, they become adults. Adults must interact with a fallen world on a regular basis. Firm in their faith, adult Christians need to negotiate contrasting worldviews with their own beliefs intact. At some point, and you will know when it happens, your child will be ready to "become a man" (or woman) and move forward into adult life. That life may include college.

PREPARE YOUR STUDENT

Therefore, train up your children in the way they should go, and when they become adult, allow them to engage the culture in order to change the world. In Mark 16:15, Jesus says, "Go into all the world and preach the gospel to all creation." Jesus doesn't say, "Go into all the world, but not college." If college is in your children's future, prepare them to face it as mature adults, grounded in their faith. Together with them, choose a college carefully, weighing the options, and praying through the decisions. Jesus also exhorts us in Matthew 10:16, "I am sending you out like sheep among wolves. Therefore be as shrewd as snakes and as innocent as doves."

At some point, your child will be ready to be an adult and live in an adult world.

Don't be afraid of college—prepare for it! It doesn't have to be a place that undermines your student's faith. It can be the proving ground for the training you have lovingly and carefully instilled during your homeschool years.

"Despite its hazards, college can be a major positive influence in your life," says Engineering Professor Don Peter. Christian college is an important consideration as well, as Bryan Jones, Associate Director of Undergraduate Admissions explains. "I personally believe strongly in Christian higher education. No Christian university is perfect or can guarantee a student won't walk away from the Lord, and in fact 'Christian' schools can vary greatly in what their requirements are for faculty, staff, and students' beliefs and involvement. But I have seen it time and time again that a student who attends a public or secular private university stumbles in their faith if they are not able to find the right campus ministry, peer group, mentor etc. These things are much more readily provided at a Christian college, and a student's faith is allowed to be stretched while not being attacked or torn down, in what is often a hostile and antagonistic environment at a public or secular institution."

Most important to remember is that no matter how "perfectly" parents may raise a child, a student may still walk away from the Lord. To quote noted Christian author and psychologist Dr. John Townsend, "even the perfect parent (God the Father) ended up with children who fell away from Him (mankind), so at some point, parents also have to let go and let a child become their own adult." I believe college is the ideal time for parents to complete the transition from sheltering their children from harm to letting them develop independence. In college, a student can begin to experience independence while still having the network of support and care from family and friends.

EXECUTIVE SUMMARY FOR BUSY PARENTS

COLLEGE IS AN ACCEPTABLE NEXT STEP FOR YOUNG ADULTS

- Reasons for sheltering our children do not change.
- Children eventually become adults.
- The Great Commission says to "go into all the world" without exception.
- Prepare children for college and for life.

C H A P T E R   3 1

The End of Homeschooling

"Your beginnings will seem humble,
so prosperous will your future be."
Job 8:7

Buttercup: *"I will never doubt again."*
Westley: *"There will never be a need."*
~ The Princess Bride

Homeschoolers seem to have one thing in common—they love their children. They love having children, they love being around their children, and they love having their children live at home. Of course, homeschool children are not always perfectly behaved, and life is not always blissful. I've been a homeschool parent, so I know that isn't true! But in general, we're pretty sad when it comes time to let the kids go. But like baby birds that fly the nest, when it's time, it's just time.

SAYING GOODBYE

When you take your children to college, it's just one step on the path to independence. Other steps follow. The first summer they live away from home. The first post-college apartment. The first holiday away from home.

Saying goodbye at college is very important. It is just as important as the other goodbyes. Each step has its own emotions, ranging from tears to relief.

I did notice one thing as I said my goodbyes at college. I had no regrets. I knew without a doubt they were academically prepared. I knew they were prepared for any assault on their worldview. I knew that I had shaped and molded their character and behaviors to the best of my ability. Their life was now up to them.

All parents have deep emotions when they are sending kids to college, not just homeschoolers. When you feel a tug on your heart, it's not because you are a homeschool parent; it's because you are a parent. Your heart may hurt, but homeschooling is a healing balm. Homeschooling high school can minimize your regrets once your children are raised. With the ability to shape and mold character while educating, your children will have the best possible chance of success. Letting go can come with no regrets!

When setting your children off into the world, I have three words of advice.

WORDS OF ADVICE

First, keep your five-year plan in mind. In five years, you want to have a happy, healthy, close extended family. When conflict occurs during college, keep that five-year plan in mind. Second, step in only when kids are being life-threateningly stupid. They will make poor choices, but they can learn from them just like you and I do every day. The only time you need to step in is when they are being dangerously dumb. Believe me...it happens. Not often, but it happens. Third, remember your Scripture. One of the most common homeschooling Bible verses will still be your greatest encouragement.

> *The five-year plan: a happy, healthy, close extended family.*

Proverbs 22:6 says, "Start children off on the way they should go, and even when they are old they will not turn from it." Homeschool parents are responsible for the first portion of the verse. The Bible instructs us to "Start children off on the way they should go." The Lord promises us a reward for our work, saying, "When they are old they will not turn from it." When you send your children into the world, you are in the middle section of this verse. That's the section that has only one thing to say—a comma. A dramatic pause. There is a pause between training them up and the promise at the end. That part is the responsibility of our children. That's the part where you are letting go. You let go of your responsibility, and look with great anticipation to the "When they are old."

On a personal level, I hate that comma. I wish the promise was immediate, and that children who have been brought up in the "fear and admonition of the Lord" would never stray from the path. But you and I know that just isn't true. Grown children make bad choices. Sometimes they make an absolutely confounding string of bad choices. At that point, however, you as parents need to remember one important fact... they are now adults. Adults get to make their own bad choices. Just like we did (remember?).

FACE THE EMPTY NEST

The children are gone, and the adjustment has begun. But what about you, the homeschool parent still at home? Toward the end of homeschooling, you start to wonder about the next stage of life. What will you do when you aren't homeschooling? I can suggest what not to do. I saw a woman at the store who was talking about how bored she was with her life. She had attended four Weight Watchers meetings during the week, not because she was overweight, but because she was bored! Although I'm a big fan of Weight Watchers, I wondered about that. Is that all there is to life?

The empty nest is not an end. It's a change and a beginning.

KEYS TO A GENTLE TRANSITION

Give yourself away. Help other people. Volunteer or work at an endeavor that allows you to help people. Homeschoolers are helpers by nature. How can YOU support other homeschoolers? What can you do to make it easier for the next mother who is stressed out about homeschooling? Give yourself away in new ways, too! I began volunteering regularly at our local clothing bank. It's a wonderful feeling to do something so concrete and physical that will help truly needy people. And there is nothing that can take your mind away from your own problems more than helping people with even bigger troubles!

> *Homeschool parents are helpers by nature. Give yourself away. Help other people.*

Get what you always wanted. When I was homeschooling, so many times I had to say "no" to fun things. I had kids at home, I had to get dinner on the table, and there were 13 soccer practices to attend each week! When the kids are gone, now is your time to say "YES!" to the fun things you have put off! My husband and I started singing in our church choir. Evening practices aren't a hassle at all when you don't have to find a babysitter!

Make a list. While you are homeschooling high school, list all the things you wish you could do. Think back on the past few years. What would have been fun to do? Your turn is coming soon, so creating a "bucket list" makes sense. Make a list of things or volunteer positions that sound like fun. List homeschool organizations you would like to help. If you had plenty of time, how would you like to serve your community and your church?

Be good to yourself. After graduation, you also have time to take care of yourself. Do you have a box of photos and no time for scrapbooking? Clutter around the house, with no time to organize? Think of all the great crafts you'll have time for! And when you retire from homeschooling, you can take care of yourself and finally be able to exercise. Just think, you can take a walk AND stop to smell the roses!

Avoid heartache. You hear about the empty nest feeling when your children go to college. It's true—and it's probably unavoidable. But you can lessen the effects by being active in your church and community. Give yourself away. Soon it will be your turn to volunteer, serve, and have fun! Your turn is coming, and you can make the best of it!

THE FOUR SEASONS OF HOMESCHOOLING

Homeschool parents assume four primary roles throughout their children's lives: that of caretaker, teacher, mentor, and friend. The last season of homeschooling—which promises to last the longest—is the season of friendship. Finally, you and your kids are equals. You may find yourself learning as much or more from them as they do from you. When the kids are grown and gone, take a deep breath and relax. You have a wonderful, life-long friendship to look forward to. The key to enjoying that friendship is up to you. You need to stop homeschooling this child. Provide guidance and counsel when asked, but hold back on unsolicited advice. Enjoy their friendship. You deserve it.

Job well done!

EXECUTIVE SUMMARY FOR BUSY PARENTS

KEYS TO HANDLING THE EMPTY NEST

- Expect deep emotions when children leave home.
- Focus on the 5-year plan: a happy, healthy, close extended family.
- Step in when behavior is life-threateningly stupid.
- Empty feelings indicate the beginning of your next stage.
- Volunteer, do activities you enjoy, and take care of yourself.
- Form life-long friendships with your grown children.

CHAPTER 32

Shaping Genuine Jewels

"Being confident of this, that he who began a good work in you will carry it on to completion until the day of Christ Jesus."

Philippians 1:6

"Let me explain. No, there is too much. Let me sum up."

Inigo Montoya, ~ *The Princess Bride*

Homeschooling is about learning, not money or prestige. It's about your child becoming the person God intends for them to be. If you combine learning and pursuing your child's specialization, the results will often be college scholarships. At a certain point, however, you have to take a deep breath and let it go. Remember the important things: education, passion, character, and work ethic. These things really matter. Remember, homeschoolers have the advantage, because we have absolute control over the curriculum in our school. We can allow time for specialization, even if it means that one day a week our students don't "go to school." We can emphasize integrity in everything.

Help your children become like diamonds. Diamonds are valued according to their cut, color, clarity, and carat weight. Think about each of these characteristics in your children.

The **CUT** of your child is who they are as a person. Are they honest? Are they hard working? Do they exhibit wisdom and character? You want them to reflect all of these values.

The **COLOR** is their uniqueness, their area of passion or specialization. Some diamonds are yellow and some are blue. Even if they look perfect to the untrained eye, each one has flaws and each is different. Your child is unique. You want them to have the perfect color that demonstrates their uniqueness.

Their **CLARITY** includes how and what they communicate. First, teach them to communicate clearly in person and in writing. Second, and more importantly, encourage them to become a genuine individual, someone who is straightforward and has a good sense of themselves.

Their **CARAT WEIGHT** is their academic preparation, the rigor of their academic life. Are they well-prepared for the academic rigors of college? Do they know how to apply themselves to their work?

Remember that you, the parent, are the jeweler. You influence the cut, color, clarity, and carat weight of your children. So go out there and present your child as a jewel, a jewel that colleges will eagerly desire to have on campus. All the time and effort you put into it will be worth it, and your family will be so much richer as a result of that work. Richer in every sense of the word!

> *You are a jeweler, carefully shaping the characteristics of your children.*

EXECUTIVE SUMMARY FOR BUSY PARENTS

CREATE DIAMONDS: CHILDREN WITH CHARACTER

- Instill hard work and honesty.
- Cultivate genuine and unique interests.
- Teach and model clear communication.
- Provide rigorous academic preparation.

Resources

The HomeScholar Planning Guide

SUBJECT	9TH GRADE	10TH GRADE	11TH GRADE	12TH GRADE	COMMENTS
English					4 years literature, writing, composition, speech
Math					3-4 years - algebra, geometry, algebra 2, trigonometry, pre-calculus or calculus
Social Studies					3 -4 years world history, US history, economics and government
Science					3 years - 1 with lab usually biology, chemistry and physics
Foreign Language					2-3 years of a single language
Physical Education					2 years ½ credit per year
Fine Arts					At least 1 year Music, theater, art, dance
Electives					Bible, driver's ed, keyboarding, logic, computer science *specialization*
Advising		Optional: October PSAT-for fun?	October PSAT, spring SAT or ACT, and visit colleges	Fall: college essays, college applications January FAFSA	AP or SAT 2 Subject Tests if needed after each course complete

Usual graduation requirements: 19 credits. Usual college preparation requirements: 24 credits or more

The HomeScholar Guide to College Costs

A. Cost of Attendance	College 1	College 2	College 3
Tuition			
Fees			
Books			
Extra Course Fees			
Other fees (parking, etc)			
TOTAL Cost of Attendance			

B. Cost of Housing	College 1	College 2	College 3
Housing, Room and Board			
Meals			
Travel or Transportation			
Incidentals (laundry, recreation)			
Other Individual Expenses			
Other costs			
Total Cost of Housing			

C. Financial Aid	College 1	College 2	College 3
Institutional Scholarship			
Institutional Grant			
Private Scholarship			
Work/Work Study			
Other			
Total Financial Aid			

Actual College Cost	College 1	College 2	College 3
A Total Cost of Attendance			
B Total Cost of Housing			
C Total Financial Aid			
Actual College Cost (A+B) −C			

Funding Actual Costs	College 1	College 2	College 3
College Budget and Savings			
Student Loan			
Parent Loan			

The HomeScholar College Application Check List

Name of College _____

Task	Date Sent	Date Received
Application		
Essay 1		
Essay 2		
Essay 3		
School Specific Supplement		
Official Homeschool Transcript		
Homeschool Supplement		
Athletic Supplement		
Art Supplement		
Other Transcript 1		
Other Transcript 2		
Community College Transcript		
Letter of Recommendation 1		
Letter of Recommendation 2		
Letter of Recommendation 3		
Midyear Grades		
FAFSA Estimate January		
FAFSA Final April		
CSS/School Profile		
Sent Reply to College		
Deposit		
Thank You Note to Interviewer		
Final Transcript June		

The HomeScholar College Bound Reading List

The HomeScholar reading list for college bound students is a selection of books drawn from a variety of different reading lists. These are books I am both familiar with and feel comfortable recommending to college-bound students.

It's not possible (or even desirable!) for any student to read all the books on every college-bound reading list, and not every book will be appropriate for every child. However, reading from a broad cross-section of both American and World literature will help prepare your students to understand a variety of different cultures and times, and strengthen their knowledge and understanding of great literature. We hope you enjoy this selection!

AMERICAN LITERATURE

Angelou, Maya   *I Know Why the Caged Bird Sings*
Two children are abandoned by their mother and sent to live with their devout, self-sufficient grandmother in a small Southern town.

Cooper, James Fenimore   *The Deerslayer*
A young white hunter, brought up in the Delaware Indian tribe, has to defend settlers before returning to the Iroquois who have allowed him parole.

Cooper, James Fenimore   *Last of the Mohicans*
The story of the adopted son of the Mohicans and the daughter of a British colonel during the French and Indian War.

Crane, Stephen   *The Red Badge of Courage*
A teenager enlists with the Union Army during the Civil War in the hopes of fulfilling his dreams of glory.

Douglass, Frederick   *Narrative of the Life of Frederick Douglass*
This famous narrative written by a former slave was an influential book during the abolitionist movement of the early 19th century.

Fitzgerald, F. Scott   *The Great Gatsby*
A portrait of the 1920's in America, this is the story of money, greed, excess, and a man in love.

Frank, Pat   *Alas, Babylon*
A survival after a nuclear attack destroys all civilization except for a small Florida town.

Franklin, Benjamin   *The Autobiography of Benjamin Franklin*
Written initially to guide his son, Franklin's autobiography is a lively, spellbinding account of his unique and eventful life.

Haley, Alex   *Roots*
This book chronicles several generations of a slave family, from a West African youth captured by slave raiders and shipped to America in the 1700's, and concluding with the Civil War.

Hawthorne, Nathaniel   *The Scarlet Letter*
Set in Puritan Boston, this book tells the story of a woman who conceives a daughter through an adulterous affair and struggles to create a new life of dignity and repentance.

Hemingway, Ernest   *A Farewell to Arms*
The life of an American soldier and a British nurse against the backdrop of the First World War, cynical soldiers, fighting and the displacement of populations.

Keller, Helen   *The Story of My Life*
A young woman overcomes the challenges of being both deaf and blind, with the help of her devoted teacher Anne Sullivan.

Kennedy, John F.   *Profiles in Courage*
John F. Kennedy profiles eight of his historical colleagues for their acts of astounding integrity in the face of overwhelming opposition.

Lee, Harper   *To Kill a Mockingbird*
An exploration of civil rights and racism in the segregated southern United States of the 1930's.

Lewis, Sinclair   *Main Street*
The story of a sophisticated young woman who moves to a small town in the American Midwest in 1912, and struggles against the small-minded culture of the citizens who live there.

London, Jack   *Call of the Wild*
In the 19th-century Klondike Gold Rush, a domesticated dog is snatched and sold into a brutal life as a sled dog.

Malcom X, with Alex Haley   *The Autobiography of Malcom X*
A narrative of spiritual conversion that outlines a controversial Black Muslim's philosophy of black pride, black nationalism, and pan-Africanism.

Miller, Arthur   *Death of a Salesman*
This is a play about a traveling salesman and his family.

Melville, Herman   *Moby Dick*
The adventures of a wandering sailor and his voyage on a whale ship commanded by Captain Ahab, whose one purpose is to seek out a great white whale.

Paine, Thomas   *Common Sense*
Paine's daring prose paved the way for the Declaration of Independence and the Revolutionary War.

Poe, Edgar Allan   *Great Tales and Poems*
One of the most famous creators of detective stories and supernatural tales.

Potok, Chaim   *The Chosen*
Traces the friendship between two Jewish boys growing up in Brooklyn at the end of World War II.

Sinclair, Upton   *The Jungle*
Explores the workingman's lot at the turn of the century: the backbreaking labor, the injustices of "wage-slavery," and the bewildering chaos of urban life.

Steinbeck, John   *The Grapes of Wrath*
This is the tale of a poor family of tenant farmers driven from their Oklahoma home by drought, economic hardship, and the Great Depression.

Stowe, Harriet Beecher   *Uncle Tom's Cabin*
A slave, whose child is to be sold, escapes her beloved home on a plantation in Kentucky and heads north, avoiding hired slave catchers, aided by the Underground Railroad.

Twain, Mark   *The Adventures of Huckleberry Finn*
Huck Finn and his old friend Jim journey down the Mississippi river together.

Twain, Mark   *The Adventures of Tom Sawyer*
A humorous and nostalgic book depicting the carefree days of boyhood in a small Midwestern town during the mid-1800's.

Twain, Mark   *Innocents Abroad*
An acerbic account of the author's travels in Europe and the Near East, humorously describing both the places he visited and his fellow passengers on the voyage

Walker, Alice   *The Color Purple*
The story of two African-American sisters, a missionary in Africa, and a child-wife living in the South, told through their letters to each other.

Washington, Booker T.   *Up From Slavery*
This is an autobiography of an influential spokesman and former slave, who became a major figure in the struggle for equal rights.

Wilder, Thornton   *Our Town*
A study of life, love, and death in a New England town at the turn of the 20th century.

WORLD LITERATURE

Austen, Jane   *Pride and Prejudice*
English country life is described in this much-loved English romance novel set in a society obsessed with profitable marriage contracts.

Austen, Jane   *Sense and Sensibility*
This tale of manners and courtship in the 19th-century English countryside follows two sisters, one sensible, and the other impetuous.

Bronte, Charlotte   *Jane Eyre*
In this romance and suspense novel, the orphaned governess Jane Eyre has a brooding, moody, wealthy employer with a terrible secret.

Bronte, Emily   *Wuthering Heights*
A masterpiece of English romanticism, tells the story of love and revenge.

Carroll, Lewis   *Alice's Adventures in Wonderland*
A fantasy about young Alice, who follows a white rabbit down a rabbit hole.

Cervantes, Miguel de   *Don Quixote*
An eccentric old gentleman from La Mancha convinces himself that he is a knight. With his portly peasant squire, he sets out "tilting at windmills" to right the wrongs of the world.

Conrad, Joseph   *Heart of Darkness*
Recounts a journey into the Congo and reveals the extent to which greed can corrupt a good man.

Defoe, Daniel   *Robinson Crusoe*
An English sailor is marooned on a desert island for nearly three decades. He struggles to survive in extraordinary circumstances, and wrestles with fate and the nature of God.

Dickens, Charles   *Great Expectations*
Traces the development of Pip from a boy of shallow aspirations to a man of depth and character.

Dickens, Charles   *David Copperfield*
David Copperfield lives through trials and tribulations, first at a boys' school and then as a young man in London before he goes to live with his great-aunt and eventually finds happiness.

Dickens, Charles   *Tale of Two Cities*
Set during the French Revolution in the cities of Paris and London, a French aristocrat is accused of spying.

Dostoyevsky, Fyodor   *The Gambler*
At a casino in Germany, a Russian family awaits news that a wealthy relative has died, but to their dismay, she arrives and begins gambling away their inheritance.

Dostoevsky, Fyodor   *Crime and Punishment*
A poverty-stricken young man is faced with an opportunity to solve his financial problems with one simple but horrifying act.

Frank, Anne   *The Diary of a Young Girl*
Traces the life of the Jewish girl who hid with seven other people in an attic for two years in Nazi-occupied Holland, and chronicles her day-to-day life in a diary.

Golding, William   *Lord of the Flies*
A group of schoolboys stranded on an island soon revert to the state of primitive man, and engage in a struggle between savagery and civilization.

Hamilton, Edith   *Mythology*
Discover the thrilling, enchanting, and fascinating world of Western mythology, from Odysseus's adventure-filled journey to the Norse god Odin's effort to postpone the final day of doom.

Homer   *The Iliad*
An epic poem about Achilles' vengeance against Agamemnon and the city of Troy at the end of the Trojan War.

Homer   *The Odyssey*
The story of Odysseus' difficulties in returning home after the Trojan War.

Huxley, Aldous   *Brave New World*
This futuristic novel warns of the dangers of sacrificing freedom and individuality for scientific progress and social stability.

Kafka, Franz   *Metamorphosis*
A seemingly typical man wakes up one morning to discover he has been transformed into a gigantic insect.

L'Engle, Madeleine   *A Wrinkle in Time*
The story of friends on a dangerous and fantastic journey that will threaten their lives and universe.

Lewis, C.S.   *The Screwtape Letters*

This satirical piece portrays human life from the vantage point of Screwtape, and his correspondence with a novice demon in charge of the damnation of an ordinary young man.

Machiavelli, Niccolo   *The Prince*

The world's most famous master plan for seizing and holding power. A disturbingly realistic and prophetic work on what it takes to be a prince...a king...a president.

Marlowe, Christopher   *Doctor Faustus*

A well-respected German scholar grows dissatisfied with the limits of traditional forms of knowledge—logic, medicine, law, and religion—and decides that he wants to learn to practice magic.

Milton, John   *Paradise Lost*

Often considered the greatest epic in any modern language, this is the story of the revolt of Satan, his banishment from Heaven, and the fall of man and his expulsion from Eden.

Orwell, George   *Animal Farm*

Domesticated animals stage a revolt against their cruel master. They soon find they have succeeded in exchanging one form of tyranny for another.

Plato   *The Republic*

A monumental work of moral and political philosophy, presented as a dialogue between Socrates and others discussing the notion of a perfect community and the ideal individuals within it.

Remarque, Erich Maria   *All Quiet on the Western Front*

Through the eyes and mind of a German private, the reader shares life on the battlefield during World War I.

Scott, Sir Walter   *Ivanhoe*

Returning from fighting in the Crusades, the young Saxon knight Ivanhoe must fight to regain the woman he loves, and to protect the social order and monarchy of England.

Shelley, Mary W.   *Frankenstein*

Tampering with life and death, Dr. Frankenstein pieces together salvaged body parts to create a human monster.

Shakespeare, William   *Romeo and Juliet*

The tale of two young star-crossed lovers and their families, who are caught in a destructive web of hatred.

Shakespeare, William   *Twelfth Night*

After a shipwreck, twin siblings Viola and Sebastian wash up on the shores of Illyria.   A story of mistaken identity and love entanglements.

Solzhenitsyn, Alexander   *One Day in the Life of Ivan Denisovich*

This novel describes the oppression of totalitarian regimes, and the terrors of Stalin's prison camps.

Sophocles   *Antigone*

Antigone defies her uncle, the new ruler, which enacts a conflict between young and old, woman and man, individual and ruler, family and state.

Stevenson, Robert Louis   *The Strange Case of Dr. Jekyll and Mr. Hyde*

Dr Jekyll wants to rid his soul of evil, and in doing so creates the monstrous alter ego Mr. Hyde.

Swift, Jonathan   *Gulliver's Travels*

A shipwrecked castaway encounters the petty, diminutive Lilliputians.

Tocqueville, Alexis de   *Democracy in America*

Covering America's call for a free press to its embrace of the capitalist system, this book enlightens, entertains, and endures as a brilliant study of our national government and character.

Tolstoy, Leo   *Anna Karenina*

Set against the backdrop of Moscow and St. Petersburg high society in the latter half of the nineteenth century, a woman forsakes her husband for a dashing count and brief happiness.

Tolkien, J.R.R   *The Hobbit*
Bilbo Baggins, a respectable, well-to-do hobbit, lives comfortably in his hobbit-hole until the day the wandering wizard Gandalf chooses him to share in an adventure from which he may never return.

Tolstoy, Leo   *War and Peace*
Tracks the evolution of five aristocratic families during the Napoleonic wars.

Wells, H.G.   *The Time Machine*
A time traveler steps out of his time-transport machine in the year 802,700 to find Earth populated by a race of people supported by a slave class.

Wells, H.G.   *War of the Worlds*
The first modern tale of alien invasion, this is a story of tentacled Martians attacking the Earth.

Wilde, Oscar   *The Importance of Being Earnest*
This is a play about two men who bend the truth in order to add excitement to their lives.

RELUCTANT READERS

For reluctant readers, focus on very short classic books. There are many great literary works that are remarkably short. Consider reading aloud the first chapter, to get them started with the story and pronunciation of character names.

Crane, Stephen   *The Red Badge of Courage* (Instead of *War and Peace*)
The story of Henry Fleming, a teenager who enlists with the Union Army in the hopes of fulfilling his dreams of glory

Dostoyevsky, Fyodor   *The Gambler*
At a casino in Germany, a Russian family awaits news that a wealthy relative has died, but to their dismay, she arrives and begins gambling away their inheritance at an alarming rate.

Hawthorne, Nathaniel   *The Scarlet Letter* (Instead of *Sense and Sensibility*)
Set in Puritan Boston, tells the story of a woman who conceives a daughter through an adulterous affair and struggles to create a new life of dignity and repentance.

Hemingway, Ernest   *Old Man and the Sea* (Instead of *Moby Dick*)

The exciting story of an old Cuban fisherman and his supreme ordeal: a relentless, agonizing battle with a giant marlin far out in the Gulf Stream.

London, Jack   *Call of the Wild*

Set in Yukon Territory during the 19th-century Klondike Gold Rush, a domesticated dog is snatched and sold into a brutal life as a sled dog, where he struggles to survive.

Melville, Herman   *Billy Budd* (Instead of *Moby Dick*)

The story of an innocent young man unable to defend himself against a wrongful accusation.

Shelley, Mary   *Frankenstein*

Frankenstein is a young man fascinated by science, who attempts to unlock the secrets of life and death.

Steinbeck, John   *Of Mice and Men*

In Depression-era California, two migrant workers dream of better days on a spread of their own, until an act of unintentional violence leads to tragic consequences.

Steinbeck, John   *The Pearl*

A young, strong, and poor Mexican-Indian pearl diver must find a way to pay the town doctor to cure his son. Then he discovers an enormous pearl the size of a seagull's egg when out diving.

KINESTHETIC LEARNERS

For children who learn best through movement, focus on books with active main characters. Again, short books may be helpful, but it's even more important to choose active main characters, rather than primarily pensive characters. Here are just a few examples.

London, Jack   *Call of the Wild*

In the extreme conditions of the Yukon during the 19th-century Klondike Gold Rush, a domesticated dog is snatched and sold into a brutal life as a sled dog, where he struggles to adjust and survive the cruel treatment he receives from humans, other dogs, and nature.

Twain, Mark   *The Adventures of Tom Sawyer*

A humorous and nostalgic book depicting the carefree days of boyhood in a small Midwestern town during the mid-1800's.

Twain, Mark   *The Adventures of Huckleberry Finn*

The young Huck Finn flees with his old friend Jim, and they journey down the Mississippi River.

PROLIFIC READERS

Voracious readers can sometimes use encouragement to feed their book hunger with quality literature rather than junk. If you have a literary lover at your house, you can increase their intake of great books by simply offering "collections" rather than individual books. Here are some examples that my prolific readers loved.

Austen, Jane   Jane Austen Four Novels

Four of her best-loved novels: *Sense and Sensibility, Pride and Prejudice, Emma,* and *Northanger Abbey*

Tolkien, J. R. R.   J.R.R. Tolkien Boxed Set (*The Hobbit* and *The Lord of the Rings*)

Four novels: *The Hobbit, The Fellowship of the Ring, The Two Towers, The Return of the King*

Dickens, Charles   Major Works of Charles Dickens (Penguin Classics set)

Great Expectations; Hard Times; Oliver Twist; A Christmas Carol; Bleak House; A Tale of Two Cities

POPULAR LITERATURE

A variety of colleges have said that homeschool applicants may have an over-emphasis on classic literature, and that reading lists should include popular literature. Some colleges have mentioned that inclusion of current literature shows "socialization." You may want to include some popular fiction in your student's reading list. For example, this recent book has become a modern classic.

Stockett, Kathryn   *The Help*
   The story of black maids raising white children in Mississippi during the 1960's civil rights movement.

WORD OF CAUTION

All families are different, and therefore all families must decide their own standards for the books their children read. Some of these books are listed on almost every reading list, but that doesn't mean they are perfect for you. This reading list is drawn from a broad cross section of college-bound reading lists. However, parents assume all responsibility for their children's education. If you are not familiar with something on this list, please review the book first.

Activities, Leadership, and Community Service Ideas

Encourage your children to become involved in activities they love. Colleges like to see leadership, community service, and a passionate interest.

For many parents, finding an interest in their children can be a challenge. If you are trying to find something to spark their interests, this list may help. This is a brainstorming list to encourage you to think beyond the ordinary. Look at a wide variety of activities, and prioritize the ones your child finds interesting. Remember, no family could possibly do all of these! This is a starting point for bewildered and confused parents searching for ideas.

In alphabetic order, this is a partial list of activities I have seen homeschoolers enjoy during high school.

- 4-H Youth Development Organization
- 5 K walks and runs
- Adopt a Highway
- Animal shelters
- Assist elderly, handicapped, or chronically ill
- Assisted living facilities
- Awana Club
- Ballet
- Band
- Boy Scouting
- Choir
- Church volunteer doing office work or maintenance
- Clothing banks
- Community or beach clean up
- Community service clean up and planting
- Congressional Award program www.congressionalaward.org
- Costumed interpreter for history village
- Disaster response organizations
- Docent at local zoo
- DoSomething.org
- Eagle Scout
- Election workers
- First Lego League
- Food pantry
- Hand bells

- History museums
- Homeschool orchestra or band
- Hospital volunteer
- Humane Society or animal shelter
- Inner city school tutor or Bible lessons
- Library after-school tutoring programs
- Library crafts or reading programs
- Lions Club, Rotary, Kiwanis
- Local community access cable station
- Local homeless shelters
- Local libraries
- Local park summer camp programs
- Locate needy families through church
- Martial Arts
- Math clubs
- Meals on Wheels
- Mission trips
- Nursing homes
- Operation Christmas Child
- Orchestra
- Organized musical groups
- Organized sports
- Organized theater groups
- Play music for food banks, churches
- Play music for retirement homes
- Political campaign
- Public school "reading buddy" programs
- Raise and train service dogs
- Red Cross
- Robotics League
- Salvation Army
- Science fairs
- Science Olympiad
- Sound and light crew at churches and playhouses
- Speech and debate clubs
- State parks volunteer
- Teach lessons in an instrument or activity
- Teach what you love to other homeschoolers
- Teen ambassador groups
- Teen Court

- Theater groups
- Therapeutic horse riding program
- United Way
- USA Computing Olympiad
- Vacation Bible School
- Volunteermatch.org
- Volunteers for tour guides
- YMCA teen leaders program
- Youth groups

College Application Lexicon

College applications have their own unique vocabulary. As you begin learning about college admission, you'll notice there are many different application choices and terms. Listed here are the terms used by the National Association for College Admission Counseling (NACAC), including the different kinds of application plans. If you need a primer on what "application" means, this is for you.

ADMISSION TERMS BY NACAC

- **Non-Restrictive Application Plans** are plans that allow students to wait until May 1 to confirm enrollment.

- **Regular Decision** is the application process in which a student submits an application to an institution by a specified date and receives a decision within a reasonable and clearly stated period of time. A student may apply to other institutions without restriction.

- **Rolling Admission** is the application process in which an institution reviews applications as they are completed and renders admission decisions to students throughout the admission cycle. A student may apply to other institutions without restriction.

- **Early Action (EA)** is the application process in which students apply to an institution of preference and receives a decision well in advance of the institution's regular response date. Students who are admitted under Early Action are not obligated to accept the institution's offer of admission or to submit a deposit prior to May 1. Under non-restrictive Early Action, a student may apply to other colleges. Restrictive Application Plans are plans that allow institutions to limit students from applying to other early plans.

- **Early Decision (ED)** is the application process in which students make a commitment to a first-choice institution where, if admitted, they definitely will enroll. While pursuing admission under an Early Decision plan, students may apply to other institutions, but may have only one Early Decision application pending at any time. Should a student who applies for financial aid not be offered an award that makes attendance possible, the student may decline the offer of admission and be released from the Early Decision commitment.

The institution must notify the applicant of the decision within a reasonable and clearly stated period of time after the Early Decision deadline. Usually, a nonrefundable deposit must be made well in advance of May 1. The institution will respond to an application for financial aid at or near the time of an offer of admission. Institutions with Early Decision plans may restrict students from applying to other early plans. Institutions will clearly articulate their specific policies in their Early Decision agreement.

- **Restrictive Early Action (REA)** is the application process in which students make application to an institution of preference and receive a decision well in advance of the institution's regular response date. Institutions with Restrictive Early Action plans place restrictions on student applications to other early plans. Institutions will clearly articulate these restrictions in their Early Action policies and agreements with students. Students who are admitted under Restrictive Early Action are not obligated to accept the institution's offer of admission or to submit a deposit prior to May 1.

What Can The HomeScholar do for You?

You can find extra encouragement and additional resources online that will supplement *The HomeScholar Guide to College Admission and Scholarships: Homeschool Secrets to Getting Ready, Getting In, and Getting Paid.* Find Online Resources and Links at **www.TheHomeScholar.com/CollegeAdmissionBook.**

Preparing students for college admission is a lot like being a juggler. You can be successful if you don't drop a ball! Each spring, I get frantic phone calls from parents, asking for help getting their kids into college. Their Suzie or Jimmy wants to go to Harvard, has never taken math, and didn't hear about SAT testing, and they want to know what I can do to help. At that point, there really isn't much I can do!

I encourage people to plan ahead, and don't drop the ball. In my newsletter, I have calendar reminders to help you remember things as you go along. Reading those reminders will help you stay on track. It just takes a little bit of attention, just once in a while, to make sure those balls stay in the air! Keep it up; you can do it! Register for my free newsletter at **www.TheHomeScholar. com**.

On my website, I offer multiple free webinars and instruction to help you successfully homeschool high school. For encouraging support and valuable tools, go to my Freebies page at **www.TheHomeScholar.com/Freebies**.

You can find my other books on Amazon (**amazon.com/author/leebinz.**) If you have enjoyed this book, you will love *Setting the Records Straight: How to Craft Homeschool Transcripts and Course Descriptions for College Admission and Scholarships.* My Coffee Break Books are designed especially for parents who don't want to spend hours reading a long book on homeschooling high school, this series combines a practical and friendly approach with detailed, but easy-to-digest information, perfect to read over a cup of coffee at your favorite coffee shop. Never overwhelming, always accessible and manageable, each book in the series will give parents the tools they need to tackle the tasks of homeschooling high school, one warm sip at a time.

The Total Transcript Solution (**www.TotalTranscriptSolution.com**) is a complete resource for creating your student's high school transcripts, and will give you the confidence and tools required to get the job done. You will save money, time and frustration by doing it yourself instead of relying on accreditation agencies and certified teachers, and the results will be professional and impressive.

My Comprehensive Record Solution (**www.ComprehensiveRecordSolution. com**) will guide you step-by-step through the process of creating beautiful and professional high school records, such as course descriptions and awards lists that colleges will love and appreciate!

The helpful resources in my Parent Training A la Carte series (**www. HomeschoolThruHighSchool.com**) will help you feel completely confident in your ability to homeschool your child through graduation and into college and career. This series includes all my online training webinars, which cover all the difficult topics you'll encounter while homeschooling middle and high school.

Lastly, my popular Gold Care Club (**www.TheHomeScholar.com/Gold-Care.php**) is my exclusive membership site that provides extensive training, templates, resources, and personal coaching to hold your hand all the way through the high school years. You will never be without the help you need!

All of these resources and much more, can be found on my website at www.TheHomeScholar.com

REAL PARENTS RESPOND

You have been a tremendous blessing to me! My daughter was awarded the highest academic scholarships from the four private colleges she applied to. She competed for full-tuition scholarships at two of those colleges, receiving full tuition from one. Had it not been for your wonderful advice, my daughters would not be in the position they are today.

~ Kathleen Mueller, Homeschooling Parent in California

Thank you for the encouragement you provided as my daughter applied to colleges this fall. Her scholarships will be paying for four years of tuition, out-of-state fees, room/board, book stipends, and $5,000 toward a summer abroad program. Thank you again for all that I learned through your services. There are so many parents that worry about college and scholarships. You are providing a service much needed by many of them.

~ Renee Gardiner, Homeschool Parent in Alabama

Just wanted you to know that our daughter got accepted to her first choice college today. Though we still do not know about "all" the financial aid/scholarships yet, we were so thrilled to know that even when we homeschooled all the way through high school and used "mommy grades," my daughter is wanted by the university she desires most to go to! I could not have done it without your website helps and your wonderful book, *Setting the Records Straight*! We are looking forward to hearing from other colleges as we go through this process. Thank you so much for all your help!

~ Mechelle Wong, Homeschool Parent in Washington

I hope that other parents who are considering homeschooling high school will realize that it can be done! My greatest fear was that I would mess up his life forever, and he would not have the opportunities that other students would have. Well, that was just simply wrong! Jacob was able to study at his own pace and accomplish quite a bit along the way. My daughter Sara was fortunate to receive a nomination to the US Naval Academy from our representative, and a nomination to the US Air Force Academy from one of our senators. Sara also applied for an Air Force ROTC scholarship, and received a full tuition scholarship!

I can't thank you enough for helping me pull it all together and cheering us across the finish line! That will be an entirely different experience, but I am sure with your materials and support it will be much easier. You have really made a difference in our lives, and helped two young people achieve their dreams by helping their mom, so our family thanks you from the bottom of our hearts!

~ Cassie Fishbein, Homeschool Parent in Ohio

CPSIA information can be obtained at www.ICGtesting.com
Printed in the USA
LVOW05s1524141113

361321LV00005B/293/P

Published by the WHITE HOUSE HISTORICAL ASSOCIATION
With the cooperation of the NATIONAL GEOGRAPHIC SOCIETY, Washington, D. C.

The First Ladies

By Margaret Brown Klapthor

THE FIRST LADIES

By *Margaret Brown Klapthor,* Curator Emeritus, Division of Political History, National Museum of American History, Smithsonian Institution

PRODUCED BY THE NATIONAL GEOGRAPHIC SOCIETY AS A PUBLIC SERVICE
Gilbert M. Grosvenor, President and Chairman of the Board
Reg Murphy, Executive Vice President
Michela A. English, Senior Vice President
PREPARED BY THE BOOK DIVISION
William R. Gray, Vice President and Director
Charles Kogod, Assistant Director
STAFF FOR THE FIRST EDITION:
Mary Ann Harrell, Managing Editor
Susan C. Burns, Jennifer Urquhart, Researchers
Geraldine Linder, Picture Editor
Ursula Perrin Vosseler, Art Director
PHOTOGRAPHY: *Steve Adams, Joseph H. Bailey, Sean Baldwin, J. Bruce Baumann, Victor R. Boswell, Jr., David S. Boyer, Sisse Brimberg, Nelson H. Brown, Dan J. Dry, Thomas Hooper, Larry D. Kinney, Erik Kvalsvik, Bates Littlehales, George F. Mobley, Robert S. Oakes, Martin Rogers, James E. Russell, Joseph J. Scherschel, David Valdez, Volkmar Wentzel*
STAFF FOR THE EIGHTH EDITION: *Jane H. Buxton,* Managing Editor; *Richard M. Crum,* Text Editor; *Melanie Patt-Corner,* Researcher; *Elizabeth G. Jevons, Sandra F. Lotterman, Peggy J. Oxford,* Staff Assistants
MANUFACTURING AND QUALITY MANAGEMENT: *George V. White,* Director; *Robert W. Messer,* Manager; *Clifton M. Brown III,* Assistant Manager/Film Archivist

White House staff members who assisted in the preparation of this edition: *Rex Scouten,* Curator; *Betty Monkman,* Associate Curator; *William Allman,* Assistant Curator; *Lydia S. Tederick,* Curatorial Assistant

First Lady Caroline Harrison, who enjoyed painting for recreation, created watercolors such as Flowering Dogwood. *She also held china-painting classes at the White House.*

COVER: *Portrait of Martha Washington, painted by Eliphalet F. Andrews in 1878, hangs in the East Room of the White House as a companion piece for the Gilbert Stuart portrait of her husband.*
PAGE 1: *Hand-colored engraving* The President's House, Washington *gives an idyllic view of the White House during the Jacksonian age, around 1833.*
PAGES 2-3: *George and Martha Washington appear at right in an unknown artist's painting "Reception at Mount Vernon." Its style suggests a fictionalized illustration for a 19th-century popular magazine. Previously unpublished, the painting hangs in the headquarters of the National Society of the Daughters of the American Revolution, in Washington, D. C., on loan from the Rhode Island Society.*

Foreword

The American people have made the role of First Lady one of the most important jobs in the country. It happened because each First Lady from Martha Washington onward contributed to her husband's historical reputation. It is a tribute to American women that, coming from different social and economic backgrounds, from many different geographical regions, and with diverse educational preparation, each First Lady served our country so well. Each left her own mark, and each teaches us something special about our history.

The White House Historical Association has published *The First Ladies* to give us an opportunity to know these fascinating women better. The biographies were written by Margaret B. Klapthor, Curator Emeritus of the Smithsonian Institution. Mrs. Klapthor has spent 50 years studying our First Ladies, and her findings put each woman into perspective. She highlights their individual achievements as well as the qualities that make them similar. As we learn about them, we begin to see that these women usually reflect the time in which they lived, so much so that a look at their lives becomes a panorama of women's history in America. Managing the social life at the White House and the personal welfare of the President and their families, the First Ladies set a standard for the women of their day. In addition, they brought their own interests to the same wide audience.

From the relative obscurity of the earliest First Ladies, a few shine like stars. We see Abigail Adams passionate in her love for John Adams, in her patriotism, and in her political and social beliefs. Dolley Madison dazzles Washington with her social skills and also proves to be an especially astute politician who aids her husband's presidential activities. Sarah Polk also assists her husband's political career. Acting as the President's private secretary, she enjoys politics more than entertaining.

The period beginning with the Civil War brought First Ladies who saw in their role an opportunity for service to the less fortunate. Mary Todd Lincoln spent hours visiting with wounded Civil War soldiers. Lucy Webb Hayes deeply touched the nation with her compassion for the poor and less privileged. Edith Roosevelt sewed for the needy.

With the 20th century, the role of First Lady included women with professional careers. Ellen Wilson was an accomplished artist; Grace Goodhue Coolidge taught the deaf; and Lou Henry Hoover was a geologist. Others, such as Eleanor Roosevelt, used their positions to speak out for peace, justice, equality for women, and "the needs of the common people."

I take courage from reading *The First Ladies*, and I hope that, like me, all of you who read these brief profiles will be motivated to learn more about this interesting group of Americans.

Hillary Rodham Clinton

In the East Room of the White House, President Abraham Lincoln greets Gen. Ulysses S. Grant, who presents his wife. To the President's left, Mary Todd Lincoln turns toward Gen. Winfield Scott, a military hero since the War of 1812. This detail from an oil painting of around 1867 draws on the actual chamber to portray an imaginary reception and famous persons of the times.

Contents

Martha Dandridge Custis Washington
1731-1802

"I think I am more like a state prisoner than anything else, there is certain bounds set for me which I must not depart from. . . ." So in one of her few surviving letters, Martha Washington confided to a niece that she did not entirely enjoy her role as first of First Ladies. She once conceded that "many younger and gayer women would be extremely pleased" in her place; she would "much rather be at home."

But when George Washington took his oath of office in New York City on April 30, 1789, and assumed the new duties of President of the United States, his wife brought to their position a tact and discretion developed over 58 years of life in Tidewater Virginia society.

Oldest daughter of John and Frances Dandridge, she was born June 2, 1731, on a plantation near Williamsburg. Typical for a girl in an 18th-century family, her education was almost negligible except in domestic and social skills, but she learned all the arts of a well-ordered household and how to keep a family contented.

As a girl of 18—about five feet tall, dark-haired, gentle of manner—she married the wealthy Daniel Parke Custis. Two babies died; two were hardly past infancy when her husband died in 1757.

From the day Martha married George Washington in 1759, her great concern was the comfort and happiness of her husband and her children. When his career led him to the battlegrounds of the Revolutionary War and finally to the Presidency, she followed him bravely. Her love of private life equaled her husband's; but, as she wrote to her friend Mercy Otis Warren, "I cannot blame him for having acted according to his ideas of duty in obeying the voice of his country." As for herself, "I am still determined to be cheerful and to be happy, in whatever situation I may be; for I have also learned from experience that the greater part of our happiness or misery depends upon our dispositions, and not upon our circumstances."

At the President's House in temporary capitals, New York and Philadelphia, the Washingtons chose to entertain in formal style, deliberately emphasizing the new republic's wish to be accepted as the equal of the established governments of Europe. Still, Martha's warm hospitality made her guests feel welcome and put strangers at ease. She took little satisfaction in "formal compliments and empty ceremonies," and declared that "I am fond only of what comes from the heart." Abigail Adams, who sat at her right during parties and receptions, praised her as "one of those unassuming characters which create Love & Esteem."

In 1797 the Washingtons said farewell to public life and returned to their beloved Mount Vernon, to live surrounded by kinfolk, friends, and a constant stream of guests eager to pay their respects to the celebrated couple. Martha's daughter Patsy had died at 17, her son Jack at 26, but Jack's children figured in the household. After George Washington died in 1799, Martha assured a final privacy by burning their letters; she died of a "severe fever" on May 22, 1802. Both lie buried at Mount Vernon, where Washington himself had planned an unpretentious tomb for them.

"Dear Patsy" to her husband, Martha Washington had this miniature painted by Charles Willson Peale about 1776; through the rest of the Revolutionary War, the general wore it in a gold locket. "Lady Washington," some admiring Americans called her; in a modest reference to her domestic skill, she described herself as an "old-fashioned Virginia house-keeper." "A most becoming pleasentness sits upon her countanance...," wrote Abigail Adams in 1789.

Abigail Adams considered it beneath her dignity to be painted bareheaded, so she chose a demure cap when she sat for this likeness, rendered by Gilbert Stuart— one of the young Republic's finest portraitists. The canvas depicts Mrs. Adams in 1800 at age 56. A few days after Stuart sketched her, she received the following written comments from a friend: "Your likeness has attracted . . . as many admirers as spectators. Stewart [sic] says, he wishes to god, he could have taken Mrs. Adams when she was young, he believes he should have a perfect Venus." When President Adams learned of this remark, he wholeheartedly agreed.

Abigail Smith Adams
1744-1818

Inheriting New England's strongest traditions, Abigail Smith was born in 1744 at Weymouth, Massachusetts. On her mother's side she was descended from the Quincys, a family of great prestige in the colony; her father and other forebears were Congregational ministers, leaders in a society that held its clergy in high esteem.

Like other women of the time, Abigail lacked formal education; but her curiosity spurred her keen intelligence, and she read avidly the books at hand. Reading created a bond between her and young John Adams, Harvard graduate launched on a career in law, and they were married in 1764. It was a marriage of the mind and of the heart, enduring for more than half a century, enriched by time.

The young couple lived on John's small farm at Braintree or in Boston as his practice expanded. In ten years she bore three sons and two daughters; she looked after family and home when he went traveling as circuit judge. "Alass!" she wrote in December 1773, "How many snow banks devide thee and me. . . ."

Long separations kept Abigail from her husband while he served the country they loved, as delegate to the Continental Congress, envoy abroad, elected officer under the Constitution. Her letters—pungent, witty, and vivid, spelled just as she spoke—detail her life in times of revolution. They tell the story of the woman who stayed at home to struggle with wartime shortages and inflation; to run the farm with a minimum of help; to teach four children when formal education was interrupted. Most of all, they tell of her loneliness without her "dearest Friend." That "one single expression," she said, "dwelt upon my mind and playd about my Heart. . . ."

In 1784, she joined him at his diplomatic post in Paris, and observed with interest the manners of the French. After 1785, she filled the difficult role of wife of the first United States Minister to Great Britain, and did so with dignity and tact. They returned happily in 1788 to Massachusetts and the handsome house they had just acquired in Braintree, later called Quincy, home for the rest of their lives.

As wife of the first Vice President, Abigail became a good friend to Mrs. Washington and a valued help in official entertaining, drawing on her experience of courts and society abroad. After 1791, however, poor health forced her to spend as much time as possible in Quincy. Illness or trouble found her resolute; as she once declared, she would "not forget the blessings which sweeten life."

When John Adams was elected President, she continued a formal pattern of entertaining—even in the primitive conditions she found at the new capital in November 1800. The city was wilderness, the President's House far from completion. Her private complaints to her family provide blunt accounts of both, but for her three months in Washington she duly held her dinners and receptions.

The Adamses retired to Quincy in 1801, and for 17 years enjoyed the companionship that public life had long denied them. Abigail died in 1818, and is buried beside her husband in United First Parish Church. She leaves her country a most remarkable record as patriot and First Lady, wife of one President and mother of another.

Jefferson's daughter Martha ("Patsy") posed for this oil-on-ivory miniature in 1789, at age 17; "a delicate likeness of her father," a friend called her during the White House years when she sometimes served as his hostess. Of her mother, whose name she bore, no portrait of any kind has survived.

Martha Wayles Skelton Jefferson
1748-1782

When Thomas Jefferson came courting, Martha Wayles Skelton at 22 was already a widow, an heiress, and a mother whose firstborn son would die in early childhood. Family tradition says that she was accomplished and beautiful — with slender figure, hazel eyes, and auburn hair — and wooed by many. Perhaps a mutual love of music cemented the romance; Jefferson played the violin, and one of the furnishings he ordered for the home he was building at Monticello was a "forte-piano" for his bride.

They were married on New Year's Day, 1772, at the bride's plantation home "The Forest," near Williamsburg. When they finally reached Monticello in a late January snowstorm to find no fire, no food, and the servants asleep, they toasted their new home with a leftover half-bottle of wine and "song and merriment and laughter." That night, on their own mountaintop, the love of Thomas Jefferson and his bride seemed strong enough to endure any adversity.

The birth of their daughter Martha in September increased their happiness. Within ten years the family gained five more children. Of them all, only two lived to grow up: Martha, called Patsy, and Mary, called Maria or Polly.

The physical strain of frequent pregnancies weakened Martha Jefferson so gravely that her husband curtailed his political activities to stay near her. He served in Virginia's House of Delegates and as governor, but he refused an appointment by the Continental Congress as a commissioner to France. Just after New Year's Day, 1781, a British invasion forced Martha to flee the capital in Richmond with a baby girl a few weeks old — who died in April. In June the family barely escaped an enemy raid on Monticello. She bore another daughter the following May, and never regained a fair measure of strength. Jefferson wrote on May 20 that her condition was dangerous. After months of tending her devotedly, he noted in his account book for September 6, "My dear wife died this day at 11-45 A.M."

Apparently he never brought himself to record their life together; in a memoir he referred to ten years "in unchequered happiness." Half a century later his daughter Martha remembered his sorrow: "the violence of his emotion . . . to this day I dare not describe to myself." For three weeks he had shut himself in his room, pacing back and forth until exhausted. Slowly that first anguish spent itself. In November he agreed to serve as commissioner to France, eventually taking "Patsy" with him in 1784 and sending for "Polly" later.

When Jefferson became President in 1801, he had been a widower for 19 years. He had become as capable of handling social affairs as political matters. Occasionally he called on Dolley Madison for assistance. And it was Patsy — now Mrs. Thomas Mann Randolph, Jr. — who appeared as the lady of the President's House in the winter of 1802-1803, when she spent seven weeks there. She was there again in 1805-1806, and gave birth to a son named for James Madison, the first child born in the White House. It was Martha Randolph with her family who shared Jefferson's retirement at Monticello until he died there in 1826.

Dolley Payne Todd Madison
1768-1849

For half a century she was the most important woman in the social circles of America. To this day she remains one of the best known and best loved ladies of the White House—though often referred to, mistakenly, as Dorothy or Dorothea.

She always called herself Dolley; and by that name the New Garden Monthly Meeting of the Society of Friends, in piedmont North Carolina, recorded her birth to John and Mary Coles Payne, settlers from Virginia. In 1769 John Payne took his family back to his home colony, and in 1783 he moved them to Philadelphia, city of the Quakers. Dolley grew up in the strict discipline of the Society, but nothing muted her happy personality and her warm heart.

John Todd, Jr., a lawyer, exchanged marriage vows with Dolley in 1790. Just three years later he died in a yellow-fever epidemic, leaving his wife with a small son.

By this time Philadelphia had become the capital city. With her charm and her laughing blue eyes, fair skin, and black curls, the young widow attracted distinguished attention. Before long Dolley was reporting to her best friend that "the great little Madison has asked. . . . to see me this evening."

Although Representative James Madison of Virginia was 17 years her senior, and Episcopalian in background, they were married in September 1794. The marriage, though childless, was notably happy; "our hearts understand each other," she assured him. He could even be patient with Dolley's son, Payne, who mishandled his own affairs—and, eventually, mismanaged Madison's estate.

Discarding the somber Quaker dress after her second marriage, Dolley chose the finest of fashions. Margaret Bayard Smith, chronicler of early Washington social life, wrote: "She looked a Queen. . . . It would be *absolutely impossible* for any one to behave with more perfect propriety than she did."

Blessed with a desire to please and a willingness to be pleased, Dolley made her home the center of society when Madison began, in 1801, his eight years as Jefferson's Secretary of State. She assisted at the White House when the President asked her help in receiving ladies, and presided at the first inaugural ball in Washington when her husband became Chief Executive in 1809.

Dolley's social graces made her famous. Her political acumen, prized by her husband, is less renowned, though her gracious tact smoothed many a quarrel. Hostile statesmen, difficult envoys from Spain or Tunisia, warrior chiefs from the west, flustered youngsters—she always welcomed everyone. Forced to flee from the White House by a British army during the War of 1812, she returned to find the mansion in ruins. Undaunted by temporary quarters, she entertained as skillfully as ever.

At their plantation Montpelier in Virginia, the Madisons lived in pleasant retirement until he died in 1836. She returned to the capital in the autumn of 1837, and friends found tactful ways to supplement her diminished income. She remained in Washington until her death in 1849, honored and loved by all. The delightful personality of this unusual woman is a cherished part of her country's history.

Already a hostess of outstanding success, Dolley Madison sat for this portrait by Gilbert Stuart in 1804. As wife of the Secretary of State, she began her long career of official hospitality; she sustained it for eight years as First Lady. Her manners, said a contemporary, "would disarm envy itself." Widowed, impoverished, and old, she never lost her charm or dignity; she enjoyed the deepening respect of her friends and country to the last.

Invariably elegant, Elizabeth Monroe chose an ermine scarf to complement her black velvet Empire-style gown for this portrait attributed to John Vanderlyn. Although she had traveled with her husband on diplomatic missions, delicate health limited her activities – and enjoyment – in her eight years as First Lady.

Elizabeth Kortright Monroe
1768-1830

Romance glints from the little that is known of Elizabeth Kortright's early life. She was born in New York City in 1768, daughter of an old New York family. Her father, Lawrence, had served the Crown by privateering during the French and Indian War and made a fortune. He took no active part in the War of Independence; and James Monroe wrote to his friend Thomas Jefferson in Paris in 1786 that he had married the daughter of a gentleman "injured in his fortunes" by the Revolution.

Strange choice, perhaps, for a patriot veteran with political ambitions and little money of his own; but Elizabeth was beautiful, and love was decisive. They were married in February 1786, when the bride was not yet 18.

The young couple planned to live in Fredericksburg, Virginia, where Monroe began his practice of law. His political career, however, kept them on the move as the family increased by two daughters and a son who died in infancy.

In 1794, Elizabeth Monroe accompanied her husband to France when President Washington appointed him United States Minister. Arriving in Paris in the midst of the French Revolution, she took a dramatic part in saving Lafayette's wife, imprisoned and expecting death on the guillotine. With only her servants in her carriage, the American Minister's wife went to the prison and asked to see Madame Lafayette. Soon after this hint of American interest, the prisoner was set free. The Monroes became very popular in France, where the diplomat's lady received the affectionate name of *la belle Américaine*.

For 17 years Monroe, his wife at his side, alternated between foreign missions and service as governor or legislator of Virginia. They made the plantation of Oak Hill their home after he inherited it from an uncle, and appeared on the Washington scene in 1811 when he became Madison's Secretary of State.

Elizabeth Monroe was an accomplished hostess when her husband took the Presidential oath in 1817. Through much of the administration, however, she was in poor health and curtailed her activities. Wives of the diplomatic corps and other dignitaries took it amiss when she decided to pay no calls — an arduous social duty in a city of widely scattered dwellings and unpaved streets.

Moreover, she and her daughter Eliza changed White House customs to create the formal atmosphere of European courts. Even the White House wedding of her daughter Maria was private, in "the New York style" rather than the expansive Virginia social style made popular by Dolley Madison. A guest at the Monroes' last levee, on New Year's Day in 1825, described the First Lady as "regal-looking" and noted details of interest: "Her dress was superb black velvet; neck and arms bare and beautifully formed; her hair in puffs and dressed high on the head and ornamented with white ostrich plumes; around her neck an elegant pearl necklace. Though no longer young, she is still a very handsome woman."

In retirement at Oak Hill, Elizabeth Monroe died on September 23, 1830; and family tradition says that her husband burned the letters of their life together.

Louisa Catherine Johnson Adams
1775-1852

Only First Lady born outside the United States, Louisa Catherine Adams did not come to this country until four years after she had married John Quincy Adams. Political enemies sometimes called her English. She was born in London to an English mother, Catherine Nuth Johnson, but her father was American—Joshua Johnson, of Maryland—and he served as United States consul after 1790.

A career diplomat at 27, accredited to the Netherlands, John Quincy developed his interest in charming 19-year-old Louisa when they met in London in 1794. Three years later they were married, and went to Berlin in course of duty. At the Prussian court she displayed the style and grace of a diplomat's lady; the ways of a Yankee farm community seemed strange indeed in 1801 when she first reached the country of which she was a citizen. Then began years divided among the family home in Quincy, Massachusetts, their house in Boston, and a political home in Washington, D. C. When the Johnsons had settled in the capital, Louisa felt more at home there than she ever did in New England.

She left her two older sons in Massachusetts for education in 1809 when she took two-year-old Charles Francis to Russia, where Adams served as Minister. Despite the glamour of the tsar's court, she had to struggle with cold winters, strange customs, limited funds, and poor health; an infant daughter born in 1811 died the next year. Peace negotiations called Adams to Ghent in 1814 and then to London. To join him, Louisa had to make a forty-day journey across war-ravaged Europe by coach in winter; roving bands of stragglers and highwaymen filled her with "unspeakable terrors" for her son. Happily, the next two years gave her an interlude of family life in the country of her birth.

Appointment of John Quincy as Monroe's Secretary of State brought the Adamses to Washington in 1817, and Louisa's drawing room became a center for the diplomatic corps and other notables. Good music enhanced her Tuesday evenings at home, and theater parties contributed to her reputation as an outstanding hostess.

But the pleasure of moving to the White House in 1825 was dimmed by the bitter politics of the election and by her own poor health. She suffered from deep depression. Though she continued her weekly "drawing rooms," she preferred quiet evenings—reading, composing music and verse, playing her harp. The necessary entertainments were always elegant, however; and her cordial hospitality made the last official reception a gracious occasion although her husband had lost his bid for re-election and partisan feeling still ran high.

Louisa thought she was retiring to Massachusetts permanently, but in 1831 her husband began 17 years of notable service in the House of Representatives. The Adamses could look back on a secure happiness as well as many trials when they celebrated their fiftieth wedding anniversary at Quincy in 1847. He was fatally stricken at the Capitol the following year; she died in Washington in 1852, and today lies buried at his side in the family church at Quincy.

"Try as she might, the Madam could never be Bostonian, and it was her cross in life," wrote Henry Adams of his London-born grandmother. Nor did Louisa Johnson Adams feel at ease in what she called the "Bull Bait" of Washington's political life. Gilbert Stuart painted her portrait in 1821.

With the devotion that always marked their marriage, Andrew Jackson once assured Rachel: "recollection never fails me of your likeness." Nearly heartbroken by her death, he wore a miniature of her daily and kept it on his bedside table every night. Family tradition held that the portrait above was the very memento he carried, and attributed it to Anna C. Peale. Current scholarship identifies it as the work of Louisa Catherine Strobel, who was in France from 1815 to 1830; she probably copied a study from life, for one of "Aunt Rachel's" relatives.

Rachel Donelson Jackson
1767-1828

Wearing the white dress she had purchased for her husband's inaugural ceremonies in March 1829, Rachel Donelson Jackson was buried in the garden at The Hermitage, her home near Nashville, Tennessee, on Christmas Eve in 1828. Lines from her epitaph —"A being so gentle and so virtuous slander might wound, but could not dishonor" —reflected his bitterness at campaign slurs that seemed to precipitate her death.

Rachel Donelson was a child of the frontier. Born in Virginia, she journeyed to the Tennessee wilderness with her parents when only 12. At 17, while living in Kentucky, she married Lewis Robards, of a prominent Mercer County family. His unreasoning jealousy made it impossible for her to live with him; in 1790 they separated, and she heard that he was filing a petition for divorce.

Andrew Jackson married her in 1791; and after two happy years they learned to their dismay that Robards had not obtained a divorce, only permission to file for one. Now he brought suit on grounds of adultery. After the divorce was granted, the Jacksons quietly remarried in 1794. They had made an honest mistake, as friends well understood, but whispers of adultery and bigamy followed Rachel as Jackson's career advanced in both politics and war. He was quick to take offense at, and ready to avenge, any slight to her.

Scandal aside, Rachel's unpretentious kindness won the respect of all who knew her—including innumerable visitors who found a comfortable welcome at The Hermitage. Although the Jacksons never had children of their own, they gladly opened their home to the children of Rachel's many relatives. In 1809 they adopted a nephew and named him Andrew Jackson, Jr. They also reared other nephews; one, Andrew Jackson Donelson, eventually married his cousin Emily, one of Rachel's favorite nieces.

Jackson's hostess Emily Donelson: by his friend and portraitist Ralph E. W. Earl.

When Jackson was elected President, he planned to have young Donelson for private secretary, with Emily as company for Rachel. After losing his beloved wife he asked Emily to serve as his hostess.

Though only 21 when she entered the White House, she skillfully cared for her uncle, her husband, four children (three born at the mansion), many visiting relatives, and official guests. Praised by contemporaries for her wonderful tact, she had the courage to differ with the President on issues of principle. Frail throughout her lifetime, Emily died of tuberculosis in 1836.

During the last months of the administration, Sarah Yorke Jackson, wife of Andrew Jackson, Jr., presided at the mansion in her stead.

Hannah Hoes Van Buren
1783-1819

Cousins in a close-knit Dutch community, Hannah Hoes and Martin Van Buren grew up together in Kinderhook, New York. Evidently he wanted to establish his law practice before marrying his sweetheart—they were not wed until 1807, when he was 24 and his bride just three months younger. Apparently their marriage was a happy one, though little is known of Hannah as a person.

Van Buren omitted even her name from his autobiography; a gentleman of that day would not shame a lady by public references. A niece who remembered "her loving, gentle disposition" emphasized "her modest, even timid manner." Church records preserve some details of her life; she seems to have considered formal church affiliation a matter of importance.

Angelica Singleton Van Buren: daughter-in-law and hostess of the widower President.

She bore a son in Kinderhook, three others in Hudson, where Martin served as county surrogate; but the fourth son died in infancy. In 1816 the family moved to the state capital in Albany. Soon the household included Martin's law partner and three apprentices; relatives came and went constantly, and Hannah could return their visits. Contemporary letters indicate that she was busy, sociable, and happy. She gave birth to a fifth boy in January 1817.

But by the following winter her health was obviously failing, apparently from tuberculosis. Not yet 36, she died on February 5, 1819. The Albany *Argus* called her "an ornament of the Christian faith."

Her husband never remarried; he moved into the White House in 1837 as a widower with four bachelor sons. Now accustomed to living in elegant style, he immediately began to refurbish a mansion shabby from public use under Jackson. Across Lafayette Square, Dolley Madison reigned as matriarch of Washington society; when her young relative-by-marriage Angelica Singleton came up from South Carolina for a visit, Dolley took her to the White House to pay a call.

Angelica's aristocratic manners, excellent education, and handsome face won the heart of the President's eldest son, Abraham. They were married in November 1838; next spring a honeymoon abroad polished her social experience. Thereafter, while Abraham served as the President's private secretary, Angelica presided as lady of the house. The only flaw in her pleasure in this role was the loss of a baby girl. Born at the White House, she lived only a few hours. In later years, though spending much time in South Carolina and in Europe, Angelica and her husband made their home in New York City; she died there in 1878.

"Jannetje," Martin Van Buren called his wife, in the Dutch language of their ancestors. An unknown artist painted two portraits of her: one for her husband, one for her niece Maria Hoes Cantine. Initials on the back of the gold brooch indicate that this belonged to the niece; an inset holds a plaited lock of reddish-brown hair, probably a memento of "Aunt Hannah." Prolonged illness, almost certainly tuberculosis, claimed Hannah Van Buren at age 35: years later, Maria remembered "the perfect composure" of her deathbed farewell to her children, and her wish that money usually spent on gifts to pallbearers "should be given to the poor."

Anna Tuthill Symmes Harrison
1775-1864

Anna Harrison was too ill to travel when her husband set out from Ohio in 1841 for his inauguration. It was a long trip and a difficult one even by steamboat and railroad, with February weather uncertain at best, and she at age 65 was well acquainted with the rigors of frontier journeys.

As a girl of 19, bringing pretty clothes and dainty manners, she went out to Ohio with her father, Judge John Cleves Symmes, who had taken up land for settlement on the "north bend" of the Ohio River. She had grown up a young lady of the East, completing her education at a boarding school in New York City.

A clandestine marriage on November 25, 1795, united Anna Symmes and Lt.

Hostess for a single month: Jane Irwin Harrison, portrayed by an unknown artist.

William Henry Harrison, an experienced soldier at 22. Though the young man came from one of the best families of Virginia, Judge Symmes did not want his daughter to face the hard life of frontier forts; but eventually, seeing her happiness, he accepted her choice.

Though Harrison won fame as an Indian fighter and hero of the War of 1812, he spent much of his life in a civilian career. His service in Congress as territorial delegate from Ohio gave Anna and their two children a chance to visit his family at Berkeley, their plantation on the James River. Her third child was born on that trip, at Richmond in September 1800. Harrison's appointment as governor of Indiana Territory took them even farther into the wilderness; he built a handsome house at Vincennes that blended fortress and plantation mansion. Five more children were born to Anna.

Facing war in 1812, the family went to the farm at North Bend. Before peace was assured, she had borne two more children. There, at news of her husband's landslide electoral victory in 1840, home-loving Anna said simply: "I wish that my husband's friends had left him where he is, happy and contented in retirement."

When she decided not to go to Washington with him, the President-elect asked his daughter-in-law Jane Irwin Harrison, widow of his namesake son, to accompany him and act as hostess until Anna's proposed arrival in May. Half a dozen other relatives happily went with them. On April 4, exactly one month after his inauguration, he died, so Anna never made the journey. She had already begun her packing when she learned of her loss.

Accepting grief with admirable dignity, she stayed at her home in North Bend until the house burned in 1858; she lived nearby with her last surviving child, John Scott Harrison, until she died in February 1864 at the age of 88.

Dressed in mourning, Anna Harrison posed for Cornelia Stuart Cassady in 1843—possibly at the Ohio home she had not left during her husband's Presidency. Her health precarious in 1841, she had temporarily entrusted the duties of White House hostess to her widowed daughter-in-law, Jane Irwin Harrison; before she could assume them herself, her husband died.

Heirloom portrait survived Civil War hazards to record the tranquil charm of Letitia Tyler for her descendants. An unknown artist painted it sometime before a paralytic stroke crippled her in 1839. At the White House she lived in seclusion. Her first daughter-in-law, Priscilla Cooper Tyler, assumed the duties of hostess until 1844, when she moved to Philadelphia. Between Letitia Tyler's death in 1842 and her husband's second marriage, the role of First Lady passed briefly to her second daughter, Letitia Tyler Semple.

Letitia Christian Tyler
1790-1842

Letitia Tyler had been confined to an invalid's chair for two years when her husband unexpectedly became President. Nobody had thought of that possibility when he took his oath of office as Vice President on March 4, 1841; indeed, he had planned to fill his undemanding duties from his home in Williamsburg where his wife was most comfortable, her Bible, prayer book, and knitting at her side.

Born on a Tidewater Virginia plantation in the 18th century, Letitia was spiritually akin to Martha Washington and Martha Jefferson. Formal education was no part of this pattern of life, but Letitia learned all the skills of managing a plantation, rearing a family, and presiding over a home that would be John Tyler's refuge during an active political life. They were married on March 29, 1813 — his twenty-third birthday. Thereafter, whether he served in Congress or as Governor of Virginia, she attended to domestic duties. Only once did she join him for the winter social season in Washington. Of the eight children she bore, seven survived; but after 1839 she was a cripple, though "still beautiful now in her declining years."

So her admiring new daughter-in-law, Priscilla Cooper Tyler, described her — "the most entirely unselfish person you can imagine. . . . Notwithstanding her very delicate health, mother attends to and regulates all the household affairs and all so quietly that you can't tell when she does it."

In a second-floor room at the White House, Letitia Tyler kept her quiet but pivotal role in family activities. She did not attempt to take part in the social affairs of the administration. Her married daughters had their own homes; the others were too young for the full responsibility of official entertaining; Priscilla at age 24 assumed the position of White House hostess, met its demands with spirit and success, and enjoyed it.

Daughter of a well-known tragedian, Priscilla Cooper had gone on the stage herself at 17. Playing Desdemona to her father's Othello in Richmond, she won the instant interest of Robert Tyler, whom she married in 1839. Intelligent and beautiful, with dark brown hair, she charmed the President's guests — from visiting celebrities like Charles Dickens to enthusiastic countrymen. Once she noted ruefully: "such hearty shakes as they gave my poor little hand too!" She enjoyed the expert advice of Dolley Madison, and the companionship of her young sister-in-law Elizabeth until she married William N. Waller in 1842.

For this wedding Letitia made her only appearance at a White House social function. "Lizzie looked surpassingly lovely," said Priscilla, and "our dear mother" was "far more attractive to me . . . than any other lady in the room," greeting her guests "in her sweet, gentle, self-possessed manner."

The first President's wife to die in the White House, Letitia Tyler ended her days peacefully on September 10, 1842, holding a damask rose in her hand. She was taken to Virginia for burial at the plantation of her birth, deeply mourned by her family. "She had everything about her," said Priscilla, "to awaken love. . . ."

Julia Gardiner Tyler
1820-1889

"I grieve my love a belle should be," sighed one of Julia Gardiner's innumerable admirers in 1840; at the age of 20 she was already famous as the "Rose of Long Island."

Daughter of Juliana McLachlan and David Gardiner, descendant of prominent and wealthy New York families, Julia was trained from earliest childhood for a life in society; she made her debut at 15. A European tour with her family gave her new glimpses of social splendors. Late in 1842 the Gardiners went to Washington for the winter social season, and Julia became the undisputed darling of the capital. Her beauty and her practiced charm attracted the most eminent men in the city, among them President Tyler, a widower since September.

Tragedy brought his courtship poignant success the next winter. Julia, her sister Margaret, and her father joined a Presidential excursion on the new steam frigate *Princeton*; and David Gardiner lost his life in the explosion of a huge naval gun. Tyler comforted Julia in her grief and won her consent to a secret engagement.

The first President to marry in office took his vows in New York on June 26, 1844. The news was then broken to the American people, who greeted it with keen interest, much publicity, and some criticism about the couple's difference in age: 30 years.

As young Mrs. Tyler said herself, she "reigned" as First Lady for the last eight months of her husband's term. Wearing white satin or black lace to obey the conventions of mourning, she presided with vivacity and animation at a series of parties. She enjoyed her position immensely, and filled it with grace. For receptions she revived the formality of the Van Buren administration; she welcomed her guests with plumes in her hair, attended by maids of honor dressed in white. She once declared, with truth: "Nothing appears to delight the President more than . . . to hear people sing my praises."

The Tylers' happiness was unshaken when they retired to their home at Sherwood Forest in Virginia. There Julia bore five of her seven children; and she acted as mistress of the plantation until the Civil War. As such, she defended both states' rights and the institution of slavery. She championed the political views of her husband, who remained for her "the President" until the end of his life.

His death in 1862 came as a severe blow to her. In a poem composed for his sixty-second birthday she had assured him that "what e'er changes time may bring, I'll love thee as thou art!"

Even as a refugee in New York, she devoted herself to volunteer work for the Confederacy. Its defeat found her impoverished. Not until 1958 would federal law provide automatic pensions for Presidential widows; but Congress in 1870 voted a pension for Mary Lincoln, and Julia Tyler used this precedent in seeking help. In December 1880 Congress voted her $1,200 a year—and after Garfield's assassination it passed bills to grant uniform amounts of $5,000 annually to Mrs. Garfield, Mrs. Lincoln, Mrs. Polk, and Mrs. Tyler. Living out her last years comfortably in Richmond, Julia died there in 1889 and was buried there at her husband's side.

"Most beautiful woman of the age and . . . most accomplished," President Tyler called his new bride, who keenly enjoyed her success as hostess at the White House. She posed for this portrait three years after leaving it.

"Time has dealt kindly with her personal charms...," declared one of many admiring citizens when Sarah Polk became First Lady. In 1846 both she and her husband posed at the White House for George P. A. Healy; three years later they took his fine portraits home to "Polk Place" in Nashville, Tennessee. In her 80th year, ladies of the state commissioned a copy of hers for the Executive Mansion; they entrusted the work to George Dury, who had already painted her at 75—still handsome and alert. Revered throughout the land, she kept her dignity of manner and her clarity of mind to the end.

Sarah Childress Polk
1803-1891

Silks and satins little Sarah took for granted, growing up on a plantation near Murfreesboro, Tennessee. Elder daughter of Captain Joel and Elizabeth Childress, she gained something rarer from her father's wealth. He sent her and her sister away to school, first to Nashville, then to the Moravians' "female academy" at Salem, North Carolina, one of the very few institutions of higher learning available to women in the early 19th century. So she acquired an education that made her especially fitted to assist a man with a political career.

James K. Polk was laying the foundation for that career when he met her. He had begun his first year's service in the Tennessee legislature when they were married on New Year's Day, 1824; he was 28, she 20. The story goes that Andrew Jackson had encouraged their romance; he certainly made Polk a political protégé, and as such Polk represented a district in Congress for 14 sessions.

In an age when motherhood gave a woman her only acknowledged career, Sarah Polk had to resign herself to childlessness. Moreover, no lady would admit to a political role of her own, but Mrs. Polk found scope for her astute mind as well as her social skills. She accompanied her husband to Washington whenever she could, and they soon won a place in its most select social circles. Constantly—but privately—Sarah was helping him with his speeches, copying his correspondence, giving him advice. Much as she enjoyed politics, she would warn him against overwork. He would hand her a newspaper—"Sarah, here is something I wish you to read. . . ."—and she would set to work as well.

A devout Presbyterian, she refused to attend horse races or the theater; but she always maintained social contacts of value to James. When he returned to Washington as President in 1845, she stepped to her high position with ease and evident pleasure. She appeared at the inaugural ball, but did not dance.

Contrasted with Julia Tyler's waltzes, her entertainments have become famous for sedateness and sobriety. Some later accounts say that the Polks never served wine, but in December 1845 a Congressman's wife recorded in her diary details of a four-hour dinner for forty at the White House—glasses for six different wines, from pink champagne to ruby port and sauterne, "formed a rainbow around each plate." Skilled in tactful conversation, Mrs. Polk enjoyed wide popularity as well as deep respect.

Only three months after retirement to their fine new home "Polk Place" in Nashville, he died, worn out by years of public service. Clad always in black, Sarah Polk lived on in that home for 42 years, guarding the memory of her husband and accepting honors paid to her as honors due to him. The house became a place of pilgrimage.

During the Civil War, Mrs. Polk held herself above sectional strife and received with dignity leaders of both Confederate and Union armies; all respected Polk Place as neutral ground. She presided over her house until her death in her 88th year. Buried beside her husband, she was mourned by a nation that had come to regard her as a precious link to the past.

Margaret Mackall Smith Taylor
1788-1852

After the election of 1848, a passenger on a Mississippi riverboat struck up a conversation with easy-mannered Gen. Zachary Taylor, not knowing his identity. The passenger remarked that he didn't think the general qualified for the Presidency—was the stranger "a Taylor man"? "Not much of a one," came the reply. The general went on to say that he hadn't voted for Taylor, partly because his wife was opposed to sending "Old Zack" to Washington, "where she would be obliged to go with him!" It was a truthful answer.

Moreover, the story goes that Margaret Taylor had taken a vow during the Mexican War: If her husband returned safely, she would never go into society again. In fact she never did, though prepared for it by genteel upbringing.

"Peggy" Smith was born in Calvert County, Maryland, daughter of Ann Mackall and Walter Smith, a major in the Revolutionary War according to family tradition. In 1809, visiting a sister in Kentucky, she met young Lieutenant Taylor. They were married the following June, and for a while the young wife stayed on the farm given them as a wedding present by Zachary's father. She bore her first baby there, but cheerfully followed her husband from one remote garrison to another along the western frontier of civilization. An admiring civilian official cited her as one of the "delicate females ... reared in tenderness" who had to educate "worthy and most interesting" children at a fort in Indian country.

Two small girls died in 1820 of what Taylor called "a violent bilious fever," which left their mother's health impaired; three girls and a boy grew up. Knowing the hardships of a military wife, Taylor opposed his daughters' marrying career soldiers— but each eventually married into the Army.

The second daughter, Knox, married Lt. Jefferson Davis in gentle defiance of her parents. In a loving letter home, she imagined her mother skimming milk in the cellar or going out to feed the chickens. Within three months of her wedding, Knox died of malaria. Taylor was not reconciled to Davis until they fought together in Mexico; in Washington the second Mrs. Davis became a good friend of Mrs. Taylor's, often calling on her at the White House.

Though Peggy Taylor welcomed friends and kinfolk in her upstairs sitting room, presided at the family table, met special groups at her husband's side, and worshiped regularly at St. John's Episcopal Church, she took no part in formal social functions. She relegated all the duties of official hostess to her youngest daughter, Mary Elizabeth, then 25 and recent bride of Lt. Col. William W. S. Bliss, adjutant and secretary to the President. Betty Bliss filled her role admirably. One observer thought that her manner blended "the artlessness of a rustic belle and the grace of a duchess."

For Mrs. Taylor, her husband's death—on July 9, 1850—was an appalling blow. Never again did she speak of the White House. She spent her last days with the Blisses, dying on August 18, 1852.

Hostess in her mother's stead, Betty Taylor Bliss probably posed for this daguerreotype about a decade after her White House days. Of Mrs. Taylor, a semi-invalid for years, no authentic likeness survives; contemporaries described her as slender and stately, a brunette in youth.

Abigail Powers Fillmore
1798-1853

First of First Ladies to hold a job after marriage, Abigail Fillmore was helping her husband's career. She was also revealing her most striking personal characteristic: eagerness to learn and pleasure in teaching others.

She was born in Saratoga County, New York, in 1798, while it was still on the fringe of civilization. Her father, a locally prominent Baptist preacher named Lemuel Powers, died shortly thereafter. Courageously, her mother moved on westward, thinking her scanty funds would go further in a less settled region, and ably educated her small son and daughter beyond the usual frontier level with the help of her husband's library.

Shared eagerness for schooling formed a bond when Abigail Powers at 21 met Millard Fillmore at 19, both students at a recently opened academy in the village of New Hope. Although she soon became young Fillmore's inspiration, his struggle to make his way as a lawyer was so long and ill paid that they were not married until February 1826. She even resumed teaching school after the marriage. And then her only son, Millard Powers, was born in 1828.

Attaining prosperity at last, Fillmore bought his family a six-room house in Buffalo, where little Mary Abigail was born in 1832. Enjoying comparative luxury, Abigail learned the ways of society as the wife of a Congressman. She cultivated a noted flower garden; but much of her time, as always, she spent in reading. In 1847, Fillmore was elected state comptroller; with the children away in boarding school and college, the parents moved temporarily to Albany.

In 1849, Abigail Fillmore came to Washington as wife of the Vice President; 16 months later, after Zachary Taylor's death at a height of sectional crisis, the Fillmores moved into the White House.

Even after the period of official mourning the social life of the Fillmore administration remained subdued. The First Lady presided with grace at state dinners and receptions; but a permanently injured ankle made her Friday-evening levees an ordeal—two hours of standing at her husband's side to greet the public. In any case, she preferred reading or music in private. Pleading her delicate health, she entrusted many routine social duties to her attractive daughter, "Abby." With a special appropriation from Congress, she spent contented hours selecting books for a White House library and arranging them in the oval room upstairs, where Abby had her piano, harp, and guitar. Here, wrote a friend, Mrs. Fillmore "could enjoy the music she so much loved, and the conversation of . . . cultivated society. . . ."

Despite chronic poor health, Mrs. Fillmore stayed near her husband through the outdoor ceremonies of President Pierce's inauguration while a raw northeast wind whipped snow over the crowd. Returning chilled to the Willard Hotel, she developed pneumonia; she died there on March 30, 1853. The House of Representatives and the Senate adjourned, and public offices closed in respect, as her family took her body home to Buffalo for burial.

Maternal dignity of a matron in middle life dominates this likeness of Abigail Fillmore record-ed by a daguerreotype. By contemporary descriptions Mrs. Fillmore had been fair of coloring and taller at 5 feet 6 inches than the average woman of her time. A snippet of Washington gossip suggests her manner as First Lady, accusing her of lacking "good form" in seeming "so motherly to her guests." In the duties of hostess her daughter Mary Abigail gave her wel-come help. "Abby," a talented young woman of poise and polish, managed the former President's household from her mother's death until her own shockingly unexpected death at age 22. Fillmore found escape from loneliness in a second happy marriage: to Caroline Carmichael McIntosh, a wealthy and childless widow who survived him.

Jane Means Appleton Pierce
1806-1863

In looks and in pathetic destiny young Jane Means Appleton resembled the heroine of a Victorian novel. The gentle dignity of her face reflected her sensitive, retiring personality and physical weakness. Her father had died—he was a Congregational minister, the Reverend Jesse Appleton, president of Bowdoin College—and her mother had taken the family to Amherst, New Hampshire. And Jane met a Bowdoin graduate, a young lawyer with political ambitions, Franklin Pierce.

Although he was immediately devoted to Jane, they did not marry until she was 28—surprising in that day of early marriages. Her family opposed the match; moreover, she always did her best to discourage his interest in politics. The death of a three-day-old son, the arrival of a new baby, and Jane's dislike of Washington counted heavily in his decision to retire at the apparent height of his career, as United States Senator, in 1842. Little Frank Robert, the second son, died the next year of typhus.

Service in the Mexican War brought Pierce the rank of brigadier and local fame as a hero. He returned home safely, and for four years the Pierces lived quietly at Concord, New Hampshire, in the happiest period of their lives. With attentive pleasure Jane watched her son Benjamin growing up.

Then, in 1852, the Democratic Party made Pierce their candidate for President. His wife fainted at the news. When he took her to Newport for a respite, Benny wrote to her: "I hope he won't be elected for I should not like to be at Washington and I know you would not either." But the President-elect convinced Jane that his office would be an asset for Benny's success in life.

On a journey by train, January 6, 1853, their car was derailed and Benny killed before their eyes. The whole nation shared the parents' grief. The inauguration on March 4 took place without an inaugural ball and without the presence of Mrs. Pierce. She joined her husband later that month, but any pleasure the White House might have brought her was gone. From this loss she never recovered fully. Other events deepened the somber mood of the new administration: Mrs. Fillmore's death in March, that of Vice President Rufus King in April.

Always devout, Jane Pierce turned for solace to prayer. She had to force herself to meet the social obligations inherent in the role of First Lady. Fortunately she had the companionship and help of a girlhood friend, now her aunt by marriage, Abigail Kent Means. Mrs. Robert E. Lee wrote in a private letter: "I have known many of the ladies of the White House, none more truly excellent than the afflicted wife of President Pierce. Her health was a bar to any great effort on her part to meet the expectations of the public in her high position but she was a refined, extremely religious and well educated lady."

With retirement, the Pierces made a prolonged trip abroad in search of health for the invalid—she carried Benny's Bible throughout the journey. The quest was unsuccessful, so the couple came home to New Hampshire to be near family and friends until Jane's death in 1863. She was buried near Benny's grave.

Treasure for a family's annals, this likeness — a photograph from about 1850 — captures the mutual devotion of Jane Pierce and Benny, last of her three sons. Two months before Pierce's inauguration, a railroad accident killed 11-year-old Benny before his parents' eyes. When his stricken mother finally brought herself to appear at White House functions, the guests who acknowledged her "winning smile" could not fail to recognize the "traces of bereavement . . . on a countenance too ingenuous for concealment. . . ."

Harriet Lane
1830-1903

Unique among First Ladies, Harriet Lane acted as hostess for the only President who never married: James Buchanan, her favorite uncle and her guardian after she was orphaned at the age of eleven. And of all the ladies of the White House, few achieved such great success in deeply troubled times as this polished young woman in her twenties.

In the rich farming country of Franklin County, Pennsylvania, her family had prospered as merchants. Her uncle supervised her sound education in private school, completed by two years at the Visitation Convent in Georgetown. By this time "Nunc" was Secretary of State, and he introduced her to fashionable circles as he had promised, "in the best manner." In 1854 she joined him in London, where he was minister to the Court of St. James's. Queen Victoria gave "dear Miss Lane" the rank of ambassador's wife; admiring suitors gave her the fame of a beauty.

In appearance "Hal" Lane was of medium height, with masses of light hair almost golden. In manner she enlivened social gatherings with a captivating mixture of spontaneity and poise.

After the sadness of the Pierce administration, the capital eagerly welcomed its new "Democratic Queen" in 1857. Harriet Lane filled the White House with gaiety and flowers, and guided its social life with enthusiasm and discretion, winning national popularity.

As sectional tensions increased, she worked out seating arrangements for her weekly formal dinner parties with special care, to give dignitaries their proper precedence and still keep political foes apart. Her tact did not falter, but her task became impossible—as did her uncle's. Seven states had seceded by the time Buchanan retired from office and thankfully returned with his niece to his spacious country home, Wheatland, near Lancaster, Pennsylvania.

From her teenage years, the popular Miss Lane flirted happily with numerous beaux, calling them "pleasant but dreadfully troublesome." Buchanan often warned her against "rushing precipitately into matrimonial connexions," and she waited until she was almost 36 to marry. She chose, with her uncle's approval, Henry Elliott Johnston, a Baltimore banker. Within the next 18 years she faced one sorrow after another: the loss of her uncle, her two fine young sons, and her husband.

Thereafter she decided to live in Washington, among friends made during years of happiness. She had acquired a sizable art collection, largely of European works, which she bequeathed to the government. Accepted after her death in 1903, it inspired an official of the Smithsonian Institution to call her "First Lady of the National Collection of Fine Arts." In addition, she had dedicated a generous sum to endow a home for invalid children at the Johns Hopkins Hospital in Baltimore. It became an outstanding pediatric facility, and its national reputation is a fitting memorial to the young lady who presided at the White House with such dignity and charm. The Harriet Lane Outpatient Clinics serve thousands of children today.

"Mischievous romp of a niece," James Buchanan once called the little tomboy who at age 26 became White House hostess for the bachelor President. Artist John Henry Brown captured her queenly beauty 21 years after Harriet Lane assumed the role of First Lady. Fun-loving and flirtatious, spending lavishly on parties and clothes, she brightened a gloomy administration as civil war threatened it, warning her guests to refrain from political discussions.

Mary Todd Lincoln
1818-1882

As a girlhood companion remembered her, Mary Todd was vivacious and impulsive, with an interesting personality—but "she now and then could not restrain a witty, sarcastic speech that cut deeper than she intended. . . ." A young lawyer summed her up in 1840: "the very creature of excitement." All of these attributes marked her life, bringing her both happiness and tragedy.

Daughter of Eliza Parker and Robert Smith Todd, pioneer settlers of Kentucky, Mary lost her mother before the age of seven. Her father remarried; and Mary remembered her childhood as "desolate" although she belonged to the aristocracy of Lexington, with high-spirited social life and a sound private education.

Just 5 feet 2 inches at maturity, Mary had clear blue eyes, long lashes, light-brown hair with glints of bronze, and a lovely complexion. She danced gracefully, she loved finery, and her crisp intelligence polished the wiles of a Southern coquette.

Nearly 21, she went to Springfield, Illinois, to live with her sister Mrs. Ninian Edwards. Here she met Abraham Lincoln—in his own words, "a poor nobody then." Three years later, after a stormy courtship and broken engagement, they were married. Though opposites in background and temperament, they were united by an enduring love—by Mary's confidence in her husband's ability and his gentle consideration of her excitable ways.

Their years in Springfield brought hard work, a family of boys, and reduced circumstances to the pleasure-loving girl who had never felt responsibility before. Lincoln's single term in Congress, for 1847-1849, gave Mary and the boys a winter in Washington, but scant opportunity for social life. Finally her unwavering faith in her husband won ample justification with his election as President in 1860.

Though her position fulfilled her high social ambitions, Mrs. Lincoln's years in the White House mingled misery with triumph. An orgy of spending stirred resentful comment. While the Civil War dragged on, Southerners scorned her as a traitor to her birth, and citizens loyal to the Union suspected her of treason. When she entertained, critics accused her of unpatriotic extravagance. When, utterly distraught, she curtailed her entertaining after her son Willie's death in 1862, they accused her of shirking her social duties.

Yet Lincoln, watching her put her guests at ease during a White House reception, could say happily: "My wife is as handsome as when she was a girl, and I . . . fell in love with her; and what is more, I have never fallen out."

Her husband's assassination in 1865 shattered Mary Todd Lincoln. The next 17 years held nothing but sorrow. With her son "Tad" she traveled abroad in search of health, tortured by distorted ideas of her financial situation. After Tad died in 1871, she slipped into a world of illusion where poverty and murder pursued her.

A misunderstood and tragic figure, she passed away in 1882 at her sister's home in Springfield—the same house from which she had walked as the bride of Abraham Lincoln, 40 years before.

Mathew Brady's camera reveals Mary Lincoln before hostile gossip, private grief, and national tragedy had marked her face—probably in 1861. Of six portraits he made that year, she found only a profile "passable."

Married at 16, Eliza McCardle Johnson taught her husband writing and arithmetic. In poor health when she went to the White House, she left the duties of First Lady to her daughter Martha Patterson (opposite), who modestly said of her family: "We are plain people, from the mountains of Tennessee, called here for a short time by a national calamity. I trust too much will not be expected of us." Byrd Venable Farioletti painted Mrs. Johnson's portrait in 1961, from a photograph taken during the White House years.

Eliza McCardle Johnson
1810-1876

"I knew he'd be acquitted; I knew it," declared Eliza McCardle Johnson, told how the Senate had voted in her husband's impeachment trial. Her faith in him had never wavered during those difficult days in 1868, when her courage dictated that all White House social events should continue as usual.

That faith began to develop many years before in east Tennessee, when Andrew Johnson first came to Greeneville, across the mountains from North Carolina, and established a tailor shop. Eliza was almost 16 then and Andrew only 17; and local tradition tells of the day she first saw him. He was driving a blind pony hitched to a small cart, and she said to a girl friend, "There goes my beau!" She married him within a year, on May 17, 1827.

Eliza was the daughter of Sarah Phillips and John McCardle, a shoemaker. Fortunately she had received a good basic education that she was delighted to share with her new husband. He already knew his letters and could read a bit, so she taught him writing and arithmetic. With their limited means, her skill at keeping a house and bringing up a family—five children, in all—had much to do with Johnson's success.

He rose rapidly, serving in the state and national legislatures and as governor. Like him, when the Civil War came, people of east Tennessee remained loyal to the Union; Lincoln sent him to Nashville as military governor in 1862. Rebel forces caught Eliza at home with part of the family. Only after months of uncertainty did they rejoin Andrew Johnson in Nashville. By 1865 a soldier son and son-in-law had died, and Eliza was an invalid for life.

Quite aside from the tragedy of Lincoln's death, she found little pleasure in her husband's position as President. At the White House, she settled into a second-floor room that became the center of activities for a large

Martha Johnson Patterson, wearing onyx earrings that Mrs. Polk had given to her.

family: her two sons, her widowed daughter Mary Stover and her children; her older daughter Martha with her husband, Senator David T. Patterson, and their children. As a schoolgirl Martha had often been the Polks' guest at the mansion; now she took up its social duties. She was a competent, unpretentious, and gracious hostess even during the impeachment crisis.

At the end of Johnson's term, Eliza returned with relief to her home in Tennessee, restored from wartime vandalism. She lived to see the legislature of her state vindicate her husband's career by electing him to the Senate in 1875, and survived him by nearly six months, dying at the Pattersons' home in 1876.

43

Julia Dent Grant
1826-1902

Quite naturally, shy young Lieutenant Grant lost his heart to friendly Julia; and he made his love known, as he said himself years later, "in the most awkward manner imaginable." She told her side of the story—her father opposed the match, saying, "the boy is too poor," and she answered angrily that she was poor herself. The "poverty" on her part came from a slave-owner's lack of ready cash.

Daughter of Frederick and Ellen Wrenshall Dent, Julia had grown up on a plantation near St. Louis in a typically Southern atmosphere. In memoirs prepared late in life—unpublished until 1975—she pictured her girlhood as an idyll: "one long summer of sunshine, flowers, and smiles. . . ." She attended the Misses Mauros' boarding school in St. Louis for seven years among the daughters of other affluent parents. A social favorite in that circle, she met "Ulys" at her home, where her family welcomed him as a West Point classmate of her brother Frederick; soon she felt lonely without him, dreamed of him, and agreed to wear his West Point ring.

Julia and her handsome lieutenant became engaged in 1844, but the Mexican War deferred the wedding for four long years. Their marriage, often tried by adversity, met every test; they gave each other a life-long loyalty. Like other army wives, "dearest Julia" accompanied her husband to military posts, to pass uneventful days at distant garrisons. Then she returned to his parents' home in 1852 when he was ordered to the West.

Ending that separation, Grant resigned his commission two years later. Farming and business ventures at St. Louis failed, and in 1860 he took his family—four children now—back to his home in Galena, Illinois. He was working in his father's leather goods store when the Civil War called him to a soldier's duty with his state's volunteers. Throughout the war, Julia joined her husband near the scene of action whenever she could.

After so many years of hardship and stress, she rejoiced in his fame as a victorious general, and she entered the White House in 1869 to begin, in her words, "the happiest period" of her life. With Cabinet wives as her allies, she entertained extensively and lavishly. Contemporaries noted her finery, jewels and silks and laces.

Upon leaving the White House in 1877, the Grants made a trip around the world that became a journey of triumphs. Julia proudly recalled details of hospitality and magnificent gifts they received.

But in 1884 Grant suffered yet another business failure and they lost all they had. To provide for his wife, Grant wrote his famous personal memoirs, racing with time and death from cancer. The means thus afforded and her widow's pension enabled her to live in comfort, surrounded by children and grandchildren, till her own death in 1902. She had attended in 1897 the dedication of Grant's monumental tomb in New York City where she was laid to rest. She had ended her own chronicle of their years together with a firm declaration: "the light of his glorious fame still reaches out to me, falls upon me, and warms me."

At Mathew Brady's studio, Julia Dent Grant adopts a characteristic pose to hide an eye defect. Grant rejected the idea of corrective surgery, teasing her gently: ''. . . I might not like you half so well with any other eyes.''

Lucy Ware Webb Hayes
1831-1889

There was no inaugural ball in 1877—when Rutherford B. Hayes and his wife, Lucy, left Ohio for Washington, the outcome of the election was still in doubt. Public fears had not subsided when it was settled in Hayes' favor; and when Lucy watched her husband take his oath of office at the Capitol, her serene and beautiful face impressed even cynical journalists.

She came to the White House well loved by many. Born in Chillicothe, Ohio, daughter of Maria Cook and Dr. James Webb, she lost her father at age two. She was just entering her teens when Mrs. Webb took her sons to the town of Delaware to enroll in the new Ohio Wesleyan University, but she began studying with its excellent instructors. She graduated from the Wesleyan Female College in Cincinnati at 18, unusually well educated for a young lady of her day.

"Rud" Hayes at 27 had set up a law practice in Cincinnati, and he began paying calls at the Webb home. References to Lucy appeared in his diary: "Her low sweet voice is very winning...a heart as true as steel.... Intellect she has too.... By George! I am in love with her!" Married in 1852, they lived in Cincinnati until the Civil War, and he soon came to share her deeply religious opposition to slavery. Visits to relatives and vacation journeys broke the routine of a happy domestic life in a growing family. Over twenty years Lucy bore eight children, of whom five grew up.

She won the affectionate name of "Mother Lucy" from men of the 23rd Ohio Volunteer Infantry who served under her husband's command in the war. They remembered her visits to camp—to minister to the wounded, cheer the homesick, and comfort the dying. Hayes' distinguished combat record earned him election to Congress, and three postwar terms as governor of Ohio. She not only joined him in Washington for its winter social season, she also accompanied him on visits to state reform schools, prisons, and asylums. As the popular first lady of her state, she gained experience in what a woman of her time aptly called "semi-public life."

Thus she entered the White House with confidence gained from her long and happy married life, her knowledge of political circles, her intelligence and culture, and her cheerful spirit. She enjoyed informal parties, and spared no effort to make official entertaining attractive. Though she was a temperance advocate and liquor was banned at the mansion during this administration, she was a very popular hostess. She took criticism of her views in good humor (the famous nickname "Lemonade Lucy" apparently came into use only after she had left the mansion). She became one of the best-loved women to preside over the White House, where the Hayeses celebrated their silver wedding anniversary in 1877, and an admirer hailed her as representing "the new woman era."

The Hayes term ended in 1881, and the family home was now "Spiegel Grove," an estate at Fremont, Ohio. There husband and wife spent eight active, contented years together until her death in 1889. She was buried in Fremont, mourned by her family and hosts of friends.

Sunny in temperament, winning in manner, firm in high principle, Lucy Hayes met both praise and gibes when White House menus omitted liquor. The Woman's Christian Temperance Union honored her with this portrait.

Intellectual Lucretia Garfield—"Crete" to the husband who depended upon her political insights—may have posed for this Brady study while still a Congressman's wife. Illness and turmoil filled her 200 days as First Lady.

Lucretia Rudolph Garfield
1832-1918

In the fond eyes of her husband, President James A. Garfield, Lucretia "grows up to every new emergency with fine tact and faultless taste." She proved this in the eyes of the nation, though she was always a reserved, self-contained woman. She flatly refused to pose for a campaign photograph, and much preferred a literary circle or informal party to a state reception.

Her love of learning she acquired from her father, Zeb Rudolph, a leading citizen of Hiram, Ohio, and devout member of the Disciples of Christ. She first met "Jim" Garfield when both attended a nearby school, and they renewed their friendship in 1851 as students at the Western Reserve Eclectic Institute, founded by the Disciples.

But "Crete" did not attract his special attention until December 1853, when he began a rather cautious courtship, and they did not marry until November 1858, when he was well launched on his career as a teacher. His service in the Union Army from 1861 to 1863 kept them apart; their first child, a daughter, died in 1863. But after his first lonely winter in Washington as a freshman Representative, the family remained together. With a home in the capital as well as one in Ohio they enjoyed a happy domestic life. A two-year-old son died in 1876, but five children grew up healthy and promising; with the passage of time, Lucretia became more and more her husband's companion.

In Washington they shared intellectual interests with congenial friends; she went with him to meetings of a locally celebrated literary society. They read together, made social calls together, dined with each other and traveled in company until by 1880 they were as nearly inseparable as his career permitted.

Garfield's election to the Presidency brought a cheerful family to the White House in 1881. Though Mrs. Garfield was not particularly interested in a First Lady's social duties, she was deeply conscientious and her genuine hospitality made her dinners and twice-weekly receptions enjoyable. At the age of 49 she was still a slender, graceful little woman with clear dark eyes, her brown hair beginning to show traces of silver.

In May she fell gravely ill, apparently from malaria and nervous exhaustion, to her husband's profound distress. "When you are sick," he had written her seven years earlier, "I am like the inhabitants of countries visited by earthquakes." She was still a convalescent, at a seaside resort in New Jersey, when he was shot by a demented assassin on July 2. She returned to Washington by special train—"frail, fatigued, desperate," reported an eyewitness at the White House, "but firm and quiet and full of purpose to save."

During the three months her husband fought for his life, her grief, devotion, and fortitude won the respect and sympathy of the country. In September, after his death, the bereaved family went home to their farm in Ohio. For another 36 years she led a strictly private but busy and comfortable life, active in preserving the records of her husband's career. She died on March 14, 1918.

Daily throughout his White House years, according to family tradition, President Chester A. Arthur had a fresh bouquet of flowers placed before this hand-tinted, silver-framed photograph of his wife. Ellen Herndon Arthur had died ten months before his election to the Vice Presidency. A sophisticated host in his own right, he asked his sister Mary McElroy to assume the role of White House hostess for form's sake, and to oversee the care of his motherless daughter, Ellen.

Ellen Lewis Herndon Arthur
1837-1880

Chester Alan Arthur's beloved "Nell" died of pneumonia on January 12, 1880. That November, when he was elected Vice President, he was still mourning her bitterly. In his own words: "Honors to me now are not what they once were." His grief was the more poignant because she was only 42 and her death sudden. Just two days earlier she had attended a benefit concert in New York City—while he was busy with politics in Albany—and she caught cold that night while waiting for her carriage. She was already unconscious when he reached her side.

Her family connections among distinguished Virginians had shaped her life. She was born at Culpeper Court House, only child of Elizabeth Hansbrough and William Lewis Herndon, U.S.N. They moved to Washington, D. C., when he was assigned to help his brother-in-law Lt. Matthew Fontaine Maury establish the Naval Observatory. While Ellen was still just a girl her beautiful contralto voice attracted attention; she joined the choir at St. John's Episcopal Church on Lafayette Square.

Then her father assumed command of a mail steamer operating from New York; and in 1856 a cousin introduced her to "Chet" Arthur, who was establishing a law practice in the city. By 1857 they were engaged. In a birthday letter that year he reminded her of "the soft, moonlight nights of June, a year ago . . . happy, happy days at Saratoga —the golden, fleeting hours at Lake George." He wished he could hear her singing.

That same year her father died a hero's death at sea, going down with his ship in a gale off Cape Hatteras. The marriage did not take place until October 1859; and a son named for Commander Herndon died when only two. But another boy was born in

Mary Arthur McElroy: youngest sister of the President, ranking lady of the Arthur administration.

1864 and a girl, named for her mother, in 1871. Arthur's career brought the family an increasing prosperity; they decorated their home in the latest fashion and entertained prominent friends with elegance. At Christmas there were jewels from Tiffany for Nell, the finest toys for the children.

At the White House, Arthur would not give anyone the place that would have been his wife's. He asked his sister Mary (Mrs. John E. McElroy) to assume certain social duties and help care for his daughter. He presented a stained-glass window to St. John's Church in his wife's memory; it depicted angels of the Resurrection, and at his special request it was placed in the south transept so that he could see it at night from the White House with the lights of the church shining through.

Frances Folsom Cleveland
1864-1947

"I detest him so much that I don't even think his wife is beautiful." So spoke one of President Grover Cleveland's political foes—the only person, it seems, to deny the loveliness of this notable First Lady, first bride of a President to be married in the White House.

She was born in Buffalo, New York, only child of Emma C. Harmon and Oscar Folsom—who became a law partner of Cleveland's. As a devoted family friend Cleveland bought "Frank" her first baby carriage. As administrator of the Folsom estate after his partner's death, though never her legal guardian, he guided her education with sound advice. When she entered Wells College, he asked Mrs. Folsom's permission to correspond with her, and he kept her room bright with flowers.

Though Frank and her mother missed his inauguration in 1885, they visited him at the White House that spring. There affection turned into romance—despite 27 years' difference in age—and there the wedding took place on June 2, 1886.

Cleveland's scholarly sister Rose gladly gave up the duties of hostess for her own career in education; and with a bride as First Lady, state entertainments took on a new interest. Mrs. Cleveland's unaffected charm won her immediate popularity. She held two receptions a week—one on Saturday afternoons, when women with jobs were free to come.

Rose Elizabeth Cleveland: her bachelor brother's hostess in 15 months of his first term of office.

After the President's defeat in 1888, the Clevelands lived in New York City, where baby Ruth was born. With his unprecedented re-election, the First Lady returned to the White House as if she had been gone but a day. Through the political storms of this term she always kept her place in public favor. People took keen interest in the birth of Esther at the mansion in 1893, and of Marion in 1895. When the family left the White House, Mrs. Cleveland had become one of the most popular women ever to serve as hostess for the nation.

She bore two sons while the Clevelands lived in Princeton, New Jersey, and was at her husband's side when he died at their home, "Westland," in 1908.

In 1913 she married Thomas J. Preston, Jr., a professor of archeology, and remained a figure of note in the Princeton community until she died. She had reached her 84th year—nearly the age at which the venerable Mrs. Polk had welcomed her and her husband on a Presidential visit to the South, and chatted of changes in White House life from bygone days.

Youngest of First Ladies, Frances Folsom Cleveland stirred the public's sentimental admiration as a White House bride at 21 and earned nationwide respect as a charming hostess, a loyal wife, and a capable mother. As President Cleveland expected, she proved "pretty level-headed." The fashionable Swedish portraitist Anders L. Zorn painted this study from life in 1899.

Caroline Lavinia Scott Harrison
1832-1892

The centennial of President Washington's inauguration heightened the nation's interest in its heroic past, and in 1890 Caroline Scott Harrison lent her prestige as First Lady to the founding of the National Society of the Daughters of the American Revolution. She served as its first President General. She took a special interest in the history of the White House, and the mature dignity with which she carried out her duties may overshadow the fun-loving nature that had charmed "Ben" Harrison when they met as teenagers.

Born at Oxford, Ohio, in 1832, "Carrie" was the second daughter of Mary Potts Neal and the Reverend Dr. John W. Scott, a Presbyterian minister and founder of the Oxford Female Institute. As her father's pupil—brown-haired, petite, witty—she infatuated the reserved young Ben, then an honor student at Miami University; they were engaged before his graduation and married in 1853.

After early years of struggle while he established a law practice in Indianapolis, they enjoyed a happy family life interrupted only by the Civil War. Then, while General Harrison became a man of note in his profession, his wife cared for their son and daughter, gave active service to the First Presbyterian Church and to an orphans' home, and extended cordial hospitality to her many friends. Church views to the contrary, she saw no harm in private dancing lessons for her daughter—she liked dancing herself. Blessed with considerable artistic talent, she was an accomplished pianist; she especially enjoyed painting for recreation.

Illness repeatedly kept her away from Washington's winter social season during her husband's term in the Senate, 1881-1887, and she welcomed their return to private life; but she moved with poise to the White House in 1889 to continue the gracious way of life she had always created in her own home.

During the administration the Harrisons' daughter, Mary Harrison McKee, her two children, and other relatives lived at the White House. The First Lady tried in vain to have the overcrowded mansion enlarged but managed to assure an extensive renovation with up-to-date improvements. She established the collection of china associated with White House history. She worked for local charities as well. With other ladies of progressive views, she helped raise funds for the Johns Hopkins University medical school on condition that it admit women. She gave elegant receptions and dinners. In the winter of 1891-1892, however, she had to battle illness as she tried to fulfill her social obligations. She died of tuberculosis at the White House in October 1892, and after services in the East Room was buried from her own church in Indianapolis.

When official mourning ended, Mrs. McKee acted as hostess for her father in the last months of his term. (In 1896 he married his first wife's widowed niece and former secretary, Mary Scott Lord Dimmick; she survived him by nearly 47 years, dying in January 1948.)

To honor the memory of their first President General, Caroline Harrison, the Daughters of the American Revolution commissioned this posthumous portrait by Daniel Huntington and presented it to the White House in 1894.

Ida Saxton McKinley
1847-1907

There was little resemblance between the vivacious young woman who married William McKinley in January 1871 — a slender bride with sky-blue eyes and fair skin and masses of auburn hair — and the petulant invalid who moved into the White House with him in March 1897. Now her face was pallid and drawn, her close-cropped hair gray; her eyes were glazed with pain or dulled with sedative. Only one thing had remained the same: love which had brightened early years of happiness and endured through more than twenty years of illness.

Ida had been born in Canton, Ohio, in 1847, elder daughter of a socially prominent and well-to-do family. James A. Saxton, a banker, was indulgent to his two daughters. He educated them well in local schools and a finishing school, and then sent them to Europe on the grand tour.

Being pretty, fashionable, and a leader of the younger set in Canton did not satisfy Ida, so her broad-minded father suggested that she work in his bank. As a cashier she caught the attention of Maj. William McKinley, who had come to Canton in 1867 to establish a law practice, and they fell deeply in love. While he advanced in his profession, his young wife devoted her time to home and husband. A daughter, Katherine, was born on Christmas Day, 1871; a second, in April 1873. This time Ida was seriously ill, and the frail baby died in August. Phlebitis and epileptic seizures shattered the mother's health; and even before little Katie died in 1876, she was a confirmed invalid.

As Congressman and then as governor of Ohio, William McKinley was never far from her side. He arranged their life to suit her convenience. She spent most of her waking hours in a small Victorian rocking chair that she had had since childhood; she sat doing fancywork and crocheting bedroom slippers while she waited for her husband, who indulged her every whim.

At the White House, the McKinleys acted as if her health were no great handicap to her role as First Lady. Richly and prettily dressed, she received guests at formal receptions seated in a blue velvet chair. She held a fragrant bouquet to suggest that she would not shake hands. Contrary to protocol, she was seated beside the President at state dinners and he, as always, kept close watch for signs of an impending seizure. If necessary, he would cover her face with a large handkerchief for a moment. The First Lady and her devoted husband seemed oblivious to any social inadequacy. Guests were discreet and newspapers silent on the subject of her "fainting spells." Only in recent years have the facts of her health been revealed.

When the President was shot by an assassin in September 1901, after his second inauguration, he thought primarily of her. He murmured to his secretary: "My wife — be careful, Cortelyou, how you tell her — oh, be careful." After his death she lived in Canton, cared for by her younger sister, visiting her husband's grave almost daily. She died in 1907, and lies entombed beside the President and near their two little daughters in Canton's McKinley Memorial Mausoleum.

Both Ida McKinley and her devoted husband posed in the private quarters of the White House for watercolor miniatures by Emily Drayton Taylor in April 1899. Despite varied illnesses, including epilepsy, she took up the role of First Lady with an indomitable determination.

With assured, cultivated taste, Edith Roosevelt approved decor for a renovated White House in 1902; she decided that the new ground-floor corridor, entryway for guests on important occasions, should display likenesses of "all the ladies ... including myself." That same year Theobald Chartran had painted her confidently posed in the South Grounds. Her firmness and prudent advice earned the deep respect of her exuberant husband, and all who knew her. Ever since her day, the corridor has served as a gallery for portraits of recent First Ladies.

Edith Kermit Carow Roosevelt
1861-1948

Edith Kermit Carow knew Theodore Roosevelt from infancy; as a toddler she became a playmate of his younger sister Corinne. Born in Connecticut in 1861, daughter of Charles and Gertrude Tyler Carow, she grew up in an old New York brownstone on Union Square — an environment of comfort and tradition. Throughout childhood she and "Teedie" were in and out of each other's houses.

Attending Miss Comstock's school, she acquired the proper finishing touch for a young lady of that era. A quiet girl who loved books, she was often Theodore's companion for summer outings at Oyster Bay, Long Island; but this ended when he entered Harvard. Although she attended his wedding to Alice Hathaway Lee in 1880, their lives ran separately until 1885, when he was a young widower with an infant daughter, Alice.

Putting tragedy behind him, he and Edith were married in London in December 1886. They settled down in a house on Sagamore Hill, at Oyster Bay, headquarters for a family that added five children in ten years: Theodore, Kermit, Ethel, Archibald, and Quentin. Throughout Roosevelt's intensely active career, family life remained close and entirely delightful. A small son remarked one day, "When Mother was a little girl, she must have been a boy!"

Public tragedy brought them into the White House, eleven days after President McKinley succumbed to an assassin's bullet. Assuming her new duties with characteristic dignity, Mrs. Roosevelt meant to guard the privacy of a family that attracted everyone's interest, and she tried to keep reporters outside her domain. The public, in consequence, heard little of the vigor of her character, her sound judgment, her efficient household management.

But in this administration the White House was unmistakably the social center of the land. Beyond the formal occasions, smaller parties brought together distinguished men and women from varied walks of life. Two family events were highlights: the wedding of "Princess Alice" to Nicholas Longworth, and Ethel's debut. A perceptive aide described the First Lady as "always the gentle, high-bred hostess; smiling often at what went on about her, yet never critical of the ignorant and tolerant always of the little insincerities of political life."

T.R. once wrote to Ted Jr. that "if Mother had been a mere unhealthy Patient Griselda I might have grown set in selfish and inconsiderate ways." She continued, with keen humor and unfailing dignity, to balance her husband's exuberance after they retired in 1909.

After his death in 1919, she traveled widely abroad but always returned to Sagamore Hill as her home. Alone much of the time, she never appeared lonely, being still an avid reader — "not only cultured but scholarly," as T.R. had said. She kept till the end her interest in the Needlework Guild, a charity which provided garments for the poor, and in the work of Christ Church at Oyster Bay. She died on September 30, 1948, at the age of 87.

Helen Herron Taft
1861-1943

As "the only unusual incident" of her girlhood, "Nellie" Herron Taft recalled her visit to the White House at 17 as the guest of President and Mrs. Hayes, intimate friends of her parents. Fourth child of Harriet Collins and John W. Herron, born in 1861, she had grown up in Cincinnati, Ohio, attending a private school in the city and studying music with enthusiasm.

The year after this notable visit she met "that adorable Will Taft," a tall young lawyer, at a sledding party. They found intellectual interests in common; friendship matured into love; Helen Herron and William Howard Taft were married in 1886. A "treasure," he called her, "self-contained, independent, and of unusual application." He wondered if they would ever reach Washington "in any official capacity" and suggested to her that they might—when she became Secretary of the Treasury!

No woman could hope for such a career in that day, but Mrs. Taft welcomed each step in her husband's: state judge, Solicitor General of the United States, federal circuit judge. In 1900 he agreed to take charge of American civil government in the Philippines. By now the children numbered three: Robert, Helen, and Charles. The delight with which she undertook the journey, and her willingness to take her children to a country still unsettled by war, were characteristic of this woman who loved a challenge. In Manila she handled a difficult role with enthusiasm and tact; she relished travel to Japan and China, and a special diplomatic mission to the Vatican.

Further travel with her husband, who became Secretary of War in 1904, brought a widened interest in world politics and a cosmopolitan circle of friends. His election to the Presidency in 1908 gave her a position she had long desired.

As First Lady, she still took an interest in politics but concentrated on giving the administration a particular social brilliance. Only two months after the inauguration she suffered a severe stroke. An indomitable will had her back in command again within a year. At the New Year's reception for 1910, she appeared in white crepe embroidered with gold—a graceful figure. Her daughter left college for a year to take part in social life at the White House, and the gaiety of Helen's debut enhanced the 1910 Christmas season.

During four years famous for social events, the most outstanding was an evening garden party for several thousand guests on the Tafts' silver wedding anniversary, June 19, 1911. Mrs. Taft remembered this as "the greatest event" in her White House experience. Her own book, *Recollections of Full Years*, gives her account of a varied life. And the capital's famous Japanese cherry trees, planted around the Tidal Basin at her request, form a notable memorial.

Her public role in Washington did not end when she left the White House. In 1921 her husband was appointed Chief Justice of the United States—the position he had desired most of all—and she continued to live in the capital after his death in 1930. Retaining to the end her love of travel and of classical music, she died at her home on May 22, 1943.

"My dearest and best critic," William Howard Taft wrote of his wife. She wore her inaugural gown and a tiara to sit for Bror Kronstrand in 1910 at her New England summer home; the artist added a White House setting.

Ellen Louise Axson Wilson
1860-1914

"I am naturally the most unambitious of women and life in the White House has no attractions for me." Mrs. Wilson was writing to thank President Taft for advice concerning the mansion he was leaving. Two years as first lady of New Jersey had given her valuable experience in the duties of a woman whose time belongs to the people. She always played a public role with dignity and grace but never learned to enjoy it.

Those who knew her in the White House described her as calm and sweet, a motherly woman, pretty and refined. Her soft Southern voice had kept its slow drawl through many changes of residence.

Ellen Louise Axson grew up in Rome, Georgia, where her father, the Reverend S. E. Axson, was a Presbyterian minister. Thomas Woodrow Wilson first saw her when he was about six and she only a baby. In 1883, as a young lawyer from Atlanta, "Tommy" visited Rome and met "Miss Ellie Lou" again—a beautiful girl now, keeping house for a bereaved father. He thought, "what splendid laughing eyes!" Despite their instant attraction they did not marry until 1885, because she was unwilling to leave her heartbroken father.

That same year Bryn Mawr College offered Wilson a teaching position at an annual salary of $1,500. He and his bride lived near the campus, keeping her little brother with them. Humorously insisting that her own children must not be born Yankees, she went to relatives in Georgia for the birth of Margaret in 1886 and Jessie in 1887. But Eleanor was born in Connecticut, while Wilson was teaching at Wesleyan University.

His distinguished career at Princeton began in 1890, bringing his wife new social responsibilities. From such demands she took refuge, as always, in art. She had studied briefly in New York, and the quality of her paintings compares favorably with professional art of the period. She had a studio with a skylight installed at the White House in 1913, and found time for painting despite the weddings of two daughters within six months and the duties of hostess for the nation.

The Wilsons had preferred to begin the administration without an inaugural ball, and the First Lady's entertainments were simple; but her unaffected cordiality made her parties successful. In their first year she convinced her scrupulous husband that it would be perfectly proper to invite influential legislators to a private dinner, and when such an evening led to agreement on a tariff bill, he told a friend, "You see what a wise wife I have!"

Descendant of slave owners, Ellen Wilson lent her prestige to the cause of improving housing in the capital's Negro slums. Visiting dilapidated alleys, she brought them to the attention of debutantes and Congressmen. Her death spurred passage of a remedial bill she had worked for. Her health failing slowly from Bright's disease, she died serenely on August 6, 1914. On the day before her death, she made her physician promise to tell Wilson "later" that she hoped he would marry again; she murmured at the end, "... take good care of my husband." Struggling grimly to control his grief, Wilson took her to Rome for burial among her kin.

First wife of Woodrow Wilson, Ellen Louise Axson shared his life from his teaching days at Bryn Mawr to the Presidency. In Washington she devoted much time to humanitarian causes, particularly better housing for Negroes. She told a cousin that she wondered "how anyone who reaches middle age can bear it if she cannot feel, on looking back, that whatever mistakes she may have made she has on the whole lived for others and not for herself." In 1913 Robert Vonnoh depicted Mrs. Wilson serving tea to her three daughters, Margaret, Eleanor, and Jessie, at the artist's home in Cornish, New Hampshire. When Ellen Wilson became gravely ill in 1914, Margaret took over as official hostess.

Solace and support for a troubled President, Edith Wilson saw him through the agonies of wartime, frustrations of protracted peace negotiations, rejection of his dream for world order, illness, and death. Adolpho Muller-Ury portrayed her soon after she had entered the White House, early in 1916.

Edith Bolling Galt Wilson
1872-1961

"Secret President," "first woman to run the government"—so legend has labeled a First Lady whose role gained unusual significance when her husband suffered prolonged and disabling illness. A happy, protected childhood and first marriage had prepared Edith Wilson for the duties of helpmate and hostess; widowhood had taught her something of business matters.

Descendant of Virginia aristocracy, she was born in Wytheville in 1872, seventh among eleven children of Sallie White and Judge William Holcombe Bolling. Until the age of 12 she never left the town; at 15 she went to Martha Washington College to study music, with a second year at a smaller school in Richmond.

Visiting a married sister in Washington, pretty young Edith met a businessman named Norman Galt; in 1896 they were married. For 12 years she lived as a contented (though childless) young matron in the capital, with vacations abroad. In 1908 her husband died unexpectedly. Shrewdly, Edith Galt chose a good manager who operated the family's jewelry firm with financial success.

By a quirk of fate and a chain of friendships, Mrs. Galt met the bereaved President, still mourning profoundly for his first wife. A man who depended on feminine companionship, the lonely Wilson took an instant liking to Mrs. Galt, charming and intelligent and unusually pretty. Admiration changed swiftly to love. In proposing to her, he made the poignant statement that "in this place time is not measured by weeks, or months, or years, but by deep human experiences...." They were married privately on December 18, 1915, at her home; and after they returned from a brief honeymoon in Virginia, their happiness made a vivid impression on their friends and White House staff.

Though the new First Lady had sound qualifications for the role of hostess, the social aspect of the administration was overshadowed by the war in Europe and abandoned after the United States entered the conflict in 1917. Edith Wilson submerged her own life in her husband's, trying to keep him fit under tremendous strain. She accompanied him to Europe when the Allies conferred on terms of peace.

Wilson returned to campaign for Senate approval of the peace treaty and the League of Nations Covenant. His health failed in September 1919; a stroke left him partly paralyzed. His constant attendant, Mrs. Wilson took over many routine duties and details of government. But she did not initiate programs or make major decisions, and she did not try to control the executive branch. She selected matters for her husband's attention and let everything else go to the heads of departments or remain in abeyance. Her "stewardship," she called this. And in *My Memoir*, published in 1939, she stated emphatically that her husband's doctors had urged this course upon her.

In 1921, the Wilsons retired to a comfortable home in Washington, where he died three years later. A highly respected figure in the society of the capital, Mrs. Wilson lived on to ride in President Kennedy's inaugural parade. She died later in 1961: on December 28, the anniversary of her famous husband's birth.

Florence Kling Harding
1860-1924

Daughter of the richest man in a small town—Amos Kling, a successful business-man—Florence Mabel Kling was born in Marion, Ohio, in 1860, to grow up in a setting of wealth, position, and privilege. Much like her strong-willed father in temperament, she developed a self-reliance rare in girls of that era.

A music course at the Cincinnati Conservatory completed her education. When only 19, she eloped with Henry De Wolfe, a neighbor two years her senior. He proved a spendthrift and a heavy drinker who soon deserted her, so she returned to Marion with her baby son. Refusing to live at home, she rented rooms and earned her own money by giving piano lessons to children of the neighborhood. She divorced De Wolfe in 1886 and resumed her maiden name; he died at age 35.

Warren G. Harding had come to Marion when only 16 and, showing a flair for newspaper work, had managed to buy the little *Daily Star*. When he met Florence a courtship quickly developed. Over Amos Kling's angry opposition they were married in 1891, in a house that Harding had planned, and this remained their home for the rest of their lives. (They had no children.)

Mrs. Harding soon took over the *Star*'s circulation department, spanking news-boys when necessary. "No pennies escaped her," a friend recalled, and the paper prospered while its owner's political success increased. As he rose through Ohio politics and became a United States Senator, his wife directed all her acumen to his career. He became Republican nominee for President in 1920 and "the Duchess," as he called her, worked tirelessly for his election. In her own words: "I have only one real hobby—my husband."

She had never been a guest at the White House; and former President Taft, meeting the President-elect and Mrs. Harding, discussed its social customs with her and stressed the value of ceremony. Writing to Nellie, he concluded that the new First Lady was "a nice woman" and would "readily adapt herself."

When Mrs. Harding moved into the White House, she opened mansion and grounds to the public again—both had been closed throughout President Wilson's illness. She herself suffered from a chronic kidney ailment, but she threw herself into the job of First Lady with energy and willpower. Garden parties for veterans were regular events on a crowded social calendar. The President and his wife relaxed at poker parties in the White House library, where liquor was available although the Eighteenth Amendment made it illegal.

Mrs. Harding always liked to travel with her husband. She was with him in the summer of 1923 when he died unexpectedly in California, shortly before the public learned of the major scandals facing his administration.

With astonishing fortitude she endured the long train ride to Washington with the President's body, the state funeral at the Capitol, the last service and burial at Marion. She died in Marion on November 21, 1924, surviving Warren Harding by little more than a year of illness and sorrow.

*"The Duchess," her husband called Florence Harding. Her drive and deter-
mination helped put the 29th President in the White House in 1921. There,
in the Queens' Bedroom, hangs this portrait from life by Philip de László.*

Grace Anna Goodhue Coolidge
1879-1957

For her "fine personal influence exerted as First Lady of the Land," Grace Coolidge received a gold medal from the National Institute of Social Sciences. In 1931 she was voted one of America's twelve greatest living women.

She had grown up in the Green Mountain city of Burlington, Vermont, only child of Andrew and Lemira B. Goodhue, born in 1879. While still a girl she heard of a school for deaf children in Northampton, Massachusetts, and eventually decided to share its challenging work. She graduated from the University of Vermont in 1902 and went to teach at the Clarke School for the Deaf that autumn.

In Northampton she met Calvin Coolidge; they belonged to the same boating, picnicking, whist-club set, composed largely of members of the local Congregational Church. In October 1905 they were married at her parents' home. They lived modestly; they moved into half of a duplex two weeks before their first son was born, and she budgeted expenses well within the income of a struggling small-town lawyer.

To Grace Coolidge may be credited a full share in her husband's rise in politics. She worked hard, kept up appearances, took her part in town activities, attended her church, and offset his shyness with a gay friendliness. She bore a second son in 1908, and it was she who played backyard baseball with the boys. As Coolidge was rising to the rank of governor, the family kept the duplex; he rented a dollar-and-a-half room in Boston and came home on weekends.

In 1921, as wife of the Vice President, Grace Coolidge went from her housewife's routine into Washington society and quickly became the most popular woman in the capital. Her zest for life and her innate simplicity charmed even the most critical. Stylish clothes—a frugal husband's one indulgence—set off her good looks.

After Harding's death, she planned the new administration's social life as her husband wanted it: unpretentious but dignified. Her time and her friendliness now belonged to the nation, and she was generous with both. As she wrote later, she was "I, and yet, not I—this was the wife of the President of the United States and she took precedence over me. . . ." Under the sorrow of her younger son's sudden death at 16, she never let grief interfere with her duties as First Lady. Tact and gaiety made her one of the most popular hostesses of the White House, and she left Washington in 1929 with the country's respect and love.

For greater privacy in Northampton, the Coolidges bought "The Beeches," a large house with spacious grounds. Calvin Coolidge died there in 1933. He had summed up their marriage in his *Autobiography*: "For almost a quarter of a century she has borne with my infirmities, and I have rejoiced in her graces." After his death she sold The Beeches, bought a smaller house, and in time undertook new ventures she had longed to try: her first airplane ride, her first trip to Europe. She kept her aversion to publicity and her sense of fun until her death in 1957. Her chief activity as she grew older was serving as a trustee of the Clarke School; her great pleasure was the family of her surviving son, John.

First as a Vice President's wife, then as First Lady, Grace Goodhue Coolidge brought to Washington society the charm and simplicity of her New England upbringing and her love of people, outdoor activity, and animals. Howard Chandler Christy portrayed her in 1924 with her famous collie Rob Roy.

Lou Henry Hoover
1874-1944

Admirably equipped to preside at the White House, Lou Henry Hoover brought to it long experience as wife of a man eminent in public affairs at home and abroad. She had shared his interests since they met in a geology lab at Leland Stanford University. She was a freshman, he a senior, and he was fascinated, as he declared later, "by her whimsical mind, her blue eyes and a broad grinnish smile."

Born in Iowa, in 1874, she grew up there for ten years. Then her father, Charles D. Henry, decided that the climate of southern California would favor the health of his wife, Florence. He took his daughter on camping trips in the hills—her greatest pleasures in her early teens. Lou became a fine horsewoman; she hunted, and preserved specimens with the skill of a taxidermist; she developed an enthusiam for rocks, minerals, and mining. She entered Stanford in 1894—"slim and supple as a reed," a classmate recalled, with a "wealth of brown hair"—and completed her course before marrying Herbert Hoover in 1899.

The newlyweds left at once for China, where he won quick recognition as a mining engineer. His career took them about the globe—Ceylon, Burma, Siberia, Australia, Egypt, Japan, Europe—while her talent for homemaking eased their time in a dozen foreign lands. Two sons, Herbert and Allan, were born during this adventurous life, which made their father a youthful millionaire.

During World War I, while Hoover earned world fame administering emergency relief programs, she was often with him but spent some time with the boys in California. In 1919 she saw construction begin for a long-planned home in Palo Alto. In 1921, however, his appointment as Secretary of Commerce took the family to Washington. There she spent eight years busy with the social duties of a Cabinet wife and an active participation in the Girl Scout movement, including service as its president.

The Hoovers moved into the White House in 1929, and the First Lady welcomed visitors with poise and dignity throughout the administration. However, when the first day of 1933 dawned, Mr. and Mrs. Hoover were away on holiday. Their absence ended the New Year's Day tradition of the public being greeted personally by the President at a reception in the Executive Mansion.

Mrs. Hoover paid with her own money the cost of reproducing furniture owned by Monroe for a period sitting room in the White House. She also restored Lincoln's study for her husband's use. She dressed handsomely; she "never fitted more perfectly into the White House picture than in her formal evening gown," remarked one secretary. The Hoovers entertained elegantly, using their own private funds for social events while the country suffered worsening economic depression.

In 1933 they retired to Palo Alto, but maintained an apartment in New York. Mr. Hoover learned the full lavishness of his wife's charities only after her death there on January 7, 1944; she had helped the education, he said, "of a multitude of boys and girls." In retrospect he stated her ideal for the position she had held: "a symbol of everything wholesome in American life."

Perfectionist of hospitality, Lou Hoover as First Lady considered formal entertaining a duty to the American people. For the White House Collection, Richard M. Brown copied a 1932 portrait from life by Philip de László.

Douglas Chandor's portrait of Eleanor Roosevelt at age 65 captures a range of moods and suggests her astonishing energy. She devoted a long career to victims of poverty, prejudice, and war. Painfully shy and self-conscious in her youth, often a controversial figure in the role of President's wife, she won international respect in later years as "First Lady of the World."

Anna Eleanor Roosevelt Roosevelt
1884-1962

A shy, awkward child, starved for recognition and love, Eleanor Roosevelt grew into a woman with great sensitivity to the underprivileged of all creeds, races, and nations. Her constant work to improve their lot made her one of the most loved — and for some years one of the most reviled — women of her generation.

She was born in New York City on October 11, 1884, daughter of lovely Anna Hall and Elliott Roosevelt, younger brother of Theodore. When her mother died in 1892, the children went to live with Grandmother Hall; her adored father died only two years later. Attending a distinguished school in England gave her, at 15, her first chance to develop self-confidence among other girls.

Tall, slender, graceful of figure but apprehensive at the thought of being a wallflower, she returned for a debut that she dreaded. In her circle of friends was a distant cousin, handsome young Franklin Delano Roosevelt. They became engaged in 1903 and were married in 1905, with her uncle the President giving the bride away. Within eleven years Eleanor bore six children; one son died in infancy. "I suppose I was fitting pretty well into the pattern of a fairly conventional, quiet, young society matron," she wrote later in her autobiography.

In Albany, where Franklin served in the state Senate from 1910 to 1913, Eleanor started her long career as political helpmate. She gained a knowledge of Washington and its ways while he served as Assistant Secretary of the Navy. When he was stricken with poliomyelitis in 1921, she tended him devotedly. She became active in the women's division of the State Democratic Committee to keep his interest in politics alive. From his successful campaign for governor in 1928 to the day of his death, she dedicated her life to his purposes. She became eyes and ears for him, a trusted and tireless reporter.

When Mrs. Roosevelt came to the White House in 1933, she understood social conditions better than any of her predecessors and she transformed the role of First Lady accordingly. She never shirked official entertaining; she greeted thousands with charming friendliness. She also broke precedent to hold press conferences, travel to all parts of the country, give lectures and radio broadcasts, and express her opinions candidly in a daily syndicated newspaper column, "My Day."

This made her a tempting target for political enemies but her integrity, her graciousness, and her sincerity of purpose endeared her personally to many — from heads of state to servicemen she visited abroad during World War II. As she had written wistfully at 14: ". . . no matter how plain a woman may be if truth & loyalty are stamped upon her face all will be attracted to her. . . ."

After the President's death in 1945 she returned to a cottage at his Hyde Park estate; she told reporters: "the story is over." Within a year, however, she began her service as American spokesman in the United Nations. She continued a vigorous career until her strength began to wane in 1962. She died in New York City that November, and was buried at Hyde Park beside her husband.

Elizabeth Virginia Wallace Truman
1885-1982

Whistle-stopping in 1948, President Harry Truman often ended his campaign talk by introducing his wife as "the Boss" and his daughter, Margaret, as "the Boss's Boss," and they smiled and waved as the train picked up steam. The sight of that close-knit family gallantly fighting against such long odds had much to do with his surprise victory at the polls that November.

Strong family ties in the southern tradition had always been important around Independence, Missouri, where a baby girl was born to Margaret ("Madge") Gates and David Wallace on February 13, 1885. Christened Elizabeth Virginia, she grew up as "Bess." Harry Truman, whose family moved to town in 1890, always kept his first impression of her—"golden curls" and "the most beautiful blue eyes." A relative said, "there never was but one girl in the world" for him. They attended the same schools from fifth grade through high school.

In recent years their daughter has written a vivid sketch of Bess as a girl: "a marvelous athlete—the best third baseman in Independence, a superb tennis player, a tireless ice skater—and she was pretty besides." She also had many "strong opinions.... and no hesitation about stating them Missouri style—straight from the shoulder."

For Bess and Harry, World War I altered a deliberate courtship. He proposed and they became engaged before Lieutenant Truman left for the battlefields of France in 1918. They were married in June 1919; they lived in Mrs. Wallace's home, where Mary Margaret was born in 1924.

When Harry Truman became active in politics, Mrs. Truman traveled with him and shared his platform appearances as the public had come to expect a candidate's wife to do. His election to the Senate in 1934 took the family to Washington. Reluctant to be a public figure herself, she always shared his thoughts and interests in private. When she joined his office staff as a secretary, he said, she earned "every cent I pay her." His wartime role as chairman of a special committee on defense spending earned him national recognition—and a place on the Democratic ticket as President Roosevelt's fourth-term running mate. Three months after their inauguration Roosevelt was dead. On April 12, 1945, Harry Truman took the President's oath of office—and Bess, who managed to look on with composure, was the new First Lady.

In the White House, its lack of privacy was distasteful to her. As her husband put it later, she was "not especially interested" in the "formalities and pomp or the artificiality which, as we had learned . . . , inevitably surround the family of the President." Though she conscientiously fulfilled the social obligations of her position, she did only what was necessary. While the mansion was rebuilt during the second term, the Trumans lived in Blair House and kept social life to a minimum.

They returned to Independence in 1953. After her husband's death in 1972, Mrs. Truman continued to live in the family home. There she enjoyed visits from Margaret and her husband, Clifton Daniel, and their four sons. She died in 1982 and was buried beside her husband in the courtyard of the Harry S. Truman Library.

Dignified and witty Bess Truman kept the original painting of this White House replica in her Missouri home. Her daughter, Margaret Truman Daniel, once described her as "a warmhearted, kind lady, with a robust sense of humor."

Mamie Geneva Doud Eisenhower
1896-1979

Mamie Eisenhower's bangs and sparkling blue eyes were as much trademarks of an administration as the President's famous grin. Her outgoing manner, her feminine love of pretty clothes and jewelry, and her obvious pride in husband and home made her a very popular First Lady.

Born in Boone, Iowa, Mamie Geneva Doud moved with her family to Colorado when she was seven. Her father retired from business, and Mamie and her three sisters grew up in a large house in Denver. During winters the family made long visits to relatives in the milder climate of San Antonio, Texas.

There, in 1915, at Fort Sam Houston, Mamie met Dwight D. Eisenhower, a young second lieutenant on his first tour of duty. She drew his attention instantly, he recalled: "a vivacious and attractive girl, smaller than average, saucy in the look about her face and in her whole attitude." On St. Valentine's Day in 1916 he gave her a miniature of his West Point class ring to seal a formal engagement; they were married at the Doud home in Denver on July 1.

For years Mamie Eisenhower's life followed the pattern of other Army wives: a succession of posts in the United States, in the Panama Canal Zone; duty in France, in the Philippines. She once estimated that in 37 years she had unpacked her household at least 27 times. Each move meant another step up the career ladder for her husband, with increasing responsibilities for her.

The first son Doud Dwight or "Icky," who was born in 1917, died of scarlet fever in 1921. A second child, John, was born in 1922 in Denver. Like his father he had a career in the Army; later he became an author and served as ambassador to Belgium.

During World War II, while promotion and fame came to "Ike," his wife lived in Washington. After he became president of Columbia University in 1948, the Eisenhowers purchased a farm at Gettysburg, Pennsylvania. It was the first home they had ever owned. His duties as commander of North Atlantic Treaty Organization forces— and hers as his hostess at a chateau near Paris— delayed work on their dream home, finally completed in 1955. They celebrated with a housewarming picnic for the staff from their last temporary quarters: the White House.

When Eisenhower had campaigned for President, his wife cheerfully shared his travels; when he was inaugurated in 1953, the American people warmly welcomed her as First Lady. Diplomacy—and air travel—in the postwar world brought changes in their official hospitality. The Eisenhowers entertained an unprecedented number of heads of state and leaders of foreign governments, and Mamie's evident enjoyment of her role endeared her to her guests and to the public.

In 1961 the Eisenhowers returned to Gettysburg for eight years of contented retirement together. After her husband's death in 1969, Mamie continued to live on the farm, devoting more of her time to her family and friends. Mamie Eisenhower died on November 1, 1979. She is buried beside her husband in a small chapel on the grounds of the Eisenhower Library in Abilene, Kansas.

Her famed and favorite pink casts a soft glow from Mrs. Eisenhower's rhinestone-studded inaugural gown. After many separations in Army life, she and the President happily resided in the White House for eight years.

Jacqueline Kennedy, portrayed by Aaron Shikler in 1970, stirred national interest in obtaining antiques and works of art for the White House. She planned the first historical guidebook of the mansion for its many visitors.

Jacqueline Lee Bouvier Kennedy Onassis
1929-1994

The inauguration of John F. Kennedy in 1961 brought to the White House and to the heart of the nation a beautiful young wife and the first young children of a President in half a century.

She was born Jacqueline Lee Bouvier, daughter of John Vernon Bouvier III and his wife, Janet Lee. Her early years were divided between New York City and East Hampton, Long Island, where she learned to ride almost as soon as she could walk. She was educated at the best of private schools; she wrote poems and stories, drew illustrations for them, and studied ballet. Her mother, who had obtained a divorce, married Hugh D. Auchincloss in 1942 and brought her two girls to "Merrywood," his home near Washington, D. C., with summers spent at his estate in Newport, Rhode Island. Jacqueline was dubbed "the Debutante of the year" for the 1947-1948 season, but her social success did not keep her from continuing her education. As a Vassar student she traveled extensively, and she spent her junior year in France before graduating from George Washington University. These experiences left her with a great empathy for people of foreign countries, especially the French.

In Washington she took a job as "inquiring photographer" for a local newspaper. Her path soon crossed that of Senator Kennedy, who had the reputation of being the most eligible bachelor in the capital. Their romance progressed slowly and privately, but their wedding at Newport in 1953 attracted nationwide publicity.

With marriage "Jackie" had to adapt herself to the new role of wife to one of the country's most energetic political figures. Her own public appearances were highly successful, but limited in number. After the sadness of a miscarriage and the stillbirth of a daughter, Caroline Bouvier was born in 1957; John Jr. was born between the election of 1960 and Inauguration Day. Patrick Bouvier, born prematurely on August 7, 1963, died two days later.

To the role of First Lady, Jacqueline Kennedy brought beauty, intelligence, and cultivated taste. Her interest in the arts, publicized by press and television, inspired an attention to culture never before evident at a national level. She devoted much time and study to making the White House a museum of American history and decorative arts as well as a family residence of elegance and charm. But she defined her major role as "to take care of the President" and added that "if you bungle raising your children, I don't think whatever else you do well matters very much."

Mrs. Kennedy's gallant courage during the tragedy of her husband's assassination won her the admiration of the world. Thereafter it seemed the public would never allow her the privacy she desired for herself and her children. She moved to New York City; and in 1968 she married the wealthy Greek businessman Aristotle Onassis, 23 years her senior, who died in March 1975. From 1978 until her death in 1994, Mrs. Onassis worked in New York City as an editor for Doubleday. At her funeral her son described three of her attributes: "love of words, the bonds of home and family, and her spirit of adventure."

Claudia Taylor (Lady Bird) Johnson
1912-

Christened Claudia Alta Taylor when she was born in a country mansion near Karnack, Texas, she received her nickname "Lady Bird" as a small child; and as Lady Bird she is known and loved throughout America today. Perhaps that name was prophetic, as there has seldom been a First Lady so attuned to nature and the importance of conserving the environment.

Her mother, Minnie Pattillo Taylor, died when Lady Bird was five, so she was reared by her father, her aunt, and family servants. From her father, Thomas Jefferson Taylor, who had prospered, she learned much about the business world. An excellent student, she also learned to love classical literature. At the University of Texas she earned bachelor's degrees in arts and in journalism.

In 1934 Lady Bird met Lyndon Baines Johnson, then a Congressional secretary visiting Austin on official business; he promptly asked her for a date, which she accepted. He courted her from Washington with letters, telegrams, and telephone calls. Seven weeks later he was back in Texas; he proposed to her and she accepted. In her own words: "Sometimes Lyndon simply takes your breath away." They were married in November 1934.

The years that followed were devoted to Lyndon's political career, with "Bird" as partner, confidante, and helpmate. She helped keep his Congressional office open during World War II when he volunteered for naval service; and in 1955, when he had a severe heart attack, she helped his staff keep things running smoothly until he could return to his post as Majority Leader of the Senate. He once remarked that voters "would happily have elected her over me."

After repeated miscarriages, she gave birth to Lynda Bird (now Mrs. Charles S. Robb) in 1944; Luci Baines (Mrs. Ian Turpin) was born three years later.

In the election of 1960, Lady Bird successfully stumped for Democratic candidates across 35,000 miles of campaign trail. As wife of the Vice President, she became an ambassador of goodwill by visiting 33 foreign countries. Moving to the White House after Kennedy's murder, she did her best to ease a painful transition. She soon set her own stamp of Texas hospitality on social events, but these were not her chief concern. She created a First Lady's Committee for a More Beautiful Capital, then expanded her program to include the entire nation. She took a highly active part in her husband's war-on-poverty program, especially the Head Start project for preschool children.

When the Presidential term ended, the Johnsons returned to Texas, where he died in 1973. Mrs. Johnson's *White House Diary*, published in 1970, and a 1981 documentary film, *The First Lady, A Portrait of Lady Bird Johnson*, give sensitive and detailed views of her contributions to the President's Great Society administration. Today Lady Bird leads a life devoted to her husband's memory, her children, and seven grandchildren. She still supports causes dear to her—notably the National Wildflower Research Center, which she founded in 1982, and The Lyndon Baines Johnson Library. She also serves on the Board of the National Geographic Society as a trustee emeritus.

Flower- and wilderness-lover, Lady Bird Johnson sponsored a beautification project that came to include the nation's cities and highways. "A woman of great depth and excellent judgment," President Johnson described her.

While First Lady, Pat Nixon traveled over the world more than any of her predecessors, alone or with her husband. She encouraged volunteer work—"individual attention and love and concern"—to help the less fortunate.

Patricia Ryan Nixon
1912-1993

Born Thelma Catherine Ryan on March 16 in Ely, Nevada, "Pat" Nixon acquired her nickname within hours. Her father, William Ryan, called her his "St. Patrick's babe in the morn" when he came home from the mines before dawn.

Soon the family moved to California and settled on a small truck farm near Los Angeles—a life of hard work with few luxuries. Her mother, Kate Halberstadt Bender Ryan, died in 1925; at 13 Pat assumed all the household duties for her father and two older brothers. At 18, she lost her father after nursing him through months of illness. Left on her own and determined to continue her education, she worked her way through the University of Southern California. She held part-time jobs on campus, as a sales clerk in a fashionable department store, and as an extra in the movies—and she graduated cum laude in 1937.

She accepted a position as a high-school teacher in Whittier; and there she met Richard Nixon, who had come home from Duke University Law School to establish a practice. They became acquainted at a Little Theater group when they were cast in the same play, and were married on June 21, 1940.

During World War II, she worked as a government economist while he served in the Navy. She campaigned at his side in 1946 when he entered politics, running successfully for Congress, and afterward. Within six years she saw him elected to the House, the Senate, and the Vice Presidency on the ticket with Dwight D. Eisenhower. Despite the demands of official life, the Nixons were devoted parents to their two daughters, Tricia (now Mrs. Edward Cox), and Julie (now Mrs. David Eisenhower).

A tireless campaigner when he ran unsuccessfully for President in 1960, she was at his side when he ran again in 1968—and won. She had once remarked succinctly, "It takes heart to be in political life."

Pat Nixon used her position as First Lady to encourage volunteer service—"the spirit of people helping people." She invited hundreds of families to nondenominational Sunday services in the East Room. She instituted a series of performances by artists in varied American traditions—from opera to bluegrass. Mrs. Nixon took quiet pride in adding 600 paintings and antiques to the White House Collection.

She had shared her husband's journeys abroad in his Vice Presidential years, and she continued the practice during his Presidency. Her travels included the historic visit to the People's Republic of China and the summit meeting in the Soviet Union. Her first solo trip was a journey of compassion to take relief supplies to earthquake victims in Peru. Later she visited Africa and South America with the unique diplomatic standing of Personal Representative of the President. Always she was a charming envoy.

Mrs. Nixon met the troubled days of Watergate with dignity. "I love my husband," she said, "I believe in him, and I am proud of his accomplishments." She died at home in Park Ridge, New Jersey, on June 22, 1993. Her husband followed her in death ten months later. She and the former President are buried at the Richard Nixon Library and Birthplace in Yorba Linda, California.

Once a professional dancer with Martha Graham and a teacher of dance to underprivileged youngsters, Betty Ford continues her support of dance and encourages the other arts. She staunchly advocates women's rights as well.

Elizabeth Bloomer Ford
1918-

In 25 years of political life, Betty Bloomer Ford did not expect to become First Lady. As wife of Representative Gerald R. Ford, she looked forward to his retirement and more time together. In late 1973 his selection as Vice President was a surprise to her. She was just becoming accustomed to their new roles when he became President upon Mr. Nixon's resignation in August 1974.

Born Elizabeth Anne Bloomer in Chicago, she grew up in Grand Rapids, Michigan, and graduated from high school there. She studied modern dance at Bennington College in Vermont, decided to make it a career, and became a member of Martha Graham's noted concert group in New York City, supporting herself as a fashion model for the John Robert Powers firm.

Close ties with her family and her hometown took her back to Grand Rapids, where she became fashion coordinator for a department store. She also organized her own dance group and taught dance to handicapped children.

Her first marriage, at age 24, ended in divorce five years later on the grounds of incompatibility. Not long afterward she began dating Jerry Ford, football hero, graduate of the University of Michigan and Yale Law School, and soon a candidate for Congress. They were married during the 1948 campaign; he won his election; and the Fords lived in the Washington area for nearly three decades thereafter.

Their four children—Michael, Jack, Steven, and Susan—were born in the next ten years. As her husband's political career became more demanding, Betty Ford found herself shouldering many of the family responsibilities. She supervised the home, did the cooking, undertook volunteer work, and took part in the activities of "House wives" and "Senate wives" for Congressional and Republican clubs. In addition, she was an effective campaigner for her husband.

Betty Ford faced her new life as First Lady with dignity and serenity. She accepted it as a challenge. "I like challenges very much," she said. She had the self-confidence to express herself with humor and forthrightness whether speaking to friends or to the public. Forced to undergo radical surgery for breast cancer in 1974, she reassured many troubled women by discussing her ordeal openly. She explained that "maybe if I as First Lady could talk about it candidly and without embarrassment, many other people would be able to as well." As soon as possible, she resumed her duties as hostess at the Executive Mansion and her role as a public-spirited citizen. She did not hesitate to state her views on controversial issues such as the Equal Rights Amendment, which she strongly supported.

From their home in California, she was equally frank about her successful battle against dependency on drugs and alcohol. She helped establish the Betty Ford Center for treatment of this problem at the Eisenhower Medical Center in Rancho Mirage.

She has described the role of First Lady as "much more of a 24-hour job than anyone would guess" and says of her predecessors: "Now that I realize what they've had to put up with, I have new respect and admiration for every one of them."

For many years, Rosalynn Carter has taken an active interest in volunteer work and in helping the mentally ill, the elderly, the handicapped, and the poor. The shy girl from Plains became a determined campaigner for her husband and called herself "more a political partner than a political wife." She used her influence as First Lady in behalf of women's rights. In 1980 the District of Columbia honored Mrs. Carter for her "commitment . . . to build a more caring society."

Rosalynn Smith Carter
1927-

"She's the girl I want to marry," Jimmy Carter told his mother after his first date with 17-year-old Rosalynn Smith, who had grown up as a friend and neighbor of the Carter family in Plains, Georgia.

Born in Plains on August 18, 1927, Rosalynn was the first of four children in the family of Allethea Murray Smith and Wilburn Edgar Smith. She grew up in a small-town atmosphere that nurtured strong ties to family and dedication to church and community. When she was 13, her father died and her mother became a dressmaker to help support the family. As the oldest child, Rosalynn worked beside her mother, helping with the sewing, the housekeeping, and the other children.

Times were difficult, but Rosalynn completed high school and enrolled in Georgia Southwestern College at Americus. In 1945, after her freshman year, she first dated Jimmy Carter, who was home from the U. S. Naval Academy at Annapolis. Their romance progressed, and in 1946 they were married.

The young couple went to Norfolk, Virginia, Ensign Carter's first duty station after graduation. The Navy kept them on the move. Their sons were born in different places: John William in Virginia, James Earl III in Hawaii, and Donnel Jeffrey in Connecticut. The Carters' only daughter, Amy Lynn, was born in Georgia in 1967.

When his father died in 1953, Jimmy left the service, and the Carters returned to Plains to run the family business. Managing the accounts of the peanut, fertilizer, and seed enterprise, Rosalynn soon found herself working full-time.

Jimmy entered politics in 1962, winning a seat in the Georgia Senate. Rosalynn, an important member of his campaign team, helped develop support for her husband's successful bid for the governorship of Georgia in 1970. During his Presidential campaigns, Rosalynn traveled independently throughout the United States. Her belief in her husband's ability to lead the nation was communicated in a quiet, friendly manner that made her an effective campaigner.

A skillful speaker and a hardworking First Lady, Mrs. Carter managed routine duties and special projects in her office in the East Wing. She attended Cabinet meetings and major briefings, frequently represented the Chief Executive at ceremonial occasions, and served as the President's personal emissary to Latin American countries.

As First Lady, she focused national attention on the performing arts. She invited to the White House leading classical artists from around the world, as well as traditional American artists. She also took a strong interest in programs to aid mental health, the community, and the elderly. From 1977 to 1978, she served as the Honorary Chairperson of the President's Commission on Mental Health.

After returning home, Mrs. Carter wrote her autobiography, *First Lady From Plains*, published in 1984. She is a director of the Carter Center, where she manages an active mental health program and works with human rights, conflict resolution, and childhood immunization. She also shares her community service talents with Habitat for Humanity, an organization that builds homes for the underprivileged.

Nancy Davis Reagan
1923-

"My life really began when I married my husband," says Nancy Reagan, who in the 1950's happily gave up an acting career for a permanent role as the wife of Ronald Reagan and mother to their children. Her story actually begins in New York City, her birthplace. She was born on July 6, 1923, according to her autobiography *Nancy*, published in 1980. When the future First Lady was six, her mother, Edith—a stage actress—married Dr. Loyal Davis, a neurosurgeon. Dr. Davis adopted Nancy, and she grew up in Chicago. It was a happy time: summer camp, tennis, swimming, dancing. She received her formal education at Girls' Latin School and at Smith College in Massachusetts, where she majored in theater.

Soon after graduation she became a professional actress. She toured with a road company, then landed a role on Broadway in the hit musical *Lute Song*. More parts followed. One performance drew an offer from Hollywood. Billed as Nancy Davis, she performed in 11 films from 1949 to 1956. Her first screen role was in *Shadow on the Wall*. Other releases included *The Next Voice You Hear* and *East Side, West Side*. In her last movie, *Hellcats of the Navy*, she played opposite her husband.

She had met Ronald Reagan in 1951, when he was president of the Screen Actors Guild. The following year they were married in a simple ceremony in Los Angeles in the Little Brown Church in the Valley. Mrs. Reagan soon retired from making movies so she "could be the wife I wanted to be. . . . A woman's real happiness and real fulfillment come from within the home with her husband and children," she says. President and Mrs. Reagan have a daughter, Patricia Ann, and a son, Ronald Prescott.

While her husband was Governor of California from 1967 to 1975, she worked with numerous charitable groups. She spent many hours visiting veterans, the elderly, and the emotionally and physically handicapped. These people continued to interest her as First Lady. She gave her support to the Foster Grandparent Program, the subject of her 1982 book, *To Love A Child*. Increasingly, she has concentrated on the fight against drug and alcohol abuse among young people. She visited prevention and rehabilitation centers, and in 1985 she held a conference at the White House for First Ladies of 17 countries to focus international attention on this problem.

Mrs. Reagan shared her lifelong interest in the arts with the nation by using the Executive Mansion as a showcase for talented young performers in the PBS television series "In Performance at the White House." In her first year in the mansion she directed a major renovation of the second- and third-floor quarters.

Now living in retirement with her husband in California, she continues to work on her campaign to teach children to "just say no" to drugs, though her husband and her home remain her first priority. In her book *My Turn*, published in 1989, she gives her own account of her life in the White House. Through the joys and sorrows of those days, including the assassination attempt on her husband, Nancy Reagan held fast to her belief in love, honesty, and selflessness. "The ideals have endured because they are right and are no less right today than yesterday."

Nancy Davis Reagan focused national attention on the problem of drug abuse in young people. Artist Aaron Shikler portrays her in the Red Room, her favorite of the White House state rooms, by a door leading into the State Dining Room.

Barbara Pierce Bush

1925-

Rarely has a First Lady been greeted by the American people and the press with the approbation and warmth accorded to Barbara Pierce Bush. Perhaps this is prompted by the image she calls "everybody's grandmother." People are comfortable with her white hair, her warm, relaxed manner, and her keen wit. With characteristic directness, she says people like her because they know "I'm fair and I like children and I adore my husband."

Barbara was born in 1925 to Pauline and Marvin Pierce, who later became president of McCall Corporation. In the suburban town of Rye, New York, she had a happy childhood. She went to boarding school at Ashley Hall in South Carolina, and it was at a dance during Christmas vacation when she was only 16 that she met George Bush, a senior at Phillips Academy in Andover, Massachusetts. They became engaged a year and a half-later, just before he went off to war as a Navy torpedo bomber pilot. By the time George returned on leave, Barbara had dropped out of Smith College. Two weeks later, on January 6, 1945, they were married.

After the war, George graduated from Yale, and they set out for Texas to start their lives together. Six children were born to them: George, Robin, Jeb, Neil, Marvin, and Dorothy. Meanwhile, George built a business in the oil industry. With Texas as home base, he then turned to politics and public service, serving as a Member of Congress, U. S. Ambassador to the United Nations, Chairman of the Republican National Committee, Chief of the U. S. Liaison Office in the People's Republic of China, Director of the Central Intelligence Agency, and later as Vice President. In those 44 years of marriage, Mrs. Bush managed 29 moves of the family.

When her husband was away, she became the family linchpin, providing everything from discipline to carpools. The death of their daughter Robin from leukemia when she was not quite four left George and Barbara Bush with a lifelong compassion. She says, "Because of Robin, George and I love every living human more."

Barbara Bush was always an asset to her husband during his campaigns for public office. Her friendly, forthright manner won her high marks from the voters and the press. As wife of the Vice President, she selected the promotion of literacy as her special cause. As First Lady, she called working for a more literate America the "most important issue we have." Involved with many organizations devoted to this cause, she became Honorary Chairman of the Barbara Bush Foundation for Family Literacy. A strong advocate of volunteerism, Mrs. Bush helped many causes—including the homeless, AIDS, the elderly, and school volunteer programs.

Today Barbara Bush lives in a home she and her husband built in Houston, Texas, where she enjoys being part of the community. Their children and grandchildren visit them often in Houston and at the family summer home in Kennebunkport, Maine. Devoted to her family, Mrs. Bush has found time to write an autobiography, to serve on the Boards of AmeriCares and the Mayo Clinic, and to continue her prominent role in the Barbara Bush Foundation.

An active volunteer for many years for the cause of literacy, Barbara Bush feels everybody should help some charitable cause. "If it worries you, then you've got to do something about it." Such sincerity has won the hearts of the nation.

Energetic First Lady Hillary Rodham Clinton juggles a heavy work agenda, ranging from performing the duties of the official White House hostess to participating in forums on women's issues. Mrs. Clinton has devoted her career to working for "America's most unprotected citizens—its children." She urges Americans "to reach across the lines that divide us not with pointing fingers but with outstretched hands. That's the kind of America I see in the future with my husband as President."

Hillary Rodham Clinton
1947-

Hillary Rodham Clinton arrived at the White House after serving as First Lady of Arkansas for 12 years. During that time she had managed many roles: wife, mother, and homemaker; full-time partner in a law firm; and chairwoman of an education committee that set public school standards in Arkansas. On many occasions Hillary Clinton has spoken about the need "to find the right balance in our lives." For her, the elements of that balance are family, work, and public service.

Hillary Diane Rodham was born in Chicago, Illinois, on October 26, 1947, daughter of Hugh and Dorothy Rodham. Her father owned a fabric store, and her mother was a full-time mother and homemaker. Mrs. Rodham encouraged Hillary to go to college and pursue a profession, even though she had never done so herself.

Hillary and her younger brothers, Hugh and Tony, grew up in Park Ridge, Illinois, as a close-knit family. Her brothers played football, while Hillary enjoyed tennis, swimming, ballet, softball, volleyball, and skating. An excellent student, she was also a Girl Scout and a member of the local Methodist youth group.

She entered Wellesley College in 1965. Graduating with honors, she moved on to Yale Law School, where she served on the Board of Editors of the *Yale Review of Law and Social Action.* While at Yale she developed her concern for protecting the interests of children and families. It was there, too, that she met Bill Clinton, a fellow student.

In 1973 Hillary became a staff attorney for the Children's Defense Fund. A year later she was recruited by the Impeachment Inquiry staff of the Judiciary Committee of the House of Representatives.

Hillary left Washington and "followed her heart to Arkansas," marrying Bill Clinton in 1975. The couple taught together on the law faculty of the University of Arkansas in Fayetteville. Their daughter, Chelsea, was born in 1980.

In Arkansas, Hillary worked tirelessly on behalf of children and families. She founded the Arkansas Advocates for Children and Families and served on the board of the Arkansas Children's Hospital. In addition to serving as chairwoman of the Arkansas Education Standards Committee, she introduced a pioneering program called the Home Instruction Program for Preschool Youngsters. It soon became a model for other states. The program sent teachers into the homes of underprivileged families to train parents to work with their children in school preparedness and literacy. In recognition of her professional and personal accomplishments, Hillary was named Arkansas' Woman of the Year in 1983 and its Young Mother of the Year in 1984.

Like her predecessors, Hillary Rodham Clinton brings her own special talents to the role of First Lady. Since her arrival at the White House, Mrs. Clinton has taken delight in using it as a showcase for the performing arts, American cuisine, and crafts. The President appointed her to head his Task Force on National Health Care Reform, one of his highest priorities on taking office. As the President remarked: "We have a First Lady of many talents…who most of all can bring people together around complex and difficult issues to hammer out consensus and get things done."

Illustrations Credits

A photographic portrait of Mrs. Clinton appears because an official painting has not yet been acquired.

Composition for *The First Ladies* by the Typographic section of National Geographic Production Services, Pre-Press Division. Printed and bound by R. R. Donnelley & Sons, Willard, Ohio.